Yezidis in Syria

Yezidis in Syria

Identity Building among a Double Minority

Sebastian Maisel

LEXINGTON BOOKS
Lanham • Boulder • New York • London

Published by Lexington Books
An imprint of The Rowman & Littlefield Publishing Group, Inc.
4501 Forbes Boulevard, Suite 200, Lanham, Maryland 20706
www.rowman.com

Unit A, Whitacre Mews, 26-34 Stannary Street, London SE11 4AB

Copyright © 2017 by Lexington Books

All rights reserved. No part of this book may be reproduced in any form or by any electronic or mechanical means, including information storage and retrieval systems, without written permission from the publisher, except by a reviewer who may quote passages in a review.

British Library Cataloguing in Publication Information Available

Library of Congress Cataloging-in-Publication Data

Names: Maisel, Sebastian, 1970- author.
Title: Yezidis in Syria : identity building among a double minority / Sebastian Maisel.
Description: Lanham, Maryland : Lexington Books, 2017. |
   Includes bibliographical references and index.
Identifiers: LCCN 2016044359 (print) | LCCN 2016052892 (ebook) |
   ISBN 9780739177747 (cloth : alk. paper) | ISBN 9780739177754 (Electronic)
Subjects: LCSH: Yezidis—Syria. | Religious minorities—Syria.
Classification: LCC BL1595 .M35 2017 (print) | LCC BL1595 (ebook) |
   DDC 299/.159—dc23
LC record available at https://lccn.loc.gov/2016044359

∞™ The paper used in this publication meets the minimum requirements of American National Standard for Information Sciences—Permanence of Paper for Printed Library Materials, ANSI/NISO Z39.48-1992.

Printed in the United States of America

Contents

List of Illustrations	vii
List of Tables	ix
Preface	xi
Note on Transliteration	xiii
1 Introduction	1
2 Minorities in Syria: Competing Hierarchies	7
3 Demystifying Yezidis: A Word About the Sources	33
4 Religious Beliefs	43
5 Historical Developments	75
6 Yezidis in the new Syria	117
7 Future Challenges	165
Appendixes	169
Bibliography	173
Index	183
About the Author	189

List of Illustrations

Figure 2.1	Map of the religious and ethnic communities of Syria and Lebanon (1935)	14
Figure 2.2	Map of Yezidi Villages in the Kurdagh/Efrin Area	18
Figure 2.3	Map of Yezidi Villages in the Jezira	23
Figure 4.1	Sheikh Adi Shrine in Beyt Far, Lebanon	45
Figure 4.2	The Melekadi Shrine in Qibare	67
Figure 5.1	Zarathustra Statue in Efrin	76
Figure 5.2	Stone Plate at Former Yezidi School in Qibare	87
Figure 5.3	First Yezidi School in Tell Khatun (1958)	105
Figure 6.1	The Syrian Yezidi Triumvirate: Lalish, Zarathustra, and Abdulla Ocalan	137

List of Tables

Table 2.1	Yezidi Villages in the Kurdagh/Efrin Area	19
Table 2.2	Yezidi Villages in the Wadi al-Jarrah	24
Table 2.3	Yezidi Villages near Amuda	24
Table 2.4	Yezidi Villages near Hasake	25
Table 2.5	Yezidi Villages near Ras al-Ayn/Sere Kaniye	26
Table 2.6	Yezidi Population in the Jezira during the Mandate and Early SAR Periods	26
Table 2.7	Decline of Yezidi Population in the Jezira	26
Table 2.8	Decline of Yezidi Population in the Wadi al-Jarrah Area	27
Table 3.1	Journals published by Markaz Lalish and their local affiliation	41
Table 4.1	Excerpt from Qewle Mezin	59
Table 4.2	Excerpt from Qewle Keniya Mara	59
Table 4.3	Taj Hillah Objects and their Guardians	65
Table 5.1	Maktum—Ajanib—National Legal Relations	101

Preface

This book is the result of two decades of interaction with Yezidis from Syria and elsewhere. Yezidis for the past centuries have been discredited, persecuted, and denied their rights to be part of our global community of ethnic and religious groups. Living in the shadows and on the periphery of society, they have endured many wrongdoings from their neighbors, compatriots, and fellow citizens. According to the Yezidis, they faced seventy-four massacres, some of which were described as genocide. They have yet to achieve equality and justice in most of their original homelands. But even under these terrible circumstances, Yezidi communities did not abandon their faith and traditions. Community leaders and religious men and laymen undertook great efforts to preserve and reinterpret Yezidism according to the conditions and challenges of the twenty-first century. And while the attacks continued and intensified, a new generation of young Yezidis seized the opportunity in the autonomous areas of Syria as well as in the diaspora to build a new identity, perhaps not very orthodox in some of their features, but certainly very assertive, inclusive, and genuine.

This scholarly contribution observed, recorded, and analyzed this process over a period of twenty years. It is meant to be a comprehensive assessment that shows the past, present and, to a lesser extent, future developments, events, and opinions that shaped the idea of what it means being Yezidi, in Syria or elsewhere. The process of identity building has not yet been completed, nor are the efforts for Syrian Yezidis to find a safe homeland where they are accepted as equal citizens and can live according to the religion of their forefathers. Ciwan Haco, the famous Kurdish singer, brought this out more clearly by saying that justice will be accomplished only when a Yezidi Kurd can one day become president of Syria.[1]

Many Yezidis shared their views about this new identity with the author, for which I am greatly indebted. Interviews were conducted in Syria, Iraq, Turkey, Armenia, the United States, and Germany. Yezidi organizations provided me with access to official documents, archival material, political statements, and many personal accounts. Special thanks are due to the Zentralrat der Yeziden in Deutschland, Hevbendiya Ezidiyen Suriye, Majlis Ezidiyin Suria, and the Ezidisches Identitätsinventar. I would like to express my gratitude to a few individuals, colleagues, and friends for their support, comments, and critiques: Chaukedin Issa, Pir Khidr Sileman, Serhan Issa, Fermaz Gharibo, Shefik Tagay, Ibrahim Kus, Sinan Shikho, Tarek Hammo, and Ali Farhan. I also wish to thank all my Yezidi informants who shared their often painful stories and memories and patiently walked me through many dark chapters of Yezidi oral history.

Over the past twenty years I have benefited from the friendship and guidance of Telim Tolan, who generously offered intellectual and spiritual support. He opened the gates of Yezidism and the doors of the Yezidis for me.

But all of this would have been impossible to accomplish without the unconditional, indefinite love and support of my family. I owe them everything.

NOTE

1. Ciwan Haco, Shivan Perwer, and other Kurdish artists support the Syrian Revolution. Uploaded by Kurdwatch.org on Feb. 6, 2012. https://www.youtube.com/watch?v=JBQtEHbQcTY, accessed August 1, 2016.

Note on Transliteration

Yezidis are multilingual, often speaking more than three languages. Many claim Kurdish as their mother tongue, which is written in three or more different letters of the alphabet. And so are the sources, oral and written, telling the Yezidis' story. Thus, in order to make the story of Yezidi identity building more accessible to readers who are unfamiliar with Kurdish and/or Arabic, Turkish, Persian, etc., foreign words have been transcribed and their spelling altered to allow for easy pronunciation and quick recognition. Equally, Kurdish and Arabic names of people, places, and objects have been transcribed and harmonized according to the most common publicized English form. In cases where both Kurdish and Arabic names are known, the form favored by Yezidis, that is, the Kurdish spelling, has been used. Transcription, may however, be slightly inconsistent, while an attempt has been made to bridge the gap between the original name and its English rendition. This can be noted by the absence of long vowel markers and other diacritical symbols.

Chapter 1

Introduction

A poster with three eye-catching images was displayed in 2013 during the Yezidi Spring festival, a religious ceremony in a small village near the Syrian-Turkish border: The temple of Lalish was flanked by Abdullah Ocalan and the Prophet Zarathustra. This captivating, although somehow contradictory, triumvirate represented the identity of these villagers who, for the longest time, were unable to express, visualize or formulate their worldview due to societal, religious, and political pressures of their environment. But now, in the wake of the recent changes and in the midst of the raging civil war, Syria's Yezidi community find themselves in a niche of opportunities. For the first time in history, they live in an area free from persecution and annihilation and find their beliefs and heritage appreciated by their neighbors. Not by all neighbors and not in every Yezidi village of course, but in those territories controlled by the Syrian Kurds.

But what are their beliefs? How can they develop historical, cultural, and doctrinal ideas when they were suppressed for generations? It appears that some ancient customs and notions survived, here symbolized in the temple of Lalish, while others transformed, such as the image of the prophet Zarathustra. And new aspects were added and incorporated into the new belief system, like that of Abdullah Ocalan, the political and spiritual leader of the PKK (Kurdish Workers Party or *Partiya Karkeren Kurdistan*). This shows how an identity can grow, how it is fluid and dynamic, but never static. Yezidis in Syria have the opportunity to develop their individual and communal profile. And while they might adopt new ideas, they will concurrently avoid and drop others. Identity evolves from that interplay of identification and differentiation. The construction of the self-image is an ongoing process, which in times of crises can lead to ambivalent decision-making. Old securities disappear, formerly strong identity markers fade away, and previous beliefs are no longer valid, leading to an identity crisis. However, those crises are not always threatening; they also offer the chance of a new beginning, growth, and progress. The Yezidis, like other minorities in Syria, reached a crossroads, not by choice but because of circumstances. They are forced to evaluate their own convictions, reassess their current position in the country's hierarchy of ethnic and religious groups, and reconstruct their identity. This book tells their story, how they emerged among the myriad of other minorities, and how they ended up venerating the three icons of Lalish, Zarathustra, and Ocalan.

The twentieth century in the Middle East was the century of minorities or better a century of various attempts to define what a minority was, which rights they possessed, and how they were to be protected or persecuted. Concurrently, the last century saw the rise of many minority groups who previously have been unable to claim status, identity, or recognition, be it for political, social, or educational reasons or the lack of it, or for simple reasons of remoteness. Toward the end of the twentieth century and concurrent with the IT revolution, special interest groups have merged into the public consciousness through a successful application of measures of identity building and self-representation.

Syria has often been described as a mosaic of various ethnic and religious minorities. Here, minorities have asserted themselves in the political landscape and gained significant rights. This is true more for religious minorities than for ethnic minorities. In theory, Article 35 of the Syrian constitution even guarantees religious freedom with some minor restrictions.[1] And in the growing sectarian civil war, the Syrian regime sees itself and is portrayed as the protector of religious minorities.[2]

The largest religious group in Syria represents the Sunni Muslims; then there are Alawites, various Christian denominations, Druzes, Twelver Shias, and Ismailis. Each group, because of its long existence and experience of working with various forms of government, has established strong and deeply rooted institutions and networks.

Syria is also a land of contrast where one of the religious minority groups seems to exert influence and control over the majority population. Much has been written about the rule of the Asad family and dominance of the Alawites over the country's political, economic, and military sector.[3] So it appears that a minority, and more so a heterodox minority group, was able to dominate the Sunni majority as well as the state institutions. This is of course only partly true. Syria's elite and ruling class includes representatives from other religious groups; even Sunnis take part in the leadership of the country. A common denominator might be the secular ideology of the Ba'th Party. Equally, not all Alawites are actually beneficiaries of the government. Thus, it serves our understanding of power, hierarchy, and elites better if we describe these groups as groups of common interest and identity. They all have to position themselves (or are sometimes forcefully placed) on the country's food chain or sociopolitical hierarchy.

Different circumstances, external influences, and changing needs and grievances force these groups to reexamine their standing over time and find ways to improve it, which usually happens at the cost of other groups that will be relegated to a lower spot on the socio-political ladder. This makes the entire system rather fluid and unstable; however, the general desire to keep the system alive in order to advance in it, guarantees its survival. The constant struggle between different interest groups over access to resources and power is a dominant theme in the evolution of Levantine and Mesopotamian societies, which is applicable to modern-day Syria and its neighboring states.

Various interest groups in the political, religious, and/or economic sector are more successful in their quest for hegemony and superiority than others. This does not exclude the possibility of low-level groups climbing the ladder and formerly influential groups falling low. The Alawites are a good example for the former and the Muslim Brotherhood for the latter. And who would have thought that the Maronites in Lebanon would eventually win their own country only to lose it later to the demographically more successful Shias! Other strong minority groups in the Syrian context are the Christians, Druze, and Kurds. Smaller communities include the Circassians and the Ismailis. And then there are political minorities, Palestinian and Iraqi refugees, as well as economic minorities, such as the nomadic Bedouin tribes in the Jezira. What is unique about Syria's majorities and minorities is the hierarchical system, which clearly defines a place for each group on the socioeconomic-political ladder. But this place is up for grabs for anyone who can afford it. The hierarchy is not written in stone, especially in times of crisis, revolution, and civil war.

Change is the only constant factor when describing the ups and downs of interest groups over the past century in Syria. The political system changed from Islamic caliphate and Ottoman Sultanate to Arab kingdom to French mandate to Arab republic. The social environment saw the traditional divide of Bedouin versus *Hadar*[4] disappear in favor of the urban versus rural divide. Gender roles changed and conflict between different generations erupted; religion lost its dominant layer of identity and regained it in the current civil war.

And then there are the Yezidis, who were resistant to change for centuries, who resided on the edges of society, and who always remained at the bottom of society. The ethno-religious minority of the Yezidis holds the lowest place in that system,[5] making them the most vulnerable and exploited community in the country. They are *the* ultimate minority, in fact a double minority, suffering and facing discrimination for being both ethnic Kurds and religious heretics.

This study seeks to investigate how the Yezidis fit into the Syrian minority context. It shows the current position of the community in the social-political-economic hierarchy. The analysis involves the perspectives of other groups on this scale, those groups that have an active interest in the affairs of the Yezidis and those groups that influence the ranking of the Yezidis, both in the positive and negative way. These groups may include other religious groups, but also ethnicities, political actors such as the government and local authorities, as well as outside and external forces like diaspora groups or foreign governments. It will be determined whether their interaction with the Yezidis is solely faith based or if it includes other common identity aspects such as gender, occupation, education, or economic status. Evaluating the relationship between the Yezidis and the other groups is a major component of this study with the ultimate goal of defining Yezidi identity vis-à-vis the identities of other Syrian interest groups.

Among the main questions for debate are: How did the Yezidis end up at the bottom of the social hierarchy? Have they always been there? Where did they come from and where will they go in the future? How did a particular Syrian Yezidi identity evolved and developed? What is the relationship between the Muslim majority and the Yezidi minority? What is the connection with non-Yezidi Kurds and their political parties? What is the Yezidi position toward the Arab Spring, the civil war, and a possible regime change?

Due to their contested current status and troubled history, little information about the Syrian Yezidi community is available. This is true not only for general, journalistic reports, but also for academic and journalistic works, which largely seem to focus on other, more prominent, minority groups, such as the Kurds and the Alawites. This study seeks to bridge this gap and to contribute to the new momentum of contemporary research on Syria that focuses on the margins of society and that is based on anthropological fieldwork.

This study also reflects the approach of the author, who spent almost twenty years working with Syrian Yezidis within the country and among the diaspora groups abroad. During this time period, the author visited the various Yezidi communities in Syria and other countries many times, conducted interviews, observed religious and nonreligious ceremonies, collected official data, and assessed social, economic, and political developments. The advantages of speaking Arabic fluently and having a good command of Kurdish allowed the gathering of first-hand information from Yezidis in Syria, Iraq, and Germany, but also from Syrian officials as well as Arab and Kurdish neighbors of Yezidi communities.

As mentioned previously, almost no literature is available about the specific conditions of Yezidis in Syria, their history, identity, or customs. Two lengthy articles about the community's identity building process in a historical context, which were based on the author's master thesis and decade-long in-country fieldwork, are the only in-depth sources.[6] Newly established Kurdish online newspapers and media centers report frequently from the three autonomous cantons in northern Syria; however, since most of them are ideologically and financially close to the dominant Kurdish political party, the PYD (Democratic Union Party or *Partiya Yekitiya Demokrat*), their biases must be recognized. But it is here where local information from the Yezidi villages is broadcasted, although often hidden among the political reports.[7]

NOTES

1. The president of the country must be a Muslim and Islamic law remains a main source of legislation.
2. For some, the Syrian regime is in fact a minority-dominated regime.
3. See for example Goldsmith 2015, Hinnebusch 2009, Lawson 2009, Lesch 2005.
4. Settled versus nomadic groups was the main conflict for much of Syria's prenation time.
5. That is of course the Yezidi perception. I found evidence that the Arab tribe of the Khawatina who lives in the border area between Syria and Iraq considered themselves lower than the Yezidis (here the Yezidis from Sinjar) and were afraid of them because of the constant harassment. In order to survive in the area they had to forge unfavorable alliances with the stronger Arab clans to protect themselves from Yezidi assaults. See Talay (2003): 167–173.
6. See Maisel (1997) and (2013).
7. The PYD has her own website (pydrojava.net) where current news from the region is broadcasted. Other news organizations include hawarnews, esyria, ANF (Ajansa Nuceyan a Firete), ezidipress.com or bahzani.net.

Chapter 2

Minorities in Syria

Competing Hierarchies

Syria is home to a plethora of ethnic and religious minorities. Labeled the cradle of civilization and melting pot of cultures, it witnessed over a time period of several millennia the rise and fall of many majorities and minorities. Before the fixture of political borders the area saw migrations from south to the north, along the rivers and from the sea. The 500-year-long rule of the Ottomans gave the Syrian land some sort of stability and connectivity; the *bilad al-sham*[1] was unique and different from other Middle Eastern regions such as the Arabian Peninsula, Egypt, and Mesopotamia. Kurdistan, or the land of the Kurds, wasn't officially part of Syria, but was certainly closely connected and the Kurds played an important political and economic part in the history of Greater Syria alongside other distinct minorities such as the various Christian groups, the Druzes, and the Alawites. Sunni Arabs dominated the political landscape until the end of World War I, when bilad al-sham was cut into zones of colonial interests and mandate territories. The creation of nation-states concurrently saw the development of new identities and power hierarchies. While Turks and Arabs gained independence, Kurds remained on the sidelines. Colonial pressures and the necessity to develop a national agenda required many smaller groups to position themselves vis-à-vis the new political realities and borders. While some groups managed to create semi-independent entities, the aspirations of others were crushed while clashing with the interests of the majority group. And the treatment of minority groups, ethnic or religious, in those newly created states was far from fair. Instead the dominant ethnic/religious group seized the opportunity to promote their majority agenda, which was and is different from the pluralistic and democratic Western approach to nation-building.

Many minority groups pre-date the creation of the modern, political Middle East and its concept of ethno-centric nation-states. Because of their transnational connections, minority groups were able to create networks of connections and support. Now that these connections were located outside the national framework, the minorities were suspicious in the eyes of the majority and often accused of treason and unpatriotic behavior. It is thus imperative to study the relations between the two groups from a historical transnational perspective.

When the *umma* ruled the land and most of the Middle East was part of the Islamic caliphate, particular religious minorities were recognized as *ahl al-kitab* or People of the Book, that is, those monotheistic religions with revealed scripture, the Jews and Christians. At other times, religious minorities were refered to as *ta'ifa* or sect.[2] Often, this overlapped with the establishment of a *millet*, an officially recognized minority community[3] with its own laws, legal system, and tax rules. Selim and Mohamed (2014) argue that the definition, as well as the historic and cultural connotations of the term 'minority', differs between the Muslim world and the West. They go even further claiming that the current word for minority, *aqaliya*, is in fact alien and a Western creation.[4] And indeed, when looking at the Syrian landscape, it appears that Western influence and ideology pushed the minority agenda over much of the country's early history. The buzz word *aqaliya* pointed to a variety of underrepresented groups, and thus must be considered a more secular, political vocabulary. *Ta'ifa* on the other hand still refers to sects or denominations within a particular religious group.

Minorities in the Middle East experienced various forms of discrimination by the majority, such as the denial of their cultural, linguistic, and religious rights or worse, violent attacks to submit them or forcefully assimilate them. However, not always has the minority group been the victim. There were strong and well-established minority groups that imposed their rule over the majority through a system of military and economic forces. Through innovative strategies they worked to covert the majority to accept their authority, belief and thinking; not literally of course, but by providing a new form of identity that suited the needs of the minority and allowed the majority to feel included.

The ethno-religious majority in the Middle East is represented by Sunni Arabs. In Syria as well as neighboring Jordan, Palestine, Kuwait, Saudi Arabia, and Egypt, they dominate the demographic landscape. As Muslims they view the world from the Sunni perspective that includes various provisions with regard to other branches and faiths. And as Arabs they have developed an identity that has put their group in the driver's seat of the national discourse. In neighboring Lebanon and Iraq, however, the majority population is represented by Shia Arabs, which differ in their religious, but not so much in their ethnic, forms of representation. Both countries are good examples of how the minority controlled the majority. Sunni Arabs participated or even dominated the political elite and ruling class. In the broader context of the Muslim nation or *umma*, Shias are considered a minority and by some even as a heretic group. However, as Arabs they enjoy some benefits of brotherly Arabness throughout the region and in the pertinent organizations and institutions, especially during times of increased secularization.[5]

The larger region is home to more than two types of minorities, that is, religious and ethnic. But given the many divisions, it is difficult, and contested, to create a classification or taxonomy of minority groups. Kumaraswamy (2003) tried it and classified contemporary Middle Eastern minorities into five broad categories, namely religious minorities, ethno-national minorities, heterodox Islamic minorities, political minorities, and majoritarian minorities.[6] Religious minorities are easy to detect and they include the Jews and various Christian dominations. Interestingly, he included Israeli Arabs as a religious minority, which must be seen in light of the current attempts of the Israeli government to make Israel a Jewish state by law and require citizens to swearing an oath of allegiance to it. The Yezidis were conspicious in their absence in his listing of religious minorities. Among the ethnic or national minorities he included the Kurds, Druze, Armenian, Circassians, Assyrians, Southern Sudanese, Berber, Turkoman, and Israeli Arabs. The inclusion of the Druze and Assyrians especially shows how fluid the borders between ethnic and religious minorities are. Again, the Yezidis would be a perfect fit for this category. Perhaps he thought of including them in the category of heterodox Islamic minorities, a label that is often given to the Yezidis. But his list includes only the Alawis, Druze, Ismailis, Baha'is, and Ahmadias.

Political minorities as a fourth category are groups like the Shias in Saudi Arabia and the Sunnis in Iran or Lebanon. And then he added a fifth column for majoritarian minorities, groups that nominally have the largest percentage of the population; however, they are not part of the country's leadership. This group includes the Shias of Bahrain, the Palestinians in Jordan, and the Sunnis in Syria. How important the numbers are can be seen in the Lebanese example, where the entire political system is built upon a proportional system of representation, which guarantees every minority group certain seats, rights, or other benefits. This balanced representation, however, is based on a census taken over fifty years ago, when Christians were nominally in the majority. Currently, Shias lead the demographic scale; however, they receive the benefits of only the third place according to their previous standing. Thus, classification and (self)-identification are important tools used by both sides to manipulate public perception.

In other cases, minorities tried to boost their numbers in order to gain additional seats in elections or win popular polls. The case of the Turkish takeover of the Sanjak of Alexandretta serves as a good example that also affected the Yezidis in Syria. Here, voters from all over Turkey were sent to the Sanjak to raise the numbers of Turkish representation.[7] Although they had a sizable presence in the region, Yezidis or Kurds were not granted any seats. Other examples are the upcoming contested referendum over the status of Kirkuk in Iraq, which is debated along ethnic (Kurdish-Arab-Turkmen) lines, and the discussion about autonomy of the Yezidi-dominated Sinjar Mountain. A strong territorial base, however, does not necessarily guarantee political success.

Minorities tend to have at least autonomous if not separatist tendencies. These are harbored usually because of the denial of certain rights by the majority population and/or government. In an autonomous region they would be able to speak their own language, practice their own religion and select their own leaders. Unfortunately, the young nation-states in the Middle East often discriminate against nonmajority segments of their society and have difficulties in granting rights or land to minorities. Thus, conflicts that relate to minorities quickly turn into territorial conflicts, which could also have economic dimensions. In Turkey, the Kurdish claim that territories have water resources; in the Israeli-occupied West Bank there is water too. In the Eastern Province of Saudi Arabia, home to the Shia minority, are all the major oil fields and industries are found. Kirkuk sits on the second largest Iraqi oilfield. Syrian Yezidis were farmers in areas close to the Turkish border and as their land ownership was considered a security risk their land was confiscated and given to Arab farmers.

As citizens of those states all people regardless of their ethnic or religious affiliation should be treated equally before the law. This is a universal pillar of the rule of law. It also implies the individuality of citizens, which does not differentiate on the basis of religion, ethnicity, gender, or class. However, in Middle Eastern countries citizenship is not primarily assigned to individuals, but citizens are recognized as members of special interest groups, such as kin groups, sects, or ethnic groups. At such, citizenship is not the most important layer of identity, because it has been used as a tool for discrimination. For many, especially minorities, it is not even in the top three. For them religious or ethnic affiliation trumps citizenship. Other regional or local expressions of identity may override citizenship as well.

As mentioned earlier, Syria's constitution claims freedom of religion as well as priority rights for Arab citizens. Later, this study discusses the right of religious freedom as a strongly contested article, especially in light of the country's secularization policies. The denial of equal rights for non-Arab citizens, however, is evident even in the country's official name: Syrian Arab Republic. Kurds and Yezidis were made second-class citizens by official decree. Often they sheer existence was denied by the authorities,; and they faced similar difficulties like the Kurdish citizens in Turkey, the Palestinian citizens in Israel, and the Shia citizens in Saudi Arabia.

On the other hand, minorities often enjoy international support and outside protection, sometimes from members of the diaspora community or the international community. Syrians emigrated all over the world, but maintained close relations with the homeland through visitations, marriages, money transfers, or ultimately burials at the old cemeteries. The Druzes are a closely connected community with groups in Syria, Lebanon, and Israel, and so are the Ismailis through the global Aga Khan network. Generally, the Syrian diaspora is a global network of migrants and their descendants, which also includes Syrians who studied at Western and Eastern universities and took up residency in those countries.

Migration and diaspora are also important issues among the Syrian Yezidis. The emigration of thousands of Yezidis from all major regions to Germany brought up new questions regarding their identity as a group and for the individual. In the past and in their homeland it was clear and obvious to be recognized and called a Kurd, a member of the Yezidi community, a tribe, or a family. Now these designations are confronted with the different living conditions in a Western country where the Yezidis no longer face the threats of religious and ethnic persecution. They don't have to hide their religion anymore, which was an important aspect of their religious understanding.

Instead they have to define religion and culture and adapt to the conditions and challenges of a modern, complex society. Some say that many of the old traditions and customs brought from Kurdistan were no longer up-to-date and thus should be disregarded or at least reformed. Otherwise, the second generation, the children of those who came to Germany in the eighties and nineties, and who were born here, would distance themselves from the religion.

The precarious situation of Yezidism is compared to a piece of sugar slowly dissolving in a cup of tea. In order to confront the loss of identity, Yezidism must be more transparent and comprehensible for the common believers. Ackermann (2001) identified three areas of conflict in the identity-building process among the Yezidis in Germany: ignorance and misconceptions about Yezidism, preservation and adjustment of Yezidi traditions, and the positioning of Yezidis in the realm of religion and politics.[8]

The definition and description as ethnic and/or religious minority is not constant. Identities shift over time and with changing circumstances. The ingredients may be the same, but the final outcome will be different. One of the most stable and common ingredients is *asabiya*.

According to the great medieval sociologist Ibn Khaldun, societies tend to create bonds on the basis of common origin forming tribal groups. Asabiya or group solidarity is the glue that keeps those groups together. With asabiya they can define themselves in contrast to other groups and create a hierarchy of power, wealth, influence, reputation, or access to resources. A very strong sense of mutual obligation and affection towards the group members can be observed. The stronger and more cohesive a group is, the more successful it will be and the higher the chances of their survival. In the Khaldunian model blood and kinship are the keys to success: we are stronger because we are related and all belong to the same family. In fact, the strongest ties are observed among the closest relatives. Kinship is thus an important marker of a person's identity. In many Middle Eastern families it is the strongest marker and the one with the deepest roots. If everything around you falls apart, you would still have your relatives to rely on.

But, as mentioned before, other markers to build a person's identity exist too. Common region, common interests, common age, common enemies, or common citizenship may work too as the glue that keeps identity groups together. And so is religion. Goldsmith convincingly argues that there is a sectarian asabiya, a common faith-based bond. He demonstrates the effectiveness of this bond with the Syrian Alawite community and their distinct religious beliefs.[9]

People tend to rely on these bonds in times of need and conflict, when it is required to position themselves. War, hunger, marginalization, discrimination, or the threat of all these are all factors that drive communities to move closer to one another looking for support and protection. The extended family may provide for this, so does religious congregation. However, religious communities tend to dig in when they feel insecure. Proud, open believers have little need for group therapy; but those religious communities that suffer from persecution, misunderstanding, and suspicious or mysterious behavior display a great sense of insecurity. These often go along with a secretive, reclusive, and isolated lifestyle. And these are common descriptors for Yezidi life during the past 200 years. But why are the Yezidis so insecure about their identity and what is the common denominator of their asabiya?

The factor that unifies all Yezidi communities is the legacy of persecution and victimhood. For various reasons, they were targeted by their neighbors. They also had to endure constant subjugation to inferiority where even educated members of the "other" group would refuse to shake hands with Yezidis or share a meal with them. So severe was the disdain for the Yezidi community that they were considered unclean and impure as a whole group. The daily humiliation added to the weak self- and group esteem, but on the other hand helped foster a cohesive group with a common interest and identity.

Where the Khaldunian model falls short is the second aspect of asabiya where the interest group eventually became successful, but then subsequently declines again. Yezidis were never successful and have no expectations of being accepted as equals, at least not in their homeland. Their communal clinging to traditions and ancient customs and the common narrative of persecution create a bond of mutual helping and togetherness.

Syrians are no exception to the common attitudes towards the Yezidis. Ignored, forgotten, or pushed aside by all elements of Syrian society, they did not fit into the mosaic of pluralistic coexistence or equal citizenship. This comes as no surprise to Syrians, who grew up and were educated along these lines. It seems thus puzzling that schoolbooks in Syria do not mention the religious diversity of the country and describe Islam as monolithic. All public schools teach Islam classes on the basis of textbooks, which clearly cater to the mainstream Sunni population. Equally, these books do not speak about interfaith dialogue or tolerance or plurality, instead all Muslim students regardless of their sectarian background, as well as the Yezidi students, have to study them.[10]

Syria has been described as a secular country, or at least a country ruled by a secular regime. This government is first and foremost interested in regime stability, and if stability is achieved by ruling with a secular agenda, it may be so. It appears that Syrians do not want to stir any religious tensions and want to maintain the current religious balance and status quo. Only if challenged, they might respond with force. While the largest religious minority group, the Christians, is allowed to run its own religious education classes, all others who belong to different beliefs and denominations whether they are Alawite, Druze, Ismaili, or Yezidi, have to pass the mandatory Sunni courses in school or at university. And with the regime becoming weaker in the five-year-long ongoing civil war, some argue that its intolerant approach toward these other groups has facilitated the creation of radical Muslim organizations such as Jabhat al-Nusra (JN) and the Islamic State (IS).

Syrian society represents a complex pattern and composition of various ethno-religious groups. The heterogenic character of the Syrian people is furthermore illustrated by the division in rural versus urban communities. All of these aspects shape the identity of the Syrian people, but they are most visible in the settlement pattern. Figure 2.1. shows how identity groups tended to live apart from other interest groups in the 1930s. Thus, we find entire villages, towns, neighborhoods, or districts inhabited by one dominant group that lived separately from other ethnic, religious, or life-style communities; for example, the town of Salamiya, which is dominated by Ismailis or the Jabal Duruz, home to the Druze community, or the Wadi al-Jarrah, a small dry river bed north-east of Qahtaniya and exclusive home to six Yezidi villages.

This has been the traditional pattern of settlement in the Middle East, but during the past decades of highlighting nationalism, urbanization, and modernization, this pattern slowly eroded, only to be reinforced during the ongoing civil war. The current situation reveals that now more than ever are groups associated with an ethnic/religious/lifestyle identity find themselves living together and distancing themselves physically and spatially from the others. The ethno-religious map of Syria can thus be easily viewed in light of the segregation of the various ethno-religious identity groups.

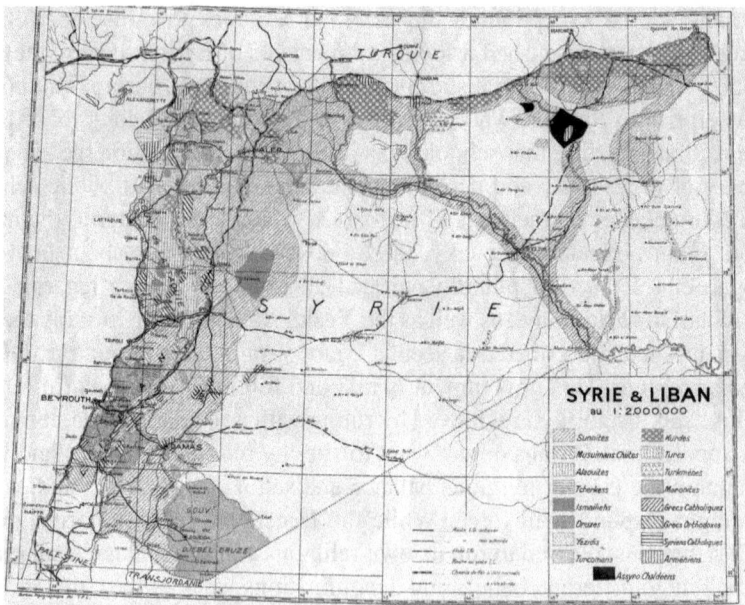

Figure 2.1 Map of the religious and ethnic communities of Syria and Lebanon (1935).
Source: Map prepared by the Bureau of Topographic French troops in the Lebanon. Public domain. http://ifpo.hypotheses.org/2753.

It has become an easy task to identify a village or neighborhood as a Kurdish, Turkmen, Yezidi, or Alawite location because all identity groups are forced to take position in the war. Multiethnic and multireligious towns are less and less recognized. Certainly, this does not apply to the country's large cities, but even within the city limits of Damascus and Aleppo, we can find quarters that are exclusively inhabited by a particular identity group; for example, Rukn al-Din in Damascus or Sheikh Maqsud in Aleppo are both well-known Kurdish neighborhoods. Bab Tuma in Damascus and Syrian al-Jadid in Aleppo are predominant Christian quarters.

As will be shown later, even the tiny minority group of the Yezidis can claim certain villages as 100 percent Yezidi, while they occupy a large section in other, mixed villages. Mixed village should not be understood as living together in one village, but rather living separately in one village, often not even sharing public institutions such as schools, baths, and cemeteries.

2.1. ETHNIC MINORITIES

Classifying people according to a shared ethnicity is a difficult undertaking. Perhaps the best common denominator is a shared language. Arabs for example have a unifying language, although expressed through various dialects. Other factors include a shared history and culture. Most of the twenty-three million Syrians are ethnic Arabs. The majority is even recognized in the country's name when she calls herself the Syrian Arab Republic, placing the Arab community on top of the citizenship hierarchy. The Kurds are thus a second-class ethnicity with roughly 10–15 percent of the population or two to three millions in real numbers. This is a smaller percentage in comparison with the neighboring countries of Iraq and Turkey where Kurds constitute almost 20 percent of the total population. Other smaller ethnic minorities include the Assyrians (400,000), Turkmen (250,000), Circassians (120,000), Armenians (100,000), and some smaller communities of Greeks. The ethnic minorities usually speak their own language, but are fluent in Arabic as well.

2.2. RELIGIOUS MINORITIES

The spectrum of religious groups is even larger than the ethnic one with two main religions and many of their denominations and sects. Islam clearly dominates the religious landscape. The Sunni branch of Islam is the most widely accepted with approximately 75 percent of Syrian Muslims adhering to it. However, let us not forget that the Syrian Muslims are of different ethnic background, mostly Arab, but they are also Kurds, Turkmen, and Circassians. Another noteworthy distinction among Sunni Muslims must be made regarding the application of a particular legal school or *madh'hab*. Among the four main Sunni schools, Hanafi, Shafi'i, Maliki, and Hanbali, Arabs and Turks usually follow the Hanafi interpretation of Shari'a law, while the Kurds prefer the Shafi'i school. On an organizational level, it shows that many Sunni Arabs used to support the Muslim Brotherhood, while among the Sunni Kurds, Sufi orders were more popular.

The remaining quarter of the Muslim population represents followers of the Alawites (about 10 percent of the total population or 2.3 million), the Druzes (ca. 3 percent or 700,000), Ismailis, and Ithna'ashariya or Twelver Shias (less than 1 percent), all of which are, in one form or another, offshoots of Shia Islam. It is very noticeable that each Muslim minority occupies a separate living area, one that is also distant from that of the Sunnis. The Alawites live mostly in the mountain range on the Mediterranean coast, the Druze in the southern Hauran Mountains, the Ismailis in the isolated towns of Salamiya, east of Hamah, and Safita and the Twelver Shias in some remote villages near Idlib.

Christianity in Syria counts for roughly 10 percent of the Syrian population and is represented by more than a dozen denominations, which differ significantly in size from one group to the other. The main division among the Christians in Syria is between the Eastern and the Uniate groups, that is, those Eastern groups that later reunited with the Roman Catholic Church.

The Eastern denominations include the largest and oldest church, the Greek Orthodox Church with some 500,000 followers, the Armenian Apostolic Church with approximately 150,000 as well as the Syrian Orthodox Church with about 90,000. The Uniate denominations include the Greek Catholic (Melkite) Church with approximately 200,000 members, the Syrian Maronite Church with roughly 50,000 followers as well as smaller groups like the Armenian Catholic Church, the Syrian Catholic Church and the Chaldean Catholic Church.

In addition, there is the Assyrian Church of the East which is largely located in north-eastern Syria and claims a different origin and identity. Some 50,000 members follow this rite.[11]

Generally, Christians in Syria were urbanites who were economically better off than Muslims and considered part of the country's elite. They are well represented in the political system and have secured religious rights for their community.

2.3. THE KURDS

Because of their special attribution, Kurds in Syria deserve special attention and should be considered separately. While describing the Syrian ethnic or religious diversity, Kurds are often placed in a separate category.[12] While sharing religious beliefs with the country's Sunni Muslim majority, they are an ethnically different and discriminated minority.

The Kurds in northern Syria are almost exclusively Sunni Muslims (with the notable exception of the Yezidi Kurds of course). They usually follow the Shafi'i legal school, while most Arabs and Turks belong to the Hanafi school. Among the Kurds, Sufism is very prominent both among the rural and the urban communities. The dominant Sufi orders are the Qadiriya, the Naqshbandiya, and the Rifa'iya and their *zawiyas* or lodges are spread all over the Kurdish villages. Often led by a charismatic sheikh, these zawiyas are at the heart of the worship, especially during the annual pilgrimages to the shrines. The shrines are often pre-Islamic sanctuaries, reappropriated by the Sufi order and rededicated to their saints. The shrines and zawiyas thus became a sacred space to discretely articulate a nonconformist identity.[13] Some sheikhs became more prominent across the region, some joined the Kurdish national movement, and some even spoke up for the Yezidis, like Sheikh Murshid Masud Khaznawi, the heir of the most prominent Sufi sheikh family in Syria.

Some scholars consider Yezidism a Sufi order.[14] Considering the obvious evolution of Yezidism as a Sufi brotherhood with similar structures and rituals, it is not surprising to note similar practices among Sunni Muslim Kurds and Yezidi Kurds in the Kurdagh, who even celebrate holidays together and worship at the same shrine. However, ultimately, Yezidism views itself as a non-Islamic religion with some shared beliefs and rituals.

2.4. OTHER MINORITIES

A number of minority groups that are not based on religion or ethnicity are worth mentioning. Classifications may also occur according to lifestyle (urban, rural, nomadic) or political affiliation (political parties other than the Ba'th party). Syria's urbanization rate before the civil war was around 55 percent, that is, with a significant rural population. The country's political and social hierarchy favors urban over rural groups, which is also reflected in the lower standard of living outside the cities.

The political landscape, however, was dominated by the Ba'th party, which allowed for smaller parties without religious or ethnic affiliation, such as nationalist, socialist, and communist parties, to continue working in the National Front. Kurdish political parties, although numerous, were only occasionally tolerated and for the most time suppressed.

The various layers of a person's identity are not exclusive and may become more important than at other times. Thus, the minority categories of urbanization and political activity relate to the Yezidis too, mostly adding to the hardship of being an ethno-religious minority. Most of the Syrian Yezidis live in rural settings and some in the larger cities, but usually not in the center. Regarding the Yezidi political identity, we must recognize the notable absence of a Yezidi political party. Their interests are partly represented by other political organizations, most of which are Kurdish parties.

2.5. DOUBLE MINORITY: THE SYRIAN YEZIDIS

Yezidis are a Kurdish-speaking religious community that mainly lives in northern Iraq. Smaller groups are living in Armenia, Germany, Syria and Georgia.[15] It seems appropriate to estimate the average number of the Yezidis at approximately 450,000 on the basis of Yezidi data (ca. 800,000) and non-Yezidi information, in this case Arab-Muslim sources, which speak of approximately 150,000. The religious center of the community is Lalish in the Sheikhan District west of Mosul in Iraq. There is the temple[16], which holds the mausoleum for the community's reformer Sheikh Adi and resting places of other important Yezidi religious figures. Yezidis travel to Lalish for several occasions, most notably for the fall festival of *Cejna Cumaya*. Ba'adhra, a small town in the vicinity of Lalish, is the residence of the leaders of the Yezidis: supreme leader Mir Tahsin Beg and the religious head, the Baba Sheikh as well as other religious dignitaries.

All Yezidis consider themselves ethnic Kurds.[17] The Yezidis of Syria are one of the smallest groups within the Syrian context of religious and ethnic minorities. Exact population data are unavailable, but it is estimated that the number of Yezidis living in Syria does not exceed 15,000. State and society recognize the Yezidis as Kurds of a different religious belief. Most Kurds of Syria are Sunni Muslims. The small number of Yezidis and subsequently the small size of their community had a negative effect on their position in the Syrian minority context. Similarly detrimental was the split up and division of their traditional settlement areas. Following the arbitrary drawing of political borders after World War I through the administration of the French mandate and territorial swaps between Syria and Turkey, the Yezidis in Syria ended up living in two isolated areas, which furthermore were cut off from the religious centers of the community and from the main settlements in northern Iraq.

2.5.1. The Yezidi communities in Efrin and Kurdagh

One of the two main Yezidi settlements in Syria is located west and northwest of Aleppo in an area that is called Jebel al-Akrad, Kurdagh, Jebel Sim'an, Guma,[18] or Jabal al-Uruba. Today this region is commonly called Efrin Area after the largest city and administrative district. The Yezidis in the Kurdagh live in a predominantly Kurdish-Muslim environment. Along with some Druzes, they are the only religious minority in the area. Since the majority of the population in the Kurdagh is Kurdish, they are not an ethnic minority there.

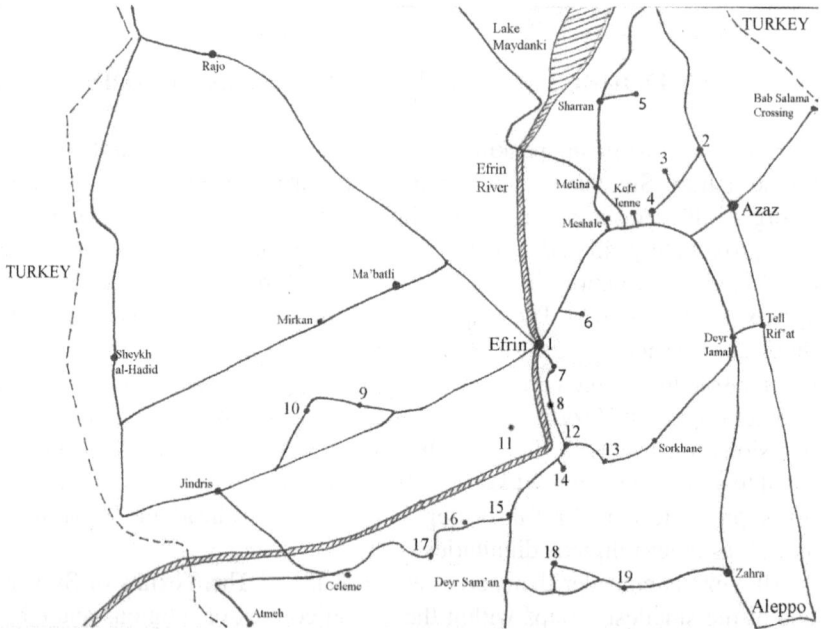

Figure 2.2 Map of Yezidi Villages in the Kurdagh/Efrin Area. *Source*: Map created by author.

The Yezidi villages are spread over the entire region, but are concentrated within three enclaves:[19]

1. The Shikak region includes the following Yezidi villages: Qestel Jindo, Baflun, Qatme, and Sinka.
2. The Guma region with the villages of Feqira, Cheqele Guma, Iskan, Shadere, Ghezewiye, Basuta, Birche Abdalo, Kefer Zeyt, Eyn Dara, Turunde, Qibare, and the city of Efrin.
3. In the Sherew region Yezidis live in the villages of Basufan, Kimar, and Gunde Mezin (Suq al-Kabir).

The Yezidis population in the Kurdagh has been small. In 1939, the Efrin (Kurdagh) region counted 1,143 Yezidis.[20] Table 2.1 lists the known population statistics for the Yezidi villages in the Kurdagh.

Table 2.1 Yezidi Villages in the Kurdagh/Efrin Area

	Kurdish Name/ Arabic Name[1]	Mandate Census, 1927–32	Local Afrin Census, 1941	M. Abdo Ali, 1995[2]	Syrian Population Census, 2004[3]	Civil Registry Afrin, 2005[4]	Gheribo, 2009[5]	MCK, 2013/ 2014[6]
1	Efrin/Afrin				36562	46031		80000[7]
2	Qestel Jindo	361	235	840	645	2094	120	2138
3	Baflun	64		350	172	593	70	602
4	Qatma	228	13	300	1215	5527	70	5749
5	Sinka	187	64	98		2776	35	2818
6	Qibare/al-Hawa	431	313	350	743	6020	70	6144
7	Turunde/al-Zhafira	139	123	120	706	3251	20	3330
8	Eyndara/Ayn Dara	22		70	248	573	20	601
9	Feqira/Ras al-Aswad	216	60	700	275	1666	100	1706
10	Ceqele Guma/Gum	24		70	346	1174	10	1205
11	Kefer Zeyd/ Kafr Zayt	57		35	727	1212	40	1266
12	Basuta	12			2389	4050		4160
13	Kimar	149	157	60	512	2131	10	2214
14	Brice Abdallo/ Burj Abdallah	115	79		1224	1908		1962
15	Ghezewiye/ Ghazawiya	219	161		1413	2086	60	2176
16	Shadere/ Sheykh al-Deyr	111	21	70	714	1259	10	1305
17	Iskan	38	20	70	1116	1757	10	1812
18	Basufan	199	245	910	901	2014	130	2059
19	Gunde Mezin/ Al-Suq al-Kabir	171	68	21		774	5	

[1] The names of many Kurdish villages were Arabized by official decree 2131, 1998.
[2] Muhammad Abdo Ali: al-Diyana al-Izidiya wa'l-Izidiyun fi Shamal Gharb Suria [The Yezidi Religion and the Yezidis in Northwest Syria], Halab: Dar Abd al-Mumin, 2008.
[3] http://www.cbssyr.sy/new web site/General_census/census_2004/NH/TAB02-15-2004.htm
[4] Ibid: pp. 54–65.
[5] Number of Yezidi families living in the village. Fermaz Gharibo: al-Izidiyun fi Suria, al-qism al-thalith, May 16, 2009, http://sherawa.com/kurdax/DIROK/YEZDI-XERIBU.htm
[6] Mausu'a Ciyaye Kurmenc, 2013 and 2014.
[7] http://www.kurdwatch.org/?cid=201&z=ar

In addition, individual Yezidi families were located in the following towns and cities: Ishkan Sharqi, Birch Hayder, Barad, Ba'iya, Ali Iqin, Quqaman, Azaz, and of course Aleppo. Only Basufan, Feqira, and Baflun were entirely Yezidi. In Basufan alone live more than 200 families of the Sheikh Nasredin lineage and thirty-five families of Sheikh Mend lineage, but no laymen or *mirids*. Qibare, Shadere, Ghezewiye, Iskan, and Qestel Jindo had a predominantly Yezidi population. A notable sign of a Yezidi majority in a particular village is the absence of a mosque in the village.

There were an estimated total of 1,000 Yezidi families living in the Kurdagh area. With an average Yezidi (and Kurdish) family usually consisting of seven members, a total number of approximately 7,000 Yezidis in northwestern Syria were estimated prior to the outbreak of the Syrian Revolution and civil war in 2011, which triggered mass migration and displacement of large populations within Syria and outside.

Kinship is an important identity marker, and Yezidi families, like their Kurdish Muslim neighbors in the Kurdagh, are organized along tribal lines and often reside together with their extended families and lineages. Among the important Yezidi tribes are the Dinadi, Reshkan, Dawudiya, Sheriqan, Khaliti, Celka, and Qopani. The first tribe, Dinadiya is split into the following branches: Hesina, Pir Omera, Xidri, Aldexi, Golki, Bolelaniya, Giraviya, Sherkiya, Xasti, Mirazi, Kemzi, Zirari, Mendomeski, and Qanxusi. And they are mirids from Sheikh Shemsani.[21] It should be mentioned that the notion of tribe and tribal cohesion among Yezidis in the Kurdagh area is still prevailing but less distinct than among the Yezidis of the Jezira.

Representatives and active members of all three castes (*mirid, sheikh,* and to a lesser extent *pir*) are found within the Kurdagh community. In order to create a more visual image of life in the Yezidi villages, some prominent towns are introduced in Table 2.1 with additional historical and cultural facts.

The Town of Qatme

Qatme used to be an important location in the Kurdagh during the mandate period. It was a station at the Baghdad Railway connecting Istanbul with Aleppo and in the 1920s turned into the administrative center of the region. Today it belongs to the Shikak district and forms a small canton of Yezidi villages with Sinka, Baflun, and Qestel Jindo. The population used to be around 6,000 people, which recently grew with the influx of refugees from neighboring Azaz and Aleppo. Qatme always had a mixed population of Muslim and Yezidi Kurds as well as a sizable Armenian group. This becomes obvious with the mosque in the town center and a church. Yezidi families, however, have been instrumental in the founding of the town, and later additional families moved to Qatme from the neighboring villages. Today no more than 30 percent of the inhabitants are Yezidis. The town kept its reputation among the various communities in the Kurdagh due to two important shrines, Sheikh Hanan and Pir Ja'far, which are located near the cemetery of Mash'ala on the outskirts of Qatme. These shrines are revered and visited by Yezidis, Muslims, and Druze alike.

The Village of Qibare (Also Arshqibar, Qibar, or al-Hawa)

The village is located in the plains of Guma, slightly elevated at 360m and has a population of approximately 6,000 inhabitants. About half of the families in Qibare are Yezidi families, and historically this has been the seat of the Darwish family, the leading Yezidi family in the area. The name Arshqibar refers to two connected villages, Arsh and Qibar. During the Arabization campaign in the 1970s the village's name was changed to al-Hawa.[22] The area around the village is rich with archaeological remnants of earlier settlements and civilizations as well as a number of caves with ancient structures and inscriptions. Three important Yezidi shrines are located adjacent to the village: the cave of Cilmera, the shrine of Melekadi, and the shrine of Hercerka Sheikh Huseyn.

The Village of Kimar

Kimar is a small village in the Sheraw region of the Efrin province. It is known for its many archaeological remains from Roman and Byzantine times. About hundred years ago it was one of the largest Yezidi villages in the area, but over the years most families converted to Islam with a few exceptions like the Nabo family. In 2004, about one hundred families lived in Kimar with a total of 512 individuals according to the Syrian census. Before the outbreak of the Syrian Revolution, the population had grown to approximately 1,500 people, but recently, the number has grown to over 5,000, most of whom are refugees from Aleppo.

Agriculture was the dominant profession with more importance given to animal husbandry than farming due to the higher altitude of the village. The village has an elementary school where the Yezidi and Muslim children learn together; however, unlike in the rest of the country, the Yezidi children in Kimar do not have attend Islam classes. A shrine called Kofak that was built on the foundations of a Byzantine temple has a cross, a sun, and a peacock inscribed to its gate. Another inscription dates the building back to the year 572. Another historic building is known for its two gates, one to the east and the other to the west, which is interpreted as a sign of a Zoroastrian temple by some Yezidis in the village.

Among the leading families in Kimar are the Khelnebok who used to be Yezidi and only recently, some thirty years ago, converted to Islam. Some of their family members are still Yezidi like the family of Khelil Alo, who himself was considered one of the most reputable men in the village for his support of the poor. He also owned some land in the neighboring village of Kefer Zeyt. There is also the Dali Hesen family, who equally used to be Yezidi, but converted to Islam in the early twentieth century. They are related to the Khelnebok family. Mr. Jamo Shahin "Abu Rif'at" was one of the best known and reputable member of this family, who encouraged his children to seek education, something that was rather uncommon in this otherwise agrarian, traditional society. The Dali Hesen family has other relatives and lands in nearby Birche Abdallo. Finally, there are Necaran and the Hiskan families.

The Village of Sokhanek

The village of Sokhenek is just three kilometers to the east of Kimar. The village has many ancient cisterns and oil presses, which indicates to its economic prosperity of the past. It represents a typical village with a population of Kurdish families who are now Muslim, but used to be Yezidis. They converted to Islam before World War I, but preserved their Yezidi heritage and constantly were looking for ways to reconnect with the Yezidi clergy for a possible return to the faith.[23] The families in Sokhanek belong to the Izoli tribe, and the leading family of the village was the Muhammad Barakat family and in particular the former mukhtar of the village, Hamud bin Huseyn Barakat and his brother al-Hajj Hassan bin Huseyn Barakat. Other members of the Barakat family who live in different villages have not converted to Islam and have remained Yezidis. It should be noted that during the 1980s almost half of the population left for Aleppo, and over the past decade, most of them returned especially after the infrastructure was improved.

The Village of Basufan

As noted earlier, Basufan is one of the few villages in the Kurdagh with a Yezidi only population. Furthermore, these Yezidi families belong to the caste of the clergy, mostly to the sheikh caste. The Sheikh Barakat family is arguably the most influential of those. The last official Syrian population census conducted in 2004 listed 156 families in the village and 909 inhabitants. This number has been changed firstly because of emigration to Germany over the past decade and secondly due to the influx of residents and relatives from other Syrian towns fleeing the conflict zones of the civil war. Basufan was affected by the war, especially by the economic blockade imposed by JN and other radical Muslim militias on the Efrin canton, where Basufan is located very close to the front line. And even the Kurdish YPG militia (*Yekineyen Parastina Gel* or People's Defense Units) extorted so-called security taxes from the inhabitants in return for protecting the village from further terror attacks. They targeted especially those presumably rich families with relatives living in Germany, demanding a tax between 75,000 and 100,000 Syrian Pounds (LS). In August 2013, clashes broke out between YPG and the radical Islamic militias that led to several casualties on both sides and physical damage and destruction due to shelling. As a consequence many villagers left for Efrin.

The village is known for its ancient churches, but it also has a shrine dedicated to Sheikh Ali, which is said to have healing powers. When Gertrude Bell visited the village in 1905, she learned that Basufan was a popular summer retreat for Christian and Jewish families from Aleppo.[24]

Sheikh Ali, a Yezidi elder from the village, explained the origin of the village which according to him was inhabited first by Yezidis from the village of Bazivan, a village in northern Kurdistan inhabited by the Khalti tribe. They were the first to move to Basufan and settle here, and over time the name has slightly changed.[25]

2.5.2. The Yezidi Communities in the Jezira

The Jezira is the second main living area of Yezidis in Syria. Spread around the two administrative centers, Hasake and Qamishli, Yezidi communities are separated in four small enclaves consisting of several dozen villages:

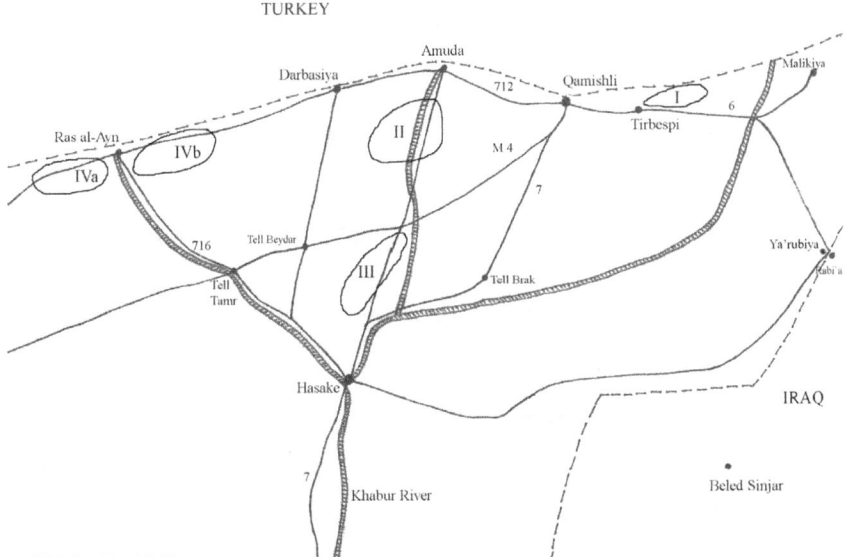

Figure 2.3 Map of Yezidi Villages in the Jezira. *Source*: Map created by author.

I. Wadi al-Jarrah northwest of Qamishli around the city of Tirbespi (also known as Qahtaniye and formerly known as Qubur Beyd) with the villages of Drechik, Mizgeft, Chelhumiye, Gurke Shemo, Tell Khatun, Otelja, and Alaresh.

Table 2.2   Yezidi Villages in the Wadi al-Jarrah (Area I on Map 3)

#	Kurdish Name/ Arabic Name[1]	Syrian Census 2004 Families/ Individuals	Number of Yezidi Families[2]	Tribal Affiliation
1	Tirbespi/Qahtaniya	2476/16946	67/50	
2	Drecik/al-Marj	88/610	24/50	Afshi
3	Mizgeft/Wahran	14/92	4/40	Nimrdani, Shifaqta, Abajani, Mahoka
4	Chelhumiye	21/171	some	
5	Gurke Shemo		some	
6	Tell Khatun	23/140	20/70	Daskan, Bajula, Bahnamniya, Khalta, Taqa, Nimrdani
7	Otelja/al-Thalja	18/111	17/30	Kiwekh, Mahoka
8	Alaresh		16/35	Kafnasa

[1] The names of many Kurdish villages were given Arabic names per official decree 2123, 1998.
[2] Issam Khuri (2006)/Baveniroda (2009)

II. Around the city of Amuda are a dozen villages: Khirbet Khazal, Khirbet Khwe, Tell Hishk, Kulye, Merkeb, Khirbet Feqira, Qislachuk, Gondor, Kerengo, Dogerki, and Chetele.[26]

Table 2.3   Yezidi Villages near Amuda (Area II on Map 3)

#	Kurdish Name/ Arabic Name	Syrian Census 2004 Families/Individuals	Yezidi Families Gharibo/Khuri	Tribal Affiliation
1	Dogerki		10/20	Sharqi, Su'ani
2	Kerengo		4	Su'ani
3	Khirbet Feqir		15	Su'ani
4	Merkeb	35/263	10/22	Su'ani
5	Qizlaçuk/Saradiq	25/183	30/17	Dina
6	Gondor	58/428	5/8	Dina
7	Çetele		10	Dina
8	Tell Ashq	8/62	5/8	Su'ani
9	Qolia/al-Lid	42/291	10	Dina
10	Khirbet Ghazal	25/175	20/77	Dina
11	Khirbet Khwey		10/13	Sheikh
12	Khirbet Jedid			Sheikh

III. North of Hasake with the villages of Khirbet Khidr, Tell Tawil, Slemaniye, Tolko, Zeydiye, Berzan, Jidale, Jdeyde, Tell Teyr, Gumar, Gumar Gharbi, Tell Aswad, Mehmudiye, Antariye, Morik, Nasriye, Khirbet Jamal, Awgira, Hasheri, Mehek, Mozko, Khirbet Dilan, and Bur Said.

Table 2.4 Yezidi Villages near Hasake (Area III on Map 3)

#	Village Name	Syrian Census 2004 Families/ individuals	Yezidi Families Gharibo/Khuri	Tribal Affiliation
1	Tell Tawil		20/16	Dina, Sharqiya
2	Tolko		100/78	Sharqiya
3	Suleymaniya	89/753	100/47	Dina
4	Barzan		100/37	Dina, Khalta
5	Tell (Khirbet) Khidr		4	Su'ani, 1 Sheikh family
6	Khirbat Jamal		4/10	Tozo (Sheikhobakr)
7	Avgira		4/6	Sheikhubakr
8	Heyshari	24/204	9/7	Sharqi, Su'ani
9	Musko		40	Su'ani
10	Mehek		9/9	Su'ani
11	Bur Sa'id		7/8	Su'ani
12	Khirbet Dilan	20/163	9/17	Su'ani, 1 Sheikh family
13	Gari Rash (Tell Aswad)	11/106	15/8	Sheikh
14	Mahmudiya (Tell Zighan)			Dina
15	Khirbet Haso Haji		10	Dina
16	Kocuk		8	Sharqi
17	Morika		/5	Dina
18	Tell Teyr		15/13	Dina
19	Zeydiya	73/563		
20	Gumar		/11	
21	Nasriye			
22	Jidala			
23	Jdeyde			
24	Antariye			

IV. Several villages west and east of the city of Ras al-Ayn/Sere Kaniye along the Khabur River: Asadiye, Tell Sakhar, Tell Beyder, Merekis, Khan Temir, Shukriye, Lizga, Chava, Derdere, Tell Eliye, Abu Jarade, Tell Naif, Khirbet Batana, and Tell Khanzir. In addition, some Yezidi families moved to the urban centers of the region.

Yezidis in the Jezira belong to the tribes of Dasikan, Bahcholan, Kiwekhi, Heverkan, Semoqa, Mihirkan, and Efshani. Many of the large Kurdish tribes, such as the Milli and Heverkan, are, however, multireligious and include Christian, Sunni, and/or Yezidi tribal groups. The number of Yezidis living in the Jezira is estimated around 7,000.[27] Finally, isolated Yezidi families originally from the Jezira can be found in the large Syrian cities of Damascus, Aleppo, Homs, and Hamah.

Table 2.5 Yezidi Villages near Ras al-Ayn/Sere Kaniye (Areas IV a and b on Map 3)

#	Village Name	Syrian Census 2004 Families/Individuals	Yezidi Families Gharibo[1]/Khuri	Tribal affiliation
1	Asadiye	135/1674	/70	
2	Cava		/30	
3	Derdere	76/579	10/10	
4	Tell Sakhr		/50	
5	Tell Beyder	38/245	/15	
6	Khan Tamr	292/2176	35/33	Khalta
7	Mreykis			
8	Shukriye	43/338	15/30	Khalta
9	Tell Khanzir	76/531	15/10	
10	Khirbet Banat		10/20	
11	Abu Jarada	176/1180	/40	
12	Tel Eliye		10	Sharqi
13	Sheikh Hmud		10	Khalta
14	Qizgi		5	Adiya
15	Jdeyda		15	
16	Lizga		/15	

[1] http://www.hekar.net/modules.php?name=News&file=print&sid=2847

Thanks to some French officials, we know how many (or few) Yezidis lived in the eastern part of Syria.[28]

Table 2.6 Yezidi Population in the Jezira during the Mandate and early SAR periods

Year	Inhabitants	Percentage of total population
1939	2150	1.36
1943	1,475	1.01
1949	Some thousand	
1953	1,749	0.75

The Yezidi Forum in Oldenburg, Germany published the results of two door-to-door surveys about the number of Yezidis in the four main regions of eastern Syria. While they counted 12,332 Yezidis in 1990, the number dropped significantly in 2000 with only 4,093 Yezidis left. This decline of 67

Table 2.7 Decline of Yezidi Population in the Jezira

Area	1990 in numbers	1990 in percent (%)	2006 in numbers	2006 in percent (%)	2008 in numbers	2008 in percent (%)
Wadi al-Jarrah	2251	18	490	12	433	13
Amuda	2178	18	792	20	664	20
Hasake	5449	45	1895	46	1641	49
Ras al-Ayn	2354	19	915	22	618	18
Total	12332		4093		3356	

Table 2.8 Decline of Yezidi Population in the Wadi al-Jarrah Area

#	Village Name	Population 1990	Population 2000	Population Decrease
1	Drecik	16	21	87%
2	Tell Khatun	1029	185	82%
3	Otelje	324	125	61%
4	Gurke Shamo	12	0	100%
5	Mizgeft	424	102	76%
6	Shalhumiye	30	0	100%
7	Alaresh	232	57	75%

percent is dramatic and reflects the growing trend to leave and escape from the unbearable situation on the Syrian ground.

In the villages of the Wadi al-Jarrah area, the decrease of Yezidi population due to mass immigration was as shown in Table 2.8.

While these numbers may help to better understand size and demographic developments, it also serves to introduce some of the Yezidi towns and villages in north-eastern Syria:

The Village of Asadiye

Asadiye is a typical Kurdish rural settlement along the main road between Ras al-Ayn and Hasake. The village was named after the former president Hafiz al-Asad in the Arabization process of eradicating the Kurdish heritage. The population of about five hundred people is mostly Yezidi from the Sherqiya tribe. They were farmers, day laborers, and small shop owners. Among the most successful farmers was Ali Sa'du Abu Aydan. Over the past decades many villagers immigrated to Europe, especially to Germany. From there, they supported the families back home with money and other supplies.

Its strategic location on the main traffic artery made the village an important target, and on August 15, 2013, militants from Jabhat al Nusra (JN) attacked the village. The villagers were able to resist until the inhabitants were able to flee. Two Yezidis, among them Ali Sa'du, were killed in the clashes, and the village was looted and destroyed after the terrorists took over.

The Town of Tirbespi

Tirbespi is located some thirty kilometers east of Qamishli. It is the administrative center for a number of Yezidi villages and was founded by Hajo Agha, the leader of the Heverkan tribe that included some Yezidi families during the early 1920s. The Yezidi families settled first in a place called Gurke Shemo, while Hajo and his Muslim followers stayed further south near the campgrounds of the Arab Jwala tribe.

The settlement policy of the French mandate authorities was sectarian driven, and every new village built was given to a particular homogenous religious or ethnic group. Qamishli was the center around which many settlements quickly emerged. But first the French built an outpost in Beyandur near the current location of Tirbespi in 1923, which was to serve as the mandate powers headquarter in the area.[29] In their attempts to take control over the local population, they arrested and killed a local Kurdish tribal leader. Hajo Agha, as the chief of the most dominant tribal group in the area, the Heverkan, joined the retaliation forces (which also included a branch of the Arab Tayy tribe) and attacked the station shortly after. Yezidi scouts helped secure the victory over the (small) French garrison. The names of Abbas Amoka, Ahmad al-Ka'ut, and Ali Bati are still remembered as the leading fighters of this campaign.[30] They succeeded in burning the place down and killing the French officer, but afterward, Hajo and his followers were forced to flee to Turkey. Because of their participation in the Sheikh Said Piran rebellion over there, they had to return in Syria in 1926 and eventually received French pardon.[31] With Hajo came those Yezidi families who were associated with the Heverkan and just recently escaped the massacre at the Bagok Mountain.[32] They then moved to the village of Doger (Dugerki), but after an incident with the Abbas family from the Sinjaqa clan they had to leave again and finally settled in the Tirbespi.

At this time, there were only a few mud houses and Bedouin tents belonging to the Hassan Ajo family from the Jotka tribe. But, Hajo's family started building concrete homes and houses. As the ruling family, they sent members of their families to supervise the nearby villages that belonged to their realm. Jamil Hajo was sent to control and collect taxes in Drechik. Jajan Hajo lived in Mizgeft, Ibrahim Hajo in Otelje, Yusuf Hajo in Diruna Qolonga, Muhammad Sharif Hajo lived in Mashuq, and Huseyn Hassan Hajo in Qatraniya. Another Yezidi village in the Tirbespi region, Tell Khatun, did not belong to the realm of the Hajo family. Instead it was owned by the Qudur Beg family. They all brought along deputies and retainers to extend their control over the entire village. Yezidis were usually not among them. The villages remained under Hajo's control until the departure of the French in 1946.

By then Tirbespi belonged to the Hasake governorate, and in 1965 it was reorganized as a municipality. During the Arabization campaign, the name of the city was changed to *Qubur al-Beyd* (the Arabic translation of the Kurdish Tirbespi) and in 1969 to *Qahtaniye*. Today it belongs to the Qamishli district in the Hasake governorate, and the municipality includes some 140 villages and farms. The city has 25,000 inhabitants, while the entire district counts 120,000 people. About 75 percent of the population is Kurdish. The Arab sector is divided into two groups: those who lived here from early on and those who were relocated to Tirbespi after the flooding of their lands in Aleppo and Raqqa in the 1960s. Some Christian families (Syriac, Assyrian, and Armenian) also live in the town; however, the majority of the Christian population has moved out, either to the city of Qamishli or abroad.

Among the influential tribes and families are the Heverkan, whose tribe includes Muslim, Christian, and Yezidi families. The leading family is the Hajo clan, and their villages stretch to the north of the city. The Sanjaqa are another prominent Kurdish tribe in the city, but their villages are to the west and the south. The leading family comes from the Abbas clan. A third Kurdish force in town is the al-Aliya tribe, settled in the east of the city under the leadership of the al-Mar'i family. There are roughly fifty Yezidi families in Tirbespi who all came from the neighboring villages hoping to find a better life in the city.

The economy of the city is based entirely on agriculture, while jobs at the nearby oilfields are reserved for skilled workers from the Syrian mainland. A spring flood in 1962 killed many inhabitants and livestock and destroyed several homes. It took another twenty years until the Jarrah Dam was built to regulate the flooding and irrigate the fields.

The Intifadah of Tell Khatun was another important event in the history of Tirbespi. On May 15, 1967, the Yezidi villagers resisted military orders to abandon their homes and get relocated in the south of the country. The order was part of the Arab Belt policies, and troops under the leadership of the deputy director Muhsin Ghabra were sent from Qamishli to the village to enforce the decision. The people's resistance was organized by Osman Sabri, the well-known fighter and political leader of the Kurdish Democratic Party in Syria (el-Party).[33]

The Village of Otelje

Otelje is a small Yezidi village in the Wadi al-Jarrah located north of the city of Tirbespi. The village was founded in 1920 by Yezidis fleeing from Turkey who were given permission to build a settlement on the land belonging to the Kurdish Muslim landlord Hajo Agha. The Yezidis belonged to the Kiwexi tribe, but Yezidis from other tribes joined them soon. A tribal elder called Zede founded a cemetery on a nearby hill, the Diyare Feleke, which soon became the main burial ground for Yezidis from the area.

In 1926, the Hajo family fled from Turkey to Syria and was given the authority over the villages in the wadi by the French Mandate authorities. For themselves they built the city of Tirbespi, but they had family members residing in each of their villages, sometimes working as the local *mukhtar* (village elder). For example, Ibrahim Hajo was the appointed mukhtar in Otelje. After the creation of the Syrian Arab Republic, the family was deprived of many of their privileged. However, unlike many of their former residents they were able to obtain Syrian passport and citizenship. As village headmen they were supposed to request the passports for the villagers, but failed to do so. As a consequence, many villagers lost the privileged associated with citizenship and became strangers in their own lands.

The Hajo family left Otelje in 1970 and moved to Tirbespi. Their former residence was transformed into a school for grades one to six. Many families immigrated to Germany which led to a sharp decline in the number of inhabitants. In 2000, only fifteen families remained with mostly older members, who continued small-scale farming and animal husbandry.

The vast majority of Syrian Yezidis still works in the agricultural sector as farmers, pastoralists, or day laborers. Only a few families in the larger cities found work in the service sector. Those families, however, had a different status than the rest of the community because they often lost the bond to their area of origin. In very few cases, they were able to enter public secular institutions such as the military or universities.

Throughout history there were almost no formal contacts between the two Syrian Yezidi communities. Informal and religious relations continued; however, they never reached the level of marital relation. The reason for this is that many conservative and traditional Yezidis of the Jezira considered their brothers in faith as deviators who no longer adhered to orthodox Yezidi doctrine. They accused them of assimilation into the Muslim environment.

However, this claim can hardly be supported. It is true that Yezidis in Efrin are economically in a better situation, and they did find a place in the social hierarchy of society at large. Due to their concentration in big villages, balanced relations between Yezidi and Muslim Kurds prevailed. Both groups lived together in stable conditions for many centuries, which created a status quo of mutual tolerance. Usually, they left each other alone and did not worry about the affairs of the others. In some economic and political issues, mostly related to problems with the authorities, they even cooperated on occasions. With regard to their religious observances, however, the community became known for not adhering to the common Yezidi dogma of endogamy of marriage within one caste.[34] The religious life in Efrin was further affected by the small number of clerics who were able to perform rituals or educate the community.[35]

NOTES

1. Land of Greater Syria.
2. Khouri (2014): 17–19.
3. Not all minorities were included in the millet roster. Alawites, Druze, or Ismailis (all of which were Shia offspring) were still subjugated to Sunni jurisdiction.
4. Selim and Mohamed (2014): 40–43.
5. Pan-Arabism was still more popular among Sunnis than Shias who in both countries, Lebanon and Iraq, were not considered equal Arab citizens. This trend is amplified in the current sectarian strife in which radical Sunnis consider the Shias, although Arabs, the bigger enemy than Christians or Jews.
6. Kumaraswamy (2003): 245–246.
7. Fisk (2007): 335.

8. Ackermann (2001): 10.
9. See Goldsmith (2011): 34–60.
10. See Monique Cardinal, "Religious Education in Syria: Unity and Difference," British Journal of Religious Education, 31, no. 2 (March 2009): 91–101.
11. Syria's beleaguered Christians, BBC.com 25. February 2015, http://www.bbc.com/news/world-middle-east-22270455, accessed June 21, 2016.
12. In Iraq, the ethnic Kurds are considered one of the country's three main populations along with the religious Sunni and Shia groups.
13. For more on the Sufi sheikhs among the Kurds in Northern Syria, see Pinto (2011).
14. See for example Pir Mamo Othman: Die Beziehungen des Sufismus zum Yezidentum. Published at http://www.yeziden.de/beziehungen_sufismus.0.html#top, accessed 8/10/2015.
15. While northern Iraq and Syria are part of the original and indigenous Yezidi homeland, countries like Armenia, Georgia, and recently Germany became centers of emigration for Yezidi communities.
16. The most detailed descriptions about the temple are found in Bachmann (1911) and Acikyildiz (2009).
17. Small, but notable exemptions of this notion are communities in Armenia, who are considered to be ethnic Yezidis(!), and in some areas in Iraq (the twin villages of Bashiqa and Bahzani as well as the Sinjari Yezidis), where Yezidis think of themselves as Arabs and speak Arabic as their native tongue.
18. If possible, Kurdish names of places and people have been transliterated according to their Arabic spelling. However, a standardized transliteration that takes both Kurdish and Arabic into account is still needed.
19. Fieldwork undertaken by the author (1995–2006), Khodeyda Sheikh Khalaf (2004): 19–20.; and Zerdesht Deshti, "Ezdiyen Kurdaxe," PIRS 6/2 (1995): 28–30. Roger Lescot, Enquête sur les Yezidis de Syrie et du Djebel Sindjar (Beyrouth: Libraire du Liban, 1938): 265–268 mentioned the following villages which are predominantly Yezidi: Qestel, Sinkelle, Baflun, Qatme, Erse Qibar, Turunde, Jdede, Basuta, Kimar, Birche Abdalo, Kefr Zet, Karabash, Ghezewiye, Sheikh Khidr, Basufan, Kibeshin, Kefr Shin, Iskan, Gunde Mezin, Bashemra, and Birch el-Qas.
20. Tejel (2007): 39.
21. On the tribal affiliation and character of Yezidi society, see Mark Sykes, "The Kurdish Tribes of the Ottoman Empire," Journal of the Anthropological Institute 38 (1908): 451–486; Lescot, Enquête (1938): 251–268; Ahmad Wasfi Zakariya, 'Asha'ir al-Sham (Damascus, 2007): 657–674; and Joseph (1919): 201–204.
22. Many Kurdish villages had their name changed to an Arabic name. Sometimes this meant only a smaller alteration or literal translation, while in other cases a completely new Arabic name was registered. Aside from Qibare (al-Hawa), this also affected the Yezidi villages of Turunde (al-Zharifa), Birche Abdalo (Burj Abdallah), Sinkarli (Sinka), Feqiran (Tell Aswad), and Ceqele Cum (Cum).
23. Information given to the author who visited the village in 1998 and 2006.
24. Bell (1907): 279–282, 292.
25. Kalo, Lokman Shamo. "Qariya Basufan al-tabi'a li-markaz (Afrin)" lokmanafrin.com; http://www.lokmanafrin.com/images/koora/basofan.htm (accessed June 5, 2016).

26. Qizlachuk, Gondor, and Dogerki are exclusive Yezidi villages; the others have a mixed population.

27. Yezidisches Forum Oldenburg Stellungnahme zu der Situation der Yeziden in Nordostsyrien auf Anfrage des VG Magdeburg, Oldenburg, 2006, 2. According to an official census from 1939, the Jezira had 158,550 inhabitants. Among them were 81,450 Muslim Kurds and 2,150 Yezidis, see Jordie Tejel, "The Terrier Plan and the emergence of a Kurdish policy under the French Mandate in Syria, 1926–1936 (Report)," International Journal of Kurdish Studies 21/1–2 (2007); Jordie Tejel, La mouvement kurde de Turquie en exil: continuites et discontinuities du nationalisme kurde sous le mandat francais en Syrie et au Liban (1925–1946) (Bern, Frankfurt, New York: Peter Lang, 2007). Gave a detailed list of Yezidi communities for the year 1939: "Selon le recensement effectue par les autorités mandataires en 1939, la communauté Yezidi se répartit comme suit: ville de Damas: 2, Caza du Kurd Dagh: 1,135; Caza d'Azaz: 8; Caza d'Hassetche: 123; Caza de Qamishli: 838." (Source: CADN, Fonds Beyrouth, Cabinet Politique, no. 8. "Inscription des Yezidis a l'état civil syrien" (Beyrouth, le 1er Octobre 1940), 1).

28. Hourani (1947): 76; Etienne, de Vaumas, "La Djézireh," Annales de Géographie [French] 65, 347 (1956): 64–80; Maurice Fevret and André Gibert, "La Djezireh syrienne et son réveil économique," Revue de géographie de Lyon [French] 28 (1953): 1–15; Centre des Archives Diplomatiques de Nantes, Fonds Beyrouth, Cabinet Politique, no. 1367, "Repartition de la population de la Haute Djezireh," (Beirut, April 1939); all cited in Tejel (2007): 95.

29. The two other outposts were in Ras al-Ayn and Malikiya, almost 200 kilometers apart from each other.

30. Majallat Roj, vol. 69 (June 2009): 13.

31. Muhammad Khalo: Beyambur—the epic of Kurdish-Arab brotherhood [in Arabic], esyria.sy/ehassakeh from April 21, 2013

32. See Issa's description (2007): 172–174.

33. Majallat Roj, vol. 68 (June 2009): 14.

34. Yezidi society is organized in three nonrelated groups of religious status: primary religious leaders (sheikh), secondary religious leaders (pir), and laymen (mirid). Marriage is allowed only within the group. Many cases of marriages between laymen and clergy are reported from Efrin.

35. During the French Mandate, a Yezidi school existed in 'Arsh Qibar (Qibare), which was financed by the local community and which had a Christian and a Yezidi teacher. The religious instruction was in the hand of a sheikh from Sinjar. The school was open for ten years only. See Roger Lescot, Enquête (1938): 89–90.

Chapter 3

Demystifying Yezidis
A Word About the Sources

The Yezidis have been accused of nearly every possible heretic sin and blasphemous transgression. These ignorant accusations culminate in the alleged descent from the highly unpopular caliph and killer of Husayn bin Ali, Yazid bin Muawiya and more so in the branding of their religion as devil worship. This resulted in general disdain among the community's neighbors and ultimately led to many attacks, sins, and transgressions against them. Misconceptions and stereotypes are hard to beat in a society that lives on the often irrational and ignorant perception of the other. Clarifications are in order, and in the following paragraphs, basic misunderstanding are debunked, once and for all.

3.1. ABOUT THE NAME "YEZIDIS"

Several names describing the community circulate in the sources, websites, publications, and even oral discussions. The name of the community is sometimes spelled Yezidis, Yazidis, Yeziden, Eziden, Ezidis, Jesiden, Ezidyan, Dasinan, Yazdan, just to name a few. Which form is the correct one, or perhaps we should ask whether there is a widely accepted correct version? Of course it depends on who you ask and the debate over the correct spelling of the name is connected with the controversial inner-Yezidi debate over identity. As mentioned earlier, most Yezidis stress their Kurdish origin. Thus, they would use the Kurdish version *Ezidi*; however, since many of them have been exposed to some form of Arabization and many of them are in fact bilingual (and publish in both languages), the *Yazidi* form may be accepted as the translated form from Arabic. On the other hand, this entails the risk of connecting the community with the caliph Yazid bin Muawiya, a connection that is strongly opposed by many, but cherished by others. With increasing opportunities to publish online and in hard print, the Ezidi form started to emerge as the most popular. However, academic scholarship is not known for its speedy and quick response to recent developments. Thus, almost all current scholars of Yezidism continue using the word Yezidi in the same way as many current Yezidi scholars who are writing in languages other than Kurdish or Arabic do.

3.2. WRITTEN SOURCES

Traditional historians rely heavily on written sources and try to create a chronological timeline tracing particular events and calendar dates over a period of time according to the slogan: if you can see it, it must be legitimate. This frantic search for written evidence led to the neglect and disregard of oral sources. But, how can we study largely illiterate societies if not on the basis of their spoken word? This is important more so when the spoken tradition remains the main component in shaping the identity of this society. How legitimate are claims to the origins and heritage of this community when they have no document, inscription, court record, or pottery to prove it? Kreyenbroek rightly pointed out that Yezidi history is topical and memorable, rather than linear or objective.[1] Thus, all periods of history occur in cycles, an approach that goes well along the Yezidi idea of reincarnation. Generally, Yezidi historical accounts differ greatly from Western scholarly accounts, with the former being evident in the scared hymns (qewls) and the latter in written sources of various qualities.

In her 2008 article about the origin and development of Yezidi Studies, Christine Allison commented plainly on the low-quality, sensationalist, and ill-informed nature of the works written by outsiders (non-Yezidis) about the community.[2] And certainly, until the 1990s, the vast majority of accounts about the Yezidis represented common trends of separate discourses, first Muslim heretic studies, Christian proselytizing efforts, Ottoman missions to civilize their citizens, the essentialist ideas of European Orientalists, colonial hegemony, to name a few; however, they largely failed to recognize or even understand Yezidi core issues. For example, the religious efforts to convert Yezidis, but also the egocentric world view of Western historians, administrators, and politicians contributed to cementing an image of the community that is far from reality. However, there is hope especially because Yezidi scholars started writing their own version and Western scholars began collaborating with Yezidi colleagues and informants.

The written historical evidence goes back to the twelfth century when the first written accounts about the Yezidis and their most important historic person, Sheikh Adi bin Musafir, were found.[3] These sources represent the controversial, polarizing debate between insiders and outsiders over the "true" nature of Yezidism. The reason why all of a sudden people became interested in this rather small and obscure group was the accusation of heresy. Famous Muslim historians, geographers, scholars, and travelers are among the popular authors documenting Yezidi history, dogma, and traditions.

The first reference to a community by the name of Yazidiya is found is Shahrastani's Book of Religions and Religious Sects, *Kitab al-Milal wa'l-Nihal*. Shahrastani, who died in 1153 and is a contemporary of Sheikh Adi, mentions the group as a kharijite-ibadi sect with some Yazid bin Unaysa as their founder. Another reference to the group comes in Sam'ani's Book of Pedigrees, *Kitab al-Ansab*. Sam'ani, who died in 1167, traces the origin of the group directly back to Yazid bin Muawiya, the second Umayyad caliph, and describes their settlement area between Hulwan and Sinjar. The former fact helped cementing the misperception of Yezidi descent from the Umayyads.

With the establishment and subsequent consolidation of the Adawiya *tariqa* (brotherhood) during the twelfth and thirteenth centuries in the Hakkari region, the number of references in Muslim sources increases as well. At times they relate simple facts and information, while other authors refer to religious practices and historic events from Lalish, the center of the community, but commonly in a pejorative way.

Among the more famous authors are Yaqut (d. 1229) who mentioned Lalish and the cult around Sheikh Adi in his Dictionary of Places, *Mu'jam al-Buldan*. Even Ibn Athir (d. 1233) talked about the death of Sheikh Adi in his Complete History, *al-Kamil fi'l-Tarikh*. More detailed information can be found in Ibn Khallikan's (d. 1282) biographical dictionary Deaths of Eminent Men and History of the Sons of the Epoch, *Wafayat al-A'yan wa-Anba' Abna' al-Zaman*, for example, an account about the life and works of Sheikh Adi, and the history of the Adawiya.

The decline of the Adawiya around 1260 also saw a reduction in the number of references and copying of past events. A noteworthy exception is the work by Bar Hebreaus (d. 1286), the legendary Syriac bishop and philosopher. As a non-Muslim writer he was not bound to the same zeal to show Yezidi heresy but instead he reported objectively about the community. We own him the important information about the survival of the community after the Mongol invasion. He was also the first to mention Yezidi life in the Jebel Sim'an region in northern Syria.

Shattanawfi (d. 1314), the biographer of the famous Sufi and founder of the Qadiriya tariqa, Abd al-Qadir al-Gilani, reported in his book The Splendor of Mysteries And Minerals of Lights, *Bahjat al-Asrar waa ma'adin al-Anwar*, many interesting biographic anecdotes about Sheikh Adi, the close friend of Gilani, like the miracles he performed and his complete name. In contrast to the praise of Sheikh Adi are the fatwas by Ibn Taymiya, who explicitly warns in his Rasa'il al-Adawiya (Letters to the Adawiya) of the extreme ideas of this heretic sect. The life of Sheikh Adi is also mentioned in Dhahabi's Short History of Islam, an entry that is later copied by Kutubi. The entry in Maqrizi's book is merely a copy of Ibn Khaliqan's account. And so is the chapter in Abd al-Rahman al-Gami's collection of Sufi biographies. Nothing new has been transmitted because there was nothing new to report. The community disappeared from the radar for almost two hundred years.

The next time further information about the community is found is in a local Kurdish chronicle, Sharafname, written by Sharaf al-Din Khan, the Emir of Bitlis, in 1597. He describes in detail the affairs of the Kurds and their tribes and includes the Yezidis as well. He introduces the seven largest Yezidi tribes and comments on their history, numbers, and distribution in the region. Equally meaningful is the travel account by Evliya Celebi, who visited the Yezidis in Sinjar and recorded his observation in his Seyahatname, Book of Travels. Both accounts have in common one factor: they describe the Yezidis as an exotic, strange group of people, and not as those who are original, indigenous, or even common.

This trend continued when a new episode in the examination of the Yezidis started in the middle of the seventeenth century, when for the first time European scholars, here French clerics, engaged with the Yezidi community near Aleppo. Although the religious component of this engagement was more important than the scientific, from now on news about the Yezidis was brought to Europe. As a result the first book about the Yezidis was published in Rome 1674. It was supplemented by the accounts of the French consul in Aleppo, J. Dupont. Sheikh Adi and Tawsi Melek were both identified correctly and further details about the number and distribution of the community in the region transmitted, and all of this without mentioning the Islamic sources! Thus, a new image was created, one free of its Muslim heretic connotations, but one that now favored a possible conversion to a Christian denomination.

It took another 150 years until the Yezidis returned to scholarly focus. This was triggered by the massacres against Christians and Yezidis during the first half of the nineteenth century in Kurdistan and surrounding areas committed by independent Muslim Kurdish emirates with tactical support of the Sublime Porte. The massacres against the Yezidis were partly justified by the writings of Muhammad al-Umari (d. 1788), who in his book Lives of the Saints, *Manhal al-Awliya*, vehemently lashed out against them and instigated the riots.[4] However, the discontent of Muslim authorities also stemmed from the missionizing activities of the Anglican and Protestant churches in the area. While they were busy converting Nestorians and Chaldeans, they collected information about the Yezidis, and their accounts proofed to be a rich illustration of Yezidi affairs.

So was the report of the British exploration of the Euphrates. The expedition corps included William Ainsworth and Christian Rassam, two prominent scholars and supports of the Yezidis in the nineteenth century.[5] With colonialism slowly but surely creeping into the Ottoman hinterland, British, French, and Russian consulates were established throughout the region and the stream of news and information about the Yezidis would never run dry. Missionaries like Asahel Grant and George Percy Badger, adventurers and scholars like August Layard and Paul Botta, and politicians like Nicolas Siouffi and Yuri Kartshow developed excellent rapport with the Yezidi communities in Sinjar and Sheikhan. And by the 1850s "discoveries" about the secret Yezidi cult, rituals, and orgies and about alleged devil worship multiplied. Certainly, not all of them were lurid, some contained solid scholarship and sharp observations. Especially the works by August Layard, the explorer and excavator of Nineveh, shaped the image of the Yezidis in the European public eyes of the nineteenth century. This was especially true for the German position where the popular writer Karl May copied Layard's text for his hugely successful book *Through Wild Kurdistan*. His description of the Yezidis has influenced the perception of generations of Germans.[6]

3.3. THE YEZIDI HOLY BOOKS

Nowhere becomes the contrast in interpreting history more obvious than in the case of the Yezidi holy books. The Western view of systemic religious history clashes with the often incoherent indigenous view and out of this clash emerges a theory or discussion that seems completely disconnected from the realities of religious life. While the West celebrated the discovery of the Yezidi scripture as a milestone for the scholarly debate over the alleged Yezidi belonging to the People of the Book, for most Yezidis this meant virtually nothing since all of their religious knowledge was transmitted orally. However, the fact is that two books, the *Kitab al-Jilwe* or *Book of Revelation* and the *Meshef Resh* or *Black Book*, appeared with some versions even written with a secret alphabet (!), and Western scholars with their orientalist fascination for the obscure and exotic jumped on the opportunity and translated, edited, interpreted, and analyzed the books and other manuscripts of equal obscure origin. Among those enthusiasts were first-class orientalists like Eduard Sachau, Carl Brockelmann, and Hugo Makas. The sudden appearance of these books seemed however suspicious, because within a short span four similar documents were published by different people. All had originated from Christian informants who claimed to have obtained the manuscript from the original Yezidi authors. Only Per Anastase received his text from a Yezidi who himself was described as some sort of an outcast.[7]

The subsequent publicity of the books made some Yezidis question their side of the story. It was tempting to thinking about the possibility to be part of the People of the Book and not to endure further discrimination. However, since the information about the books and their content was restricted to a few, educated Yezidis, the idea never gained any ground among the majority. The Yezidi masses remained illiterate, and under the spiritual influence of their clergy forgot about the sacred books. Other events, however, had a larger impact on them, and with the outbreak of World War I, the interest of European scholarship in the Yezidis was disrupted.

3.4. RECENT STUDIES

The end of the war was also the end of an era. The collapse of the Ottoman Empire, the rise of nationalism, and the creation of nation-states required a strong, well-articulated, and unified position from local groups hoping to accomplish their agendas. The new world order in the Middle East, however, did not favor the Kurds or Yezidis who were lacking this powerful voice and political vision. Instead new masters took control of Yezidi territories and with them came a new type of investigator, the administrator-scholar. Interestingly, many of those focused again on the Islamic origin of the community especially after the Sufi Sheikh Adi bin Musafir was identified historically as the founder of the community. Authors such as Lescot in Syria and Edmonds in Iraq studied the community and traveled extensively among them. However, their works still shows the typical marks of the Orientalist's and colonialist's approach. And the time when oral narratives would be considered authentic primary sources in historical studies has not arrived yet. Allison (2008) used a line from Lescot's account as a title for her analysis: "unbelievable slowness of mind." She summarized the common understanding of Yezidism during that time: "an un-Islamic Islamic faith, a descripturalized scriptural religion, a belief system incomprehensible to its own believers."[8]

Inversely, the political transformation in the Middle East brought along social change as well. Yezidis started to become more educated, and more nonelite members explored aspects of their history, religion, and identity. In the late 1970s in Armenia, the Celil brothers published oral traditions, as did Pir Khidr Sileman and Sheikh Khalil Jindi in Iraq. They represented a new generation of indigenous Yezidi scholarship that focused on Yezidi world-views and belief systems that were mostly the opposite of Western concepts.

Kreyenbroek (2008) distinguished between the two by describing the Western view as being based on provable facts and being linear and highly time-oriented, while the Yezidi view was topical and memorable.[9] And finally, towards the end of the last century, Yezidis began sharing their side of the story with the outside world. For one, the image of the secret cult has been replaced with that of an ancient, original religion. Some go ever further, calling Yezidism the original Kurdish religion, while others in their attempts to politically own the religion declare them Ummayyads or Zoroastrians.

It has become common practice to regard oral accounts, such as poems, psalms, hymns, legends, myth, folklorist stories, and life stories as equally important sources to study history, anthropology, and even psychology. While Yezidi religious and historic knowledge has been transmitted orally for centuries, the past decades saw a move towards formalization and canonization of this knowledge and both Yezidi and non-Yezidi scholars have contributed to the collecting, recording, transcribing, and analyzing of the oral narratives. Specialists from other disciplines, historians, anthropologists, and linguists collaborate with Yezidi scholars and conduct empiric research and field work mixing the outside with the local discourse.

This new attitude was sanctioned by Mir Tahsin Beg, who encouraged all to participate in this movement.[10] This indicates a shift in the perception of Yezidis Studies, which no longer are considered a Western or Muslim dominated discipline, but a vibrant and open scene that contributes to the process of formulating a new Yezidi theology.

What follows is a review of recent milestones, publications from the past twenty years, which were based on this approach and represent the small, but successful, team of scholars in Yezidis Studies.

John Guest was the first to bring the topic of the Yezidis to a Western audience. In his book *Survival among the Kurds: A History of the Yezidis* (Routledge, 1993), he traces the origin of Yezidi religion, describes the discovery of the people by Western travelers in the early nineteenth century, and details the Yezidi community's traumatic recent history and its present status. An epilogue reviews the present status of the Yezidi community, with the last chapter focusing on how the Yezidis are faring in the post-Communist Armenia in 1992.

Arguably, the most credible Western scholar about Yezidism is Philip Kreyenbroek, professor of Iranian Studies at Göttingen University. He made the studies of Yezidi theology and oral history a recognized academic subject and laid the groundwork for the exegesis of Yezidi religion in his book *Yezidism – Its Background, Observances, and Textual Tradition* (Edwin Mellen Press, 1995). During the late twentieth century, a corpus of Yezidi sacred hymns has come to light, which had previously been transmitted orally, and did not exist in written form until the late 1970s. These texts have offered a more detailed insight into the beliefs, observances, and background of the faith. The first half of Kreyenbroek' book reexamines the findings of earlier works on Yezidism in light of the author's fieldwork with the Yezidi community of northern Iraq and of insights into the history of the religions of Iranian peoples. The second part consists of text and translations of nineteen Yezidi hymns, with a commentary on points of philological and theological interest. Kreyenbroek teamed up with the notable Yezidi scholar Khalil Rashow (Jindi) for the edition of more religious texts in the book *God and Sheikh Adi are perfect – Sacred poem and religious narratives from the Yezidi tradition* (Harrassowitz, 2005). The authors continue their analysis of oral history and poetry from Yezidi tradition. They focus on structure, function, and form of the poem and provide the transcription and translation of over fifty poems, hymns, and prayers.

Another milestone in the study of Yezidi religious texts was Christine Allison's book *The Yezidi Oral Tradition in Iraqi Kurdistan* (Curzon Press, 2001). Yezidi heartland, where Lalish Temple, the Yezidis' holiest shrine, is located, is in the Badinan province of northern Iraq, and it is the communities in this area that are the main focus of this book. Allison listened to and interpreted Yezidi oral traditions, such as battle songs, and poems about love, loss, and grief. Part two of the book provides the Kurdish texts and translations. This topic was further discussed and intertwined with historic methods in Eszter Spät's rich account *Late Antique Motifs in Yezidi Oral Tradition* (Gorgias, 2010) tracing ancient religious themes in Yezidi mythology and lure.

A recent study that deals with the Yezidi community's religious practices and material and architectural culture is the book *The Yezidis – The History of a Community, Culture and Religion* (I.B. Tauris, 2010) by Birgul Acikyildiz. The book allows for interdisciplinary comparisons across political borders and historical time periods. The author attempts to answer basic and general questions on the belief system, and religious art and architecture.

Two important regional studies of Yezidi communities include Nelida Fuccaro's book *The Other Kurds: Yazidis in Colonial Iraq* (I.B. Tauris, 1999), where she offers an account—from the Kurdish perspective—of the complex Yezidi tribal society under the British Mandate in Iraq, when the Yezidis resisted integration into modern Iraq and failed to identify with the aspirations of mainstream Kurdish society and the rising Kurdish movement.

With a team of young Yezidi scholars published *Yezidism in Europe: Different Generation speak about their religion* (Harrassowitz, 2009), the first study about Yezidism in the diaspora. From the 1960s onward, an increasing number of Yezidis from Turkey, Iraq, and Syria were forced to migrate to Western Europe. After the fall of the Soviet Union, many Yezidis from Armenia and Georgia moved to Russia and the Ukraine. This work addresses the question of differences in perception of the religion between Yezidi migrants who grew up in the homeland and those who were mainly socialized in the diaspora. It is based on extensive qualitative research among Yezidis of different generations in Germany and Russia.

Several Yezidi groups and associations have started publishing their own journals, books, and online sources. The Lalish Center in Dohuk is the leading

Table 3.1 Journals published by Markaz Lalish and their local affiliation

Name of Village	Name of Journal
Bashiqa (Bashik)	Bashik Lalish
Barzan	Nur Lalish
Barbani and Binkindi	Zamzam Lalish
Sinuni (Sinjar)	Shengal Lalish
Sharia	Qebbagh
	Diwan Lalish
Sheikhan	Jaraye Lalish

organization in this field running a network of local branches in the main Iraqi settlements and regularly publishing journals and newsletters. The main branch is located in Dohuk and in charge of publishing *Lalish* journal, the oldest and most distinguished product currently in its 39th issue. The editor-in-chief is the well-known Yezidi expert and scholar Pir Khidr Sileman. They also publish the weekly *Denge Lalish* which currently had its 336th number issued. Other local branches of the Lalish Center and their irregularly published journals include those shown in Table 3.1. A more detailed bibliography, which also contains a number of articles and essays, can be found at the end of this book.

3.5. THE QEWLS

Yezidi religious meanings, dogmas, and beliefs were transmitted orally for centuries usually by trained religious men, called the qewals, who memorized the texts, psalms, hymns, and prayers and, accompanied by musical performances, recited them to laymen on various occasions. Other clerics from the Sheikh and Pir group know selected verses too, which are required to be recited at birth, baptism, weddings, or funerals. These sacred texts are referred to as sacred poems (*qewl*); prayers (*di'a* or *niza*), legends (*me'na*), or hymns (*beyt*), and they are considered the primary source of doctrinal and ritual references and the theological foundation on which Yezidism is built upon. *Me îman ji Qewl e*: Our faith comes from the sacred poems, is a common saying. It is widely believed that Sheikh Adi wrote many of the qewls; however, some seem to be of an older period while others were composed by later generations.

Written in an archaic language, some in Kurdish and others in Arabic, and coated with layers of inner meaning, the qewls are extremely difficult for laymen to understand; however, over the past two or three decades, a process to textualize, translate, and interpret them has been initiated with the help of both clergy and interested laymen. The first studies were published by two Iraqi Yezidis, Pir Khidr Sileman and Sheikh Khalil Jindi, and concurrently by the Celil brothers in Armenia.[11] Kreyenbroek based his analysis of Yezidism heavily on qewls that he collected or obtained from other sources.[12] And finally, in their seminal work, Kreyenbroek teamed up with Sheikh Khalil to discuss the genesis, evolution, and current state of Yezidism on the basis of the sacred poems.[13]

The qewls are believed to have a divine origin and were usually attributed to some of the legendary Yezidi forefathers, such as Sheikh Fekhre Adiyan, Derwish Qatan, or Abu Bakr Jezira.[14] Many go back to Sheikh Adi or his descendants. Reciting the qewls is an artistic skill that must be developed through a lot of training. Those who have mastered the art of reciting the qewls are called "qewal," and it is their responsibility to visit each Yezidi community and teach and interpret their meaning to the mirids or laymen. Historically, the qewals stemmed from the twin villages of Bahzani and Bashiqa in Iraq, and while this profession seemed to disappear, recently a school for studying the qewls has been opened in Bashiqa.

NOTES

1. Kreyenbroek (2008): 85.
2. Christine Allison, "Unbelievable Slowness of Mind: Yezidi Studies from Nineteenth to Twenty-First Century," *The Journal of Kurdish Studies* 6 (2008): 1–23.
3. Frank, 1911: 44–46
4. Siouffi dissected the work for its content on the Yezidis. See Siouffi, *Journal Asiatique*, series 8, vol. 5 (1885): 78–98.
5. Guest 1992
6. See Bach 2010
7. Guest (1987): 141–158 masterfully described the academic battle between the various discoverers and their informants.
8. Allison (2008): 13.
9. Kreyenbroek (2008): 85.
10. In an interview with Denge Ezidiya, a Yezidi periodical published in Germany, the Mir called to collect the sacred text. (Denge Ezidiya, 1997: 6–7).
11. K. Sileman and K. Jindy, *Ezdiyati, Baghdad, 1979*; O. Celil and C. Celil, *Zargotina Kurda, Yerevan*, 1978.
12. Philip G. Kreyenbroek, *Yezidism—Its Background, Observances, and Textual Tradition* (New York: Edwin Mellen Pr, 1995).
13. Philip G. Kreyenbroek and K. Jindy Rashow, *God and Sheikh Adi are Perfect: Sacred Poems and Religious Narrative from the Yezidi Tradition* (Wiesbaden: Harrassowitz, 2005).
14. For more on the role and importance of the legends and psalms, see Omerkhali (2009–2010): 199–202.

Chapter 4

Religious Beliefs

4.1. THE ORTHODOX BELIEF SYSTEM

4.1.1. Origins and the Creation Story

Yezidism is an ancient belief system with a unique and distinct genesis and divine pantheon. The creation of the world is attributed to God who lived inside a pearl. When he manifested himself as the Light, the pearl became separated. Angels existed as well and played an important role in the following stages of Yezidi evolution. After the pearl exploded, water appeared, day and night were recognized, and so were sun and moon.

The Yezidi story of the creation of mankind is equally unique and a very distinct component of Yezidi identity. Unlike other religions from the region, who describe the creation of Adam and Eve and their offspring, in Yezidism, the story highlights Adam's role in the creation of man. He and Eve argued over the right of parenthood for their children, and they decided to test who was right. They placed their seeds (or sweat) in two jars, sealed them, and waited for nine months before they opened them. When they opened them, Eve's jar had only worms in it, while from Adam's jar, a beautiful young boy emerged. This boy later married a Huri (companions in the hereafter), and their offspring were the Yezidis. As for the other children of Adam and Eve, they were considered the forefathers of the rest of humanity.[1] This exclusive birthright makes the Yezidis a special group of people and inheritors of the true religion. It also explains the strict endogamic marriage rules that forbid marital relations with non-Yezidis. As we now know, non-Yezidis are "less pure" and only the Yezidis are the "chosen people."

4.1.2. God

Yezidis believe in the existence of a super-divine power, the truth of the universe or God, in Kurdish called *khwede*.[2] God is the one spiritual creator of Yezidism and the Yezidi world. However, unlike God in the Abrahamic religions, he is rather vague and passive; and after creating the world and the humans, he is largely recognized by his manifestations: Tawsi Melek, Sheikh Adi, and Sultan Ezid. Ultimately, God became impartial and removed.[3]

4.1.3. Tawsi Melek

The most important manifestations of God come in the form of a triad, and Tawsi Melek or the Peacock Angel is the leader of the three. For many he symbolizes the faith and the community because no other religious group in the region has a similar figure. At the same time, Tawsi Melek and his subsequent association with the devil[4] is also the reason why others call the Yezidis devil worshipers, a baseless accusation that led to much suffering of the community and to their brandishing as heretics.

Tawsi Melek is best described as an angel, in fact the leader of a group of seven angels.[5] God passed on to him authority over the angels, the earth, and the humans. For many non-Yezidis, Muslims, Sufis, and Western scholars, Tawsi Melek also resembles the fallen angel, disobedient to the will of God commanding him to worship Adam. But, Yezidism as a syncretistic religion combines some attributes and narratives from other religions. And so the story of the fallen angel does exist in Yezidi lore; however with a distinct twist and explanation: When Tawsi Melek refused to bow in front of Adam, God punished him and sent him to hell. There, Tawsi Melek repented and wept for 40,000 years and eventually extinguished hell fire with his tears. Thus, God reinstated him and abolished hell. Yezidism does not know a source of eternal evil or punishment in hell.

4.1.4. Sheikh Adi

Sheikh Adi maintains a central position within the Yezidi dogma; however, his life and legacy are part of a controversial debate even among Yezidi scholars and clerics. For some, he represents an incarnation of Tawsi Melek who came to the Yezidis to reform the faith and society. For others, he was enlightened by Tawsi Melek, but remained a human. And then there are those who maintain that Sheikh Adi was a Sufi sheikh, a historical figure with a background in Sunni Islam, who may have descended from the Umayyads.

It is agreed that Sheikh Adi was born around 1075 in the Beqaa valley in a village called Beyt Far (present-day Khirbet Qanafir) and that his father and

Religious Beliefs 45

Figure 4.1 Sheikh Adi Shrine in Beyt Far, Lebanon. Photo by author.

grandfather were well-known Sufis in the area.⁶ Figure 4.1 is a recent photo taken by the author of the shrine.

The young Adi later went to Baghdad for studying under the famous Sufi teachers Abd al-Qadir al-Gilani and Ahmad al-Ghazzali. Gilani supposedly sent him to Mosul and the Hakkari Plains to proselytize among the Kurdish tribes known for their practice of sun worship.⁷

Sheikh Adi performed miracles and established a group of followers and disciples around him. Some noticed similarities with other Sufi orders and thus concluded that the Adawiya was exactly that, another Sufi order. Others claimed that he instead founded a new religious movement that was based on the local principles of sun worship and his Sufi doctrine. Regardless, his message was quite successful and caught the attention of other Muslim scholars and sheikhs. They came to visit and test him, but Sheikh Adi was able to convince them that his works were genuinely pure and pious and they left him alone.⁸ Political adversaries, here mostly the Atabegs of Mosul and the Mongols, however, felt threatened by the rise of the Adawiya movement and after Sheikh Adi's death around 1160 started to close in on the group and attacked their centers and leadership.

Genealogy of Sheikh Adi

His full name is given as Sharaf ad-Din Abu l-Fadail Adi bin Musafir bin Ismail bin Musa bin Marwan bin al-Hassan bin Marwan.⁹

Since Sheikh Adi did not have any children, the leadership of the Adawiya was given to the son of his brother Sakhr (who also came from Beyt Far). His lineage of descent looks as follows:

Sheikh Adi died in 1162 in Lalish.

His nephew Sakhr bin Sakhr Abu'l-Barakat

His son Adi bin Sakhr, executed in 1221 by the Mongols

His son Hassan bin Adi was executed by the Mongols in 1254

His son Sharaf al-Din bin Hassan died in battle against the Mongols in 1258.

His other son Fakhr al-Din bin Hassan left for Ayubid Egypt in 1276.

His other son, Shams al-Din bin Hassan, revolted against him, but was defeated and fled to Syria.

It is believed that after the Mongols crushed the Adawiya they split into two branches. The Syrian branch maintained the Islamic-Sufi tradition, while the group that survived and remained in Lalish preserved the syncretistic and more indigenous character of Sheikh Adi's original movement.

Among the changes Sheikh Adi initiated among the local Kurds was the social system of *Sed u Hed*, or confinement, the unique Yezidi caste system. By looking at Sheikh Adi from this angle, it becomes irrelevant whether he was a Muslim, Sufi or Yezidi. Because of his accomplishments and merits for reforming Yezidism, he was largely accepted as the pillar of the doctrine and the veneration for him became part of Yezidi identity. Ortac (2005) convincingly describes that there is no need to question or doubt his authority, leaving the debate over this rather meaningless side note to the scholars. He also reminds us of the debate over the acceptance of oral and written sources, and that the debate over Sheikh Adi's origin is based on two opposite and fundamentally different worldviews: the view of the Muslim historian that is based on written sources and the Yezidi view that depends on oral narratives, myths, and legends.[10] According to my observations from among Yezidi and non-Yezidi stakeholders in the debate, it seems that the issue of his origin is clearly secondary; however, it remains a popular topic and is favored among the scholars because the other primary issue, the caste system, is even more controversial and is less likely to reach a consensus.

4.2. THE CASTE SYSTEM

Yezidi society is a representing and endogamic form of social organization, one that does not actively recruit new members, discourages conversion, and strictly regulates domestic matters of interaction. Yezidism is inherited by birth, and every member has a fixed position within society. The general division of society is between clerics and laymen, mirid, whereas the clerics further divide into two castes: sheikh and pir. No mobility or marital relations between the castes exist. As early as the twelfth century, during the times of Sheikh Adi, the caste system of sed-u hed is officially recognized, although the caste of the Pirs existed already in the pre-Sheikh Adi period.

The division of the community in clerics and laymen is not unique, but can be found among other equally heterodox religious groups in the region, such as the Sufis, Alawites, Alevis, and the Druzes. Yezidi castes are, however, very static and do not allow for any mobility or marriage among them. In fact, the strict endogamic marriage rules are considered a distinct feature of Yezidism. Some argue that these rules helped the community to survive in a sea of religious intolerance, especially in light of constant Muslim pressure for conversion, while others blame the low and vulnerable status of the community on the harsh and inflexible application of ancient marriage rules.

Membership or belonging to a particular caste is predefined by birth and includes both men and women. Upon death of a pir or sheikh, the disciples are divided among his descendants. Omarkhali estimates that between 6 and 7 percent of the Yezidis belong to the cleric caste and the remaining are mirid.[11] While the service is hereditary and requires no formal training, many present-day sheikhs and pirs have a little more religious knowledge than their mirids and restrict the interaction to the observation of a few rituals and the collection of the fees.

4.2.1. The Laymen or Mirid

Most of the Yezidis are mirids, that is, those not initiated into the religious discourse nor involved in the religious leadership. In the past when the vast majority of Yezidis were illiterate, it had little consequences for them; however, with the gradual increase in education and political and spiritual self-awareness, mirids started to question age-old hierarchies. According to them, this is what was left for a mirid in terms of religious interaction: attending ceremonies during the various rites of passage (birth, baptism, circumcision, marriage, death) and celebrating the different religious holidays during the Yezid festival calendar.

Every mirid family is associated with a sheikh family and a pir family. In return for the religious mentoring, the mirids pay the clerics annual fees, *feto*, which today are of more symbolic nature. In addition to the sheikh and pir, every mirid has a special relation with a brother or sister in the hereafter and a godfather. Although less formal than the sheikh and pir relationship, these connections also do not allow marital relations between the families.

To say that the mirids are the lowest caste is misleading, because even the sheikhs and pirs must have their own mentors, that is, a sheikh needs to have a pir and a pir must have a sheikh. Even the Mir and the other high-ranking religious leaders are not exempt from this rule and they must obey the rules and restrictions like other mirids too. Issa maintains that in effect all Yezidis are mirids regardless to which caste they belong. As such, they form the backbone of Yezidi society and religion.[12]

4.2.2. The Pirs

The caste of the pirs is seemingly the oldest group of Yezidi clerics dating back to the period before Sheikh Adi. Back then, they were the sole religious leaders of the community. After the reforms initiated by Sheikh Adi, they had to share religious and political power with the sheikh caste. However, they still constitute an important cornerstone in the social and religious structure of the community.

The Kurdish word *pir* translates into a wise, old man. As such they provide mostly spiritual guidance. In addition, they have to be present at various religious and social functions for which they receive compensation from their disciples. These disciples include families from the sheikh caste; for example, the pir clan of Hasan Meman was the mentor of the Sheshims sheikh clan. Pir Afat was associated with Sheikhisn and Pir Cerwan with Sheikhobakr.

The pir caste is divided into four main clans with some forty families who can marry only within their own clan. These clans include the Hasan Meman, Pir Afat, Pir Cerwan, and Pir Haci Ali. Although the smallest in numbers, the clan of Pir Hasan Meman is considered to be the leading pir clan. The marital restrictions mean that a man finds it extremely difficult to find a suitable spouse.

4.2.3. The Sheikhs

The counterpart for the pir caste is played by the sheikhs. The Arabic word *sheikh* also translates into a wise, old man. The caste was introduced by Sheikh Adi and since then has gained the spiritual and religious leadership of the Yezidi community. For example, the families of the Mir and the Baba Sheikh both belong to the sheikh group. The duties of the sheikh are very similar to those of the pir: spiritually guiding their disciples, performing religious practices (baptisms, marriages, and funerals), visitations during religious holidays etc. Occasionally, the sheikh has to act as a mediator in case of conflict between his mirid families, and he also advises them in mundane matters of their life.

The names of the sheikh clans derive from the Arabic names of compatriots of Sheikh Adi. In contrast, the pir clans descended from Kurdish ancestors. The Sheikh caste divides into three clans: Adani, Qatani, and Shemsani. Because of the rivalry between the three clans, it is important here to mention their subclans or important families. The Adani sheikhs descended from Sheikh Hassan, the Qatani sheikhs from the four brothers of Sheikh Adi (Sheikhobakr, Sheikh Abdelqader, Sheikh Ismail, and Sheikh Abdelaziz), and the Shemsani sheikhs from the four sons of Ezdina Mir (Shemsadin, Fakhredin, Sijadin, and Nasredin). The Mir hails from the Qatani clan, while the Baba Sheikh usually comes from the Fakhredin clan. Other high-ranking religious leaders represent other sheikh clans; for example, the Sheikh el-Wezir is a Shemsani sheikh.

4.2.4. Other religious functions and titles

The Mir

For most Yezidis, including some of the Syrian Yezidis, the Mir of Sheikhan represents the highest political and religious authority. As a member of the Qatani Sheikh family, he is the legitimate successor of Sheikh Adi and sees himself as the head of all Yezidis. His influence certainly reaches the nearby communities; however, the further we move away from the center the more his power decreases. Often, the communities in Armenia, Georgia, and Syria are too distant and disconnected for the Mir to play a significant role in their daily life. While the Iraqi communities of Sheikhan and Sinjar are large and cohesive, in the periphery these isolated groups and villages have to find other forms of both secular and religious representation.

In theory, and more so in the diaspora, the Mir represents all Yezidis. He has legislative and executive powers and his decisions are binding. As the head of the spiritual council he appoints the Baba Sheikh, administers Lalish, and receives the offerings from the annual journey of the sacred objects, *sinjaq,* among the Yezidi communities. He and his family also wield some influence over Iraqi politics. For the Syrian Yezidis he is merely a distant religious figurehead who has little influence over the decision-making process in the Kurdagh or the Jezira. This is not to say that he did not try to extend his power over those communities. During the French Mandate, Mir Said sent official letters of approval and appointing the leaders of the Yezidi community in Kurdagh, Darwish Shamo, and later to his son Jamil Darwish.

The present Mir is Tahsin Said Beg, and he is in office for decades, since 1944, when his grandmother Mayan Khatun handpicked him from among his siblings. Over time, his authority was challenged by members from the junior branches of the Mir's family. But especially during the recent attacks and challenges, Mir Tahsin was able to secure approval and support from most Yezidis, because generally they recognized that only through unity they would be able to survive.

The Baba Sheikh

The Baba Sheikh is an elected official and he represents the highest religious authority among the Yezidis. Nominally, he is the head of all sheikhs and kocheks. The Baba Sheikh hails from a different sheikh lineage than the Mir: the Fakhredin family from the Shemsani branch. This practice ensures balance of power. His responsibilities include the organization of the festivals in Lalish and the annual tawaf. Furthermore, he knows all the qewls and interprets them for the clergy. He has the final word in questions of legal status and the caste system. Through the improved communication between the center and the periphery, Yezidi villages in Syria are now more aware or better informed about recent decisions taken by the Baba Sheikh or the Spiritual Council; however, it does not mean that the villagers will obey them. They were, however, influenced by his decision to cancel the annual pilgrimage to Lalish and the tawaf due to security concerns. During the current crisis in Sinjar, the Baba Sheikh Xeto Haji Ismail took the initiative and traveled to the United States in order to lobby for support and aid.

The Spiritual Council or Civata Ruhani

Another institution dominated by Iraqi Yezidis is the Spiritual Council or civata ruhani. The council offers recommendations and guidelines for the well-being of the community at large. Its meetings are held in Lalish, and among his members are all the leading clerics from Sheikhan in addition to some tribal leaders and village elders. Representatives from the distant communities are not part of the council; thus, its decisions carry little weight among them. Therefore, there is a risk that it might become irrelevant to many Yezidis because it was viewed as too slow to respond to current challenges and not willing to reform itself. The Mir and the Baba Sheikh as the two leading figures in the council were mostly exempt from this criticism; however, demands were made that the council would include additional, better educated (nonclerical) members, hold elections, provide financial support to clerics in the distant communities, and open a religious training school in Lalish.[13]

The Qewals

The qewals are members of a group of clerics who memorize, preserve, and recite the religious hymns, the qewls. Considering the importance of oral narration, the qewals have arguably the most important task in protecting and preserving the religious texts and identity. Issa calls them "the collective religious memory of the Yezidis."[14] During their annual travels, the *tawusgeran* or circulation of the peacock, they visit many Yezidi villages and thus link the various communities with the religious center. The qewals carry sacred objects, the *sinjaq*, with them and display them at each village. Qewls are recited and sacred melodies are played on the drums and flutes. Then, they distribute the *berat*, small stones from Lalish, and water from the White Spring, *kaniya sipi*. After the ritual, they answer questions and collect the fees and offerings.

These annual visits have been interrupted frequently due to political unrest and hazardous travel conditions. Some areas have not seen a qewal for many years, while in other areas the qewals just rushed through. In Sinjar, for example, the sinjaq did not tour the villages from 2005 until 2010, but in 2011 and 2012.[15]

Qewals are not part of the castes of sheikh or pir; in fact they are mirids from a particular tribe (Dimili or Hekkari) and from a particular village (Bashiqa and Bahzani in Iraq). They should be, however, dedicated and pious Yezidi men with an interest in preserving the tradition and possibly possess some talent for reciting the qewls and playing instruments. This significantly limits the number of possible candidates for the job, and it comes as no surprise that the number of qewals is dropping. It is predicted that their profession may become extinct in a couple of years. The current trend to write down religious texts and no longer rely exclusively on oral recitation contributes to the dilemma.

The Feqir

Any Yezidi who lives a humble, pious, and ascetic life and receives the calling may become a feqir. A feqir devotes his entire life to the service of religion and observes all rituals, acts, and taboos. They don't constitute a separate caste, but if the feqir hails from the clergy, he is referred to as *feqir dunav*, feqir with two honors, while the feqir from the mirids is called *feqir yeknav*, feqir with one honor. The feqir wears a distinct outfit, the *kherqe*, made from black wool, which was baptized or sealed at the White Spring in Lalish. They also wear a red belt, a copper ring, and a cap called *kulik* that symbolizes Sheikh Adi's crown. Because of this black cap, they are sometimes called Karabash or black heads. Whenever the kherqe becomes worn out, it will not be thrown away, but stored at a shrine until it decomposes. In Sheikhan, this place is naturally located in Lalish, in Sinjar at the Pir Akhayi Shrine and in the Kurdagh at the Melekadi shrine in Qibare.[16] Symbolizing religious purity, the feqir does not shave his beard and participates in many ceremonies in Lalish; for example, he represents Sheikh Adi during the procession at the Cejna Cemaya or Assembly festival and during the tawaf. In their communities, where they are highly respected elders and leaders, they work on mediation and reconciliation. Even the mukhtar and the clergy obeyed their rulings. Whenever a feqir wearing his kherqe enters a room, everyone must stand up, even the Mir or the elderly, to greet him and pay him respect.

The Kochek

This group of religious men is almost extinct, but it used to have significant influence over the minds of largely uneducated Yezidis. Kocheks have the gift or foreseeing, communicating with the dead, and interpreting dreams. Almost all of them live in Sheikhan, and in particular near Lalish, but some have gone abroad. People see them when they need advice or when they have dreams and visions and need explanations. When consulted, a Kochek usually ponders or dreams over the request or the diagnosis for a while until he determines which Yezidi saint may be useful. Certain saints are equated with healing qualities; for example, Sheikh Mend for snake bites, Sheikh Mus and Sheikh Hassan for rheumatic and lung problems, Sherfedin for skin-related issues, and Sheikh Amadin for pain in the stomach.

A Kochek may also answer questions about the dead. In case of the absence of the local pir or sheikh, he may perform some of their duties. As a pious man, he fasts the forty days in the winter and the summer and wears a special white ceremonial dress and turban. Anyone who feels that he possesses the gift may become a kochek; however, in recent times none in the younger generation has shown any interest in this position and the older kocheks pass away.

The Michewir

The michewir or custodian is the local religious worker in charge of the shrine, cemetery, and to a lesser extent, religious instruction and the preservation of religious knowledge. He often belongs to the clergy, but may be a mirid too. While the mukhtar or village elder is in charge of the government and official matters, the michewir looks after the religious affairs of the village. He organizes funerals, the annual tawaf, and keeps the shrine in order. The job is usually passed down to the generations and most michewirs are quite old. However, he has certain duties such as receiving and hosting the qewals during the annual tawaf and entertaining the locals during evening sessions with religious prose and qewls.

The Brother/Sister of the Hereafter or Biraye Akhrete

The brother or sister of the Hereafter plays an important spiritual role in the life of every Yezidi. After puberty or in early adolescence, a companion is selected who will mentor and guide the other in this life and the next, for which he or she may receive a small honorarium.[17] When a Yezidi dies, the Biraye Akhrete is supposed to be present and reveal to him the secrets of Yezidism and of the next life. Because the relationship with the brother or sister of the Hereafter excludes future marital relations between the families, they are usually selected from among the sheikh or the pir caste. Generally, it is difficult to find out more about the current application of this custom because of the personal nature of the relationship and the everlasting consequences. Yezidis believe in reincarnation and thus the relationship with the brother or sister of the Hereafter is not of this world only.[18]

The Krive

Yezidis circumcise their young boys and the person who holds the boy during the ceremony is considered his godfather or patron, *krive* in Kurdish. This creates a special bond between the two families and prohibits future marital relations between them. Thus, the krive is often selected from the clergy families or even Muslim families, which may be interpreted as a strategic choice in order to enjoy the protection of influential Muslims.

4.3. YEZIDI TRIBES

Every Yezidi belongs to a caste and a tribe. The caste describes his religious position, while the tribe defines his social status. Tribe refers to a conglomerate of individuals and their relatives who form a cohesive unit of mutual support and solidarity. They all believe in shared ancestry and usually reside together in a village. Tribal members can be mirids, pir, or sheikh, and the leadership of the tribe is usually hereditary in the hand of an influential wealthy family. The tribe provides sustenance and support to its members, protects them from aggression, and serves as the first point of contact in all private, social, and economic matters. The tribe should be seen as a socioeconomic unit and not a religious organization. This is supported by the fact that tribes and tribal confederations often included Yezidi, Muslim, and Christian groups.

All traditional Yezidi communities were organized along tribal lines, whether they lived in Armenia, Turkey, Syria, or Iraq. Due to migration, some tribes were found across several regions, but usually each region is dominated by certain tribes. In Armenia and Georgia, these include the Zuqiri, Sipki, Hesini, and Mehemdi. These tribes used to live in the Van region and later in the Kars region in present-day Turkey before they finally immigrated to Armenia.

The Yezidis in Sinjar are divided geographically in those tribes who live on the northern slope of the mountain and those on the southern side. The Yezidis in the south belong to the Khorkani and those in the north to the Jwana tribe. Each of these groups is subdivided into several tribes, and these, in turn, into several clans or subclans. For instance, the Khorkani include such subtribes as Aldekhi (Aldaghi), Adiyan, Bekran (Bekura), Jefri, Chelka, Dilkan, Heliqi, Mendikan (Menduka), Musani, Qirani, Simuqi, Sherqiyan, and so on. The Jiwana group includes Aqoshi, Chuan, Hebaban, Masekî, Khinan, Mala Khalite, etc. The Mala Khalite is comprised of the following clans: Miskora, Qicikan, Heseni, Nukri, Eldinan, Usivan, Khosi, Eli Sorka, and Khifsan.

Yezidi tribes in Sheikhan are Belesini, Birimeni, Dina, Dumili, Hekari, Heraqi, Mamusi, Qaidi, Qirnayi, Rubanishti, Khaliti, Khetari, etc. The Yezidis near Zakho are mostly Howari and those near Duhok belong to the Dinnadi tribe.

As we heard, many Yezidi villages and communities used to exist in south-east Turkey, especially in the Tur Abdin area near Mardin and Midyat, but most of them had left during several waves of migration to Russia or recently to Germany. They brought along their tribal affiliation and thus it is worthwhile mentioning that some of the important groups in Armenia are Shemmike, Sohrani, Mahmila, Bishreyeh, Khalta, and Sheriqan.

The tribal component is also visible among the Syrian Yezidis, however with various forms of cohesion. Among the Yezidis from Kurdagh the tribal layer of identity is of lesser importance than ethno-religious aspects. Tribal sentiments still exists and among the important Yezidi tribes are the Dinadi, Reshkan, Dawudiya, Sheriqan, Khaliti, and Qopani.[19] Some tribes used to be Yezidi, but were forced to convert to Islam, like the Aghawat and the Dina. It is unclear how they are regarded by those Yezidi groups who remained steadfast. It is also unknown whether the entire tribe or only selected families converted or continued Yezidism. Apparently, this is a highly controversial topic and in general, people avoid talking about it. Other Kurdish Muslim tribes incorporated some Yezidi clans without forcing them to convert, such as the Millalan as well as the Al Umo and Genc.[20]

Comparing the importance of these sentiments in the formation of local identities between the Yezidis from Kurdagh and the Jezira, one should note the greater significance of tribal values and loyalties among the Jezira communities. Yezidis in the Jezira belong to the tribes of Dasikan, Bahcolan, Kiwakhi, Heverkan, Semoqa, Mihirkan, and Efshani. Many of the Kurdish tribes, such as the Milli and Heverkan, are, however, multireligious tribes, including Christian, Sunni, and/or Yezidi tribal groups. This and their transnational connections contributed to the elevated position of tribalism among the identity of the Jezira communities. Being a member of a multiconfessional and multinational network of support has many benefits; however, the current upheaval and civil war in Syria causes the age-old system to show its durability and justification. Tribal connections are predominantly used in times of conflict when they provide another layer of security and/or protection. Tribal connections may also offer early warnings from imminent attacks, physical armed protection, possible hiding places, and the opportunity to bribe officials and authorities; they offer free and trustworthy mediators and allies for highly likely revenge attacks. That this is a two-way relationship of mutual support can be seen in many chapters of Yezidi history from World War I until today. Arguably one of the most well-known episodes is the story of Hajo Agha from the Heverkan tribe.[21]

Chief among the tribal values is a sense of shared ancestry and group solidarity. In addition to this, the tribal society (that includes Yezidis, Kurds,

Arabs, and Turks) is characterized as patriarchal (dominated by men), patrilineal (descent through the male blood line), patrilocal (wives settle in their husband's family), and endogamous (marriage within the tribal group). Especially the latter aspect adds a burden to the already difficult marriage selection process within the Yezidi community. As mentioned previously, marrying someone from a different caste (and tribe) is considered a sin. To a degree, there is an overlap between the religious and the tribal divide of society, that is, pir families may come from the same tribe, while sheikh families belong to a different tribe. Thus, it is essential to know the primordial position of each individual in the complex socioreligious hierarchy of Yezidism.

4.4. RELIGIOUS PRACTICES AND RITUALS

4.4.1. Prayer

Praying is not a religious duty for individuals or for entire communities. Although a number of daily prayers are known and are observed by some older people[22], most Yezidis do not consider praying an essential act of worship. Instead, they interact with the divine through sacrifices and offerings, that is, spiritual gifts that will help answer their requests or wishes, during visits to shrines and sanctuaries as well as during pilgrimages. Animals may be sacrificed, money and food is offered, and sacred objects are touched to receive the blessing or confirmation of one's requests. But if a person decides to pray, he would then face the sun and call upon the divine beings. Occasionally, the blessing of God, Tawsi Melek, or Sheikh Adi are evoked when performing difficult tasks or to cure the sick.

4.4.2. Fasting

Fasting, which is a custom in other religions, is also considered an act of physical and spiritual cleansing among the Yezidis. Several periods of fasting are known; however, not all of them are obligatory. The one occasion when all Yezidis, laymen and clerics, are supposed to fast is during the three days preceding the Ezid Festival, which is usually celebrated on a Friday in the second week of December. From Tuesday to Thursday Yezidis do not eat or drink during the day. Usually they get up early before sunrise and have a small breakfast, called *pashev*, and finish the fasting at sunset with a communal meal, *fitar*. On Friday, they celebrate *Eida Ezid* with relatives, friends, and neighbors, including Muslim and Christian neighbors.

Voluntary fasting periods are observed for forty days in the winter (*Chile Zivistane*) and forty days in the summer (*Chile Havine*). Aside from the religious leaders, only devoted and pious Yezidis participate in this strenuous ritual. The winter fasting period starts on January 14 and the summer period on July 14.

4.4.3. Religious Holidays

The annual calendar of Yezidi holidays is rather long and includes festivals, pilgrimages, and other gatherings. Some events are observed by all communities, others only in certain regions, and some holidays are interpreted differently among the separated groups. One may also differentiate between holidays that existed forever, while others were inaugurated during or after Sheikh Adi's time.

The three feasts that are recognized by (almost) all Yezidis are the New Year, the Assembly at Sheikh Adi, and the Ezid Feast.

Yezidi New Year, Serisal, *also called Red Wednesday,* Charshemasor

The Yezidi New Year is celebrated on the third Wednesday in April according to the Eastern—Julian—calendar (which runs two weeks behind the Western—Gregorian—calendar).[23] Yezidis believe that on this day God instructed Tawsi Melek to create earth and make it hospitable for animals, plants, and humans to live on it. Thus, Yezidis decorate their homes with flowers, greens, and colored eggs. On the evening before the holiday, Yezidi families visit the cemeteries bringing sweets, fruits, and colored eggs as offerings. Some women put together small goody bags, which they give to the poor. Qewals do recitations and musical performances. Another tradition is to tie a ribbon on the old tree that usually stands next to the cemetery or local shrine for a wish to come true. During the holidays old and young enjoy playing some traditional games, like Breaking-the-Egg, where two persons hit their eggs against the other, and the person whose egg breaks first should give the other some of his eggs.

The Assembly Festival or Cejna Cemaye

Not only for Iraqi Yezidis, but theoretically for all Yezidi communities, the autumn assembly, Cejna Cemaye Sheikh Adi, is supposed to be the most important in the annual calendar of events. For seven days in late September or early October, delegations from the various Yezidi areas come to Lalish to perform a pilgrimage at the shrine of Sheikh Adi. The event has a unifying function and strengthens the cohesion within the entire Yezidi community, because all Yezidis are strongly encouraged traveling to Lalish and participating in the event. While it has been difficult for those communities in Armenia or Syria to travel to Lalish, it is nevertheless considered an important aspect of the identity building of these groups. Stories have been told about how in earlier years some community members managed to perform the pilgrimage. Recently, after the transformation of the political landscape in Iraqi-Kurdistan, a large number of Yezidis from abroad participate in the event; but sometimes the event is canceled due to security concerns. However, the journey of the communities to Lalish and the travel of the Qewal from Lalish to the communities are the two features that help foster ties between the religious center and the periphery.

Each of the festivals's seven days has special performances and rituals that include processions, communal meals, theatrical performances, recitals of qewls, animal sacrifices, candle lighting, and other religious ceremonies. The Assembly Festival is also a joyous fair with dances, musical performances, markets, and games and offers a great opportunity for young Yezidis to meet, date, and party.

The Ezid Festival or Eida Ezid

As mentioned before, Eida Ezid is connected to the only obligatory fasting for Yezidis. After the three days of fasting in early December, the festival of Eida Ezid is celebrated among all Yezidi communities to commemorate the birth of Sultan Ezid.[24] This is usually done in a communal way, when the entire local community gets together to eat, dance, and celebrate. Often a visit to the cemetery and the recital of hymns and qewls are also part of the feast.

Other religious festivals are celebrated among the different communities who add a local touch or special interpretation to them. The most popular is the annual visit to the local shrine, which is dedicated to a holy man or mystical ancestor who possesses certain qualities such as healing illness, fulfilling wishes, and granting blessings. Once a year, the custodian of the shrine invites the community to a day of celebrations, which includes a communal meal, music, dances, and a ritual cleansing of the shrine. Since the shrine is typically located at or near the cemetery, families also take this opportunity to visit the graves of their ancestors.

Batizmi in December and Khidr Elias in February are two other popular festivals with regional importance. The annual tour of the sacred objects to the Yezidi communities, *tawusgeran*, is an event that links the religious center in Sheikhan with the distant Yezidi groups even in other countries.

4.4.4. Rites of Passage: Birth, Baptism, Circumcision, Marriage, Divorce, Death

The Yezidi life story is marked by several occasions that receive religious attention. A Yezidi is born to two Yezidi parents. The designated sheikh will then perform the *bisk* ceremony where a lock of hair is cut from boys aged five or seven months. Through this initiation ritual, the young Yezidi is given his religious identity and social status. Young boys are also circumcised with the help of a godfather. Later, after puberty, a brother (or sister) of the Hereafter is chosen. Strict marriage rules dictate who is an eligible spouse. First of all, marriage with a non-Yezidi is strictly forbidden. Next, marriage must occur only within a caste, that is, mirids can marry only other mirids, sheikhs marry sheikhs, pir marry pirs. Qewals were supposed to marry qewals, but the Baba Sheikh issued a decree allowing them to marry into the mirid caste.[25] Divorce is permissible, but discouraged. Both spouses may file for divorce and a peshimam is brought in to first mediate and later oversee the separation.[26]

When a Yezidi dies, his sheikh or pir should wash the body in the presence of the brother (sister) of the Hereafter. Berat stones are placed on his eyes, mouth, and body. The body is wrapped in a white sheet and carried to the cemetery. Qewls are recited and often a feqir gives a speech. Then, the body is laid to rest and the grave is covered with stones and a head marker. The family will visit the grave for the next three days and then again after forty days.[27] Some holidays include further visitations at the cemetery. In each region, Yezidis have developed special forms of tomb and grave stone representations, each depicting regional identity markers. Yezidi cemeteries in Syria look different from those in Iraq, Armenia, or Germany.[28] And even within Syria, the two main communities developed different cemetery cultures.

4.4.5. Afterlife

Since Yezidism is deprived of a strong, codified theological tradition, only vague and sometimes contradictory information about the Yezidi Hereafter are available.[29] Many Yezidis believe in reincarnation, while others adhere to the heaven and hell story. After death with the help of the brother (sister) of the Hereafter, they ascend to the *Sirat* Bridge where they are questioned by Sheikh Adi about their life. If they can give a satisfactory answer they are allowed to cross the bridge and enter heaven. For the majority of Yezidis it is unclear (and perhaps irrelevant) what happens next. The question whether a hell exists or whether hellfire was extinguished by Tawsi Melek is debated among the scholars and clerics. The laymen most likely believe in reincarnation, which will be repeated until the soul reaches ultimate purity and enter heaven. Some, however, believe that a soul who committed sins and crimes will not be able to enter heaven and instead will reincarnate back into earth.

4.5. SPECIAL RELIGIOUS PRACTICES AMONG THE SYRIAN YEZIDIS

4.5.1. References in the Sacred Texts

The importance of the Syrian land in the evolution of Yezidism is shown in its frequent mentioning in the sacred poems, the qewls. They refer to the physical connection of Sheikh Adi and his family, descendants, and ancestors to the land of Sham or Greater Syria.

For example in the Qewle Mezin, the longest known qewl, the legendary forefathers of Sheikh Adi and the family connection with the Umayyad caliph Muawiya and Yezid are mentioned in two verses[30] (see Table 4.1).

Table 4.1 Excerpts from Qewle Mezin

4. Mi'awi be yeke nedihate bere.	4. Muawiya could not understand this.
Bi Dimesqe kir sefere.	He traveled to Damascus.
Maka Siltan Ezi ji Shame dikete dere.	Sultan Ezi's mother left Syria.
45. Dibejin: Ezide kure Mi'awi.	45. They call me Ezid son of Muawiya.
Xudane libse keske semawi.	Lord of the heavenly green apparel.
Ez hatime ligel qadi u ekabiret.	I have come with judges and notables.
Shame bikem da'wi.	To claim Syria.

Equally, direct references to Sheikh Adi coming from Syria are found in the Qewl Keniya Mara[31] (see Table 4.2).

Table 4.2 Excerpt from Qewle Keniya Mara

34. Sheikhadi il-'ame.	34. Sheikh Adi is the sheikh of all.
Usfetet wi beri Islame.	His attributes date from before Islam.
Qedem guhastine ji Shame.	His footsteps brought him from Syria.

4.5.2. Special Observances and Rituals of Syrian Yezidis

Marriage

Yezidis from Efrin consider it less problematic to marry someone from another caste, that is, a mirid can marry a sheikh or a pir or viceversa. However, this does not apply to the entire community and there are many conservative families who uphold these marriage restrictions. Unfortunately, the Efrin community earned a bad reputation for their laxity in these matters to a degree that other communities consider them no longer Yezidis and would not enter marriage relations with them.

Fasting

The obligatory three-day fasting before Eida Ezid is extended by many Yezidi families from the Jezira. The reason is their proximity to the religious centers in Iraq where a similar practice is observed. They fast for three separate periods during this holiday season. The first three days (Tuesday to Thursday) of fasting are devoted to Sheikh Shems. After this, three days of celebrations follow from Friday to Sunday. The next cycle of fasting starts on the following Tuesday, again for three days, but this they fast in honor of the pious ancestor, *Rojiyen Khodanen*. Three days of celebration conclude this second period of fasting. The final round of fasting is dedicated to Ezi or God, which is followed by the three-day long Eida Ezid holiday. Yezidis from Efrin follow the lighter version of fasting for only three days and having a one-day celebration for Ezid.[32]

The voluntary fasting during the forty days in the summer and the winter are usually observed by Yezidis who feel a strong commitment to the religious tradition. Their decision to fast for eighty days is highly respected; however, I have not met a single Syrian Yezidi who undertook this challenging ritual. Generally, among the Syrian Yezidis and particularly among the young generation, the fasting is observed less and less.

Religious Holidays

New Year

Many Yezidis in Efrin participate in the Kurdish New Year (*Newroz*) celebrations, which falls on the Spring Equinox. Because of the belief that Zarathustra started this custom, some Yezidis see this as another sign how the two religions are identical. According to them, Zarathustra was born on this day.

Assembly of Sheikh Adi

While it has been easier for the Jezira Yezidis to travel to Lalish, only a few actually did so. Even fewer Yezidis from Efrin made the journey, and thus the event developed a somehow mystical aura. It was more likely that the qewals from Lalish would come visit the Syrian villages, than for Syrian Yezidis to perform the pilgrimage to Lalish. We also remember that the feast served to bring the community together; however, together here under one leadership, that of the Mir's family. The relations between the center and the periphery were rather loose and for many Syrian Yezidis, the pilgrimage to the local shrines was more important than the one to Lalish.

Eida Ezid

Syrian Yezidis, especially those in the Jezira, participate in a longer fast in preparation of Eida Ezid. They fast three times for three days where the first cycle is called *Rojiyen Sheshims* in honor of Sheshims. They end with the *Eida Sheshims* when families visit and congratulate each other. The next three-day cycle is called *Rojiyen Khodanen* in honor of the saintly forefathers. It also concludes with a small celebration called *Eida Khodan*. The final and most important fast is to honor God and to remind the faithful of his grace, mercy, and omnipotence. The fast ends with the grand celebration of Eida Ezid. The community usually celebrates and eats together and invites its Muslim and Christian neighbors and godfathers.

Batizmi[33]

The Batizmi festival is celebrated only among the Yezidis in the northern part of the Jezira in the villages near Tirbespi. These families are related to the former Yezidi community of Tur Abdin on the other side of the Turkish border; however, those families have all but left the area and immigrated to Germany. Still, the custom lives on among the Syrian relatives, who belong to the Chelka tribal confederation. The Chelka used to live in the larger area between Tur Abdin and Sinjar, but today are separated because of the political borders. Among the important Chelka clans are the Choli, Kelikan, Shemikan, Dasikan, and Bajolan. All of these tribes used to live in Tur Abdin, but many settled in Syria during the French Mandate.

The festival lasts for seven days in mid-December or early January and is celebrated in honor of Pirali. The legendary Yezidi saint and preacher supposedly lived before Sheikh Adi and traveled among the Yezidi villages in the plains between Tur Abdin and Sinjar in order to teach the people about Yezidism by performing miracles to save them from harm and disease. The date of the event differs from village to village on the basis of his appearance. Thus, some celebrate Batizmi during the last week of December, while others won't start until early January.[34] However, all follow the same chronology of events and rituals lasting from one Sunday to the next. It starts with the *Chil Sho* ceremony on the first Sunday, that is, the cleaning the house and clothes. On Monday and Tuesday, the *Nane Miriya* or Offering to the Deceased, they remember the dead and often fast during the day. The sheikhs and pirs normally distribute special yeast to make bread on this day. On Wednesday, *Pez Guran* or Slaughtering of the Sacrifice, animals are slaughtered. From them, seven pieces of meat are put separately. They are called *Parcha Pire Ali* and are cooked in honor of Pirali. The rest of the meat is given to the poor and needy. On the morning of the same day, women prepare a special bread called *Sewik* made from the yeast that was presented by the clergy earlier. They also prepare candles, *Chira*, from white fabric dipped into the fat of the slaughtered animals. Thursday, *Roja Gere*, is the day of visitations to friends, neighbors, and relatives. In the evening they all sit together under the candle light and at sunset they wish each other good luck and success in life. It is common to put the candle on a altar-like pedestal together with the sacrificial meat, the Sewik bread and Berat stones from Lalish. People usually stay up all night long until Friday morning. The night is spent with music and dance for the younger people and prayer and meditation for the older generations. Friday and Saturday are other days to visit relatives, friends, and neighbors. The actual Batizmi holiday is held on Sunday, and the Yezidis from this area consider this the beginning of the New Year, Serisal. A final celebration is made in honor of Sheshims with more candles lit. On this occasion a small bracelet, *Basimbar*, is made from red, yellow, and white yarn. It is worn to protect the weak and the sick, but nowadays all Chelkas wear it as a symbol of their identity.[35]

Tawusgeran

It was customary on the part of the qewals to visit the various Yezidi communities in Tur Abdin, Armenia, Aleppo, and elsewhere when no political borders or war hindered their movement. They took with them the sinjaq, the bronze statue of the peacock, of which seven originally existed; seven according to the seven main Yezidi communities. Once a year, the qewals were supposed to bring the sinjaq to the distant villages, organize celebrations, recite qewls, instruct the mirids about Yezidism, resolve quarrels and conflicts, and collect taxes and fees on behalf of the religious leadership in Iraq. Especially during times of increased persecution, the visits of the qewals boosted the moral and self-confidence of the Yezidis:

> SFS46: I remember, at night the young people gathered and asked the Qewwals questions, and they answered. I believe that we profited from this. At that time there was also spiritual profit, for we had nothing—living among Moslems and not knowing anything about Yezidism. ... At that time, with all the persecutions the Yezidis were exposed to, they hid themselves, they did not dare to say: "We are Yezidis." Then the Qewwals came and the Yezidi community would sit down: it was like a support for the people ... in our area, Kurd Dagh.[36]

The role of the qewals has changed or rather diminished over the past centuries, and now only occasional and symbolic visits take place. The political and security situation is largely to blame for the decline; however, as illustrated in the following statements, Yezidis in the periphery caught up with regard to the level of education and were often dissatisfied with the traditional performance of the equals.

> SMMi27: When we were small when they came to explain to us about the religion, they would just say, "this is so." They didn't recite the qewls for us. As children, we'd never heard of the Yezidi qewls![37]
>
> TFMi39: that qewwal, who is supposed to teach the religion. He didn't say much, and he sang in between, and what he said was mostly in Arabic. We didn't understand anything for the qewwals usually sing in Arabic.[38]

IMS44: The tours of the Tawusi Melek and the qewwals that was all organized by the Princely family to get money... they can no longer go to Turkey, Syria or the former Soviet Union. Only in Iraq do they still travel. Instead of once a year, as before, the Princely family now sends them to the same village five times a year.[39]

Obviously, the number of qewals is decreasing, and their work becomes more difficult with travel restrictions and salary cuts. Perhaps the practice of tawusgeran will lose some importance, but to this day, and especially under these difficult circumstances, the presence of the qewals, their music and sermons, and the object of worship, the peacock sinjaq will reinforce a sense of identity among the Yezidis.[40]

Tawaf

The annual pilgrimage to sacred places is for many Syrian Yezidis the most important religious event during the year. These places include the tombs of saints, buildings dedicated to them, hidden caves, large trees, and other natural objects. In the Syrian lands these official visits occur mostly between April and June.[41] However, locals regularly visit the shrines throughout the year, and they often go there with a special request, prayer, or wish. The custodian, michewir, takes care of the place, but during the tawaf the community is invited to help cleaning or repairing the building. The day is filled with festive activities, meal preparations, and lots of dancing. On this day, it is also recommended to end any quarrels or disputes.

As will be discussed below, the Kurdagh is rich with Yezidi and formerly Yezidi shrines and sacred places. Almost every village has a tomb, a cave, or sanctuary dedicated to a sheikh, pir, or religious forefather; and on his anniversary, the villagers flock to the shrine and celebrate as a community. In the Jezira this is more complicated because of the short history of settlement; the Yezidi community has no ancient roots in the area. No shrines, only some recently built cemeteries, are the only places where Yezidis can congregate during their holidays. Sinjar and Tur Abdin used to be close by and their shrines available for visits, but not any more after the demarcation of the political borders.

Taj Hilla[42]

A tradition similar to the journey of the sinjaqs called *Taj Hilla* or Crown of Clothes is observed in the Kurdagh. On the first day of the Muslim Feast of Sacrifice, *Eid al-Adha*, Yezidis who live near Muslim communities participate in a holiday called Taj Hilla. Seven pieces of woolen, dark brown clothes representing the seven angels in Yezidis cosmology[43], are considered sacred objects and called Taj Hilla. They are placed in a special container and guarded by special families. They will designate a location in the house of the guardian for the objects that are kept especially clean, and because of their content, they contain *baraka* or spiritual power. On the day of the feast, the guardian receives the clerics and laymen from the village for a communal ceremony to bless the relics. The objects are presented on an altar-like pedestal. The sacred fabric is then touched or kissed by the visitors. Sacrificing an animal is also part of the ceremony.

After the food is served, the sheikh recites a prayer and a qewl for this sacred occasion. He also explains some of the religious meanings through a sermon and offers guidance in worldly and religious matters. Before leaving, everyone would kiss the hand, head, or shoulder of the sheikh as a sign of respect and to receive blessings. The guardian of the Taj Hilla would then hide the sacred objects in a safe place until next year's Eid al-Adha.

The following legend is told about the first Taj Hilla: When Abraham slaughtered the ram that was sent to redeem his son Ishmael, he wove from its hair a dress called *kherqe*. Thus, the kherqe is considered heaven sent and the angels' dress. The garment consists of seven pieces of cloth:[44]

1. *Taj*—a crown
2. *Kulik*—a small hat worn under the crown
3. *Kemberbest*—a waist band
4. *Mezer*—a head band similar to the Iqal
5. *Chube*—a cloak with an opening at the front. This particular coat is also considered the ancient Zoroastrian dress.
6. *Keshkul* or *Zembil*—a small bag
7. *Elekani*—a belt similar to the one that Zarathustra was wearing

The number of sacred objects is seven, which is also considered a blessed number because there are seven sinjaqs representing the seven angels with Tawsi Melek at their head. And then there were seven enlightened forefathers: Sheshams, Sheikh Mend, Sheikh Nasredin, Sheikhobakr, Shekhasan, Sheikh Fakhredin, and Sheikh Sijadin. However, they are not all stored together and several copies of one object may exist. For example, in the village of Qibare, seven objects all related to one of the enlightened forefathers are stored (Table 4.3).

In Qestel Jindo two objects are stored, one at the house of Heseni Evdoke and the other at the house of Osi Evdi Chune. Os Mende has an attachment to the Taj Hille called *Chiraliq* at his house. In Feqiran the most complete set of Taj Hille is found. It includes six of the seven pieces and is stored at the house of Said Aybo Iskan. Although this sounds like a very sophisticated and well-organized ceremony, it was not observed for decades until in October 2013, when the visits to the houses of the Taj Hilla in Qibare and Feqira were revived.[45]

Table 4.3 Taj Hillah Objects and their Guardians

Name of the Forefather	Guardian of the Taj Hilla
Sheikh Mend	Mustafa Darwish
Nasredin	Hannan Hasko
Sheshams	Mannan Ja'far
Sheshams	Mahmud Kalash
?	Wahid Abdo Hassan
Sheikhobakr	Haydar Khelil
Sheikhobakr	Bakr Sheikh Nasir

4.5.3. Yezidi Shrines and Sanctuaries in the Efrin Region

For ages the Yezidis in the Kurdagh considered special locations as places of worship, which they regularly visited especially during the holidays, bringing offerings and burying their dead around them. Many legends and stories were told about them. The majority of these places are shrines for their sheikhs and pious religious men or they are places of retreat for worship and meditation. Yezidi shrines can be found in almost every village in the Kurdagh.

The oldest and most important site is Chilxane, which is very different from the other structures because as a cave it does not have a dome and nobody was buried here. However, next to the cave are same old graves, but nobody remembered who was buried here. The Kurdish word *chilxane* translates as House of the Forty. It is believed that the angels came here to fast for forty days, and so did Sheikh Adi himself. However, it is also known that some religious men came here for retreat and meditation at different times. And among them were those who fasted the forty days in the summer and in the winter.

This place is located in the Laylun Mountain about two kilometers south of the village of Qibare. It is a cave overlooking the plains of Sahl Arshi (in Kurdish *Deshta Ershe*), which stretches from the mountain all the way to Efrin. This is very a fertile agricultural land. The valley that leads to the shrine is called Wadi Chilxane. It ends into another valley called Wadi Sheikh Sifil, (in Kurdish *Geliye Sheikh Sifil*) where another shrine is located called *chilxane bicuk* or Small Chilxane.

The cave is about six meters long, two meters wide and three meters high. It has some inscriptions on the walls as well as a small square niche for oil and candles. On the floor is another square hole with water dripping from the ceiling. Around the shrine are many trees, such as olive, oak, and mulberry trees. At the gate of the cave is a tree where the visitors put little strings of cloths for making special wishes. Infertile women to make offerings and pray for a child. Also, women come here who don't have enough milk to feed their babies come here. A few steps to the north is a hoof-shaped stairway leading to a basin carved in the rock. The size is 2.5 × 1.5 m. It is mostly believed that this basin is a burial place. Some mentioned a connection to the Zoroastrians who used to put their dead up high to be completely disposed.

Yezidis in the Kurdagh visit this shrine regularly. However, there is a special day in April on a Wednesday evening where all people gather to celebrate the Yezidi New Year. They bring their offerings, sacrifice meat, and prepare the food. They repeat this visit on Friday when they come with drums and flute to dance until evening when they go back home.

Ancient stories were told about this shrine. For example it was narrated that an ascetic sheikh was wandering around the area looking for an appropriate place to perform his rituals. He settled in this cave wishing to meet his lord. The sheikh spent many years worshiping. In one of the cold winter nights a wolf attacked him and trapped him. The sheikh was crying for the help of his lord to get him out of this misery. Then a dervish appeared in a bright white dress and with his stick he chased the wolf away. Then he demanded from the sheikh to fast for forty days. After finishing this task on the fortieth day his eyes became cloudy and he saw himself in the presence of his lord.

People also narrate the story of a pregnant woman who came to the cave and gave birth to twins and died. To enable the two to stay alive, the walls of the cave and the ceiling became a well for the kids to drink from.

Some three hundred meters next to the cave and near the Yezidi cemetery is the shrine Hecherka Sheikh Huseyn. It is said that this Sheikh Huseyn was a grandchild of Sheikh Mend who came to this area from the Mountains of Reshan and fled the Ottomans in the middle of the eighteenth century. After he performed some miracles and good deeds to the people they respected him very highly and worked according to his advice. When he died people built a small shrine at a point between Qibare and the cemetery where one of his miracles appeared to them. Later they built a larger dome which they still visit frequently.

The third shrine in Qibare is dedicated to Melekadi, in reference to Sheikh Adi bin Musafir, the legendary reformer of Yezidism. It is located some three hundred meters above the cave of Chilxane and is also close to the Yezidi cemetery.

This shrine is built in a traditional style from rocks with a small dome. It does have great religious significance because it was at this location where the sacred shirt of the feqir was given its distinct dark brown color. The shirt or kherqe is made of wool and dyed with the leaves from the walnut tree. In order to complete the ritual and to seal the shirt, the *kherqe* should be dipped into the White Spring in Lalish. After the kherqe is worn out, it may not be destroyed or pitched; however, it is kept until it disintegrates. As mentioned before, every Yezidi may become a feqir provided that he is a pious person and dedicates his life to religious studies. Often the gatekeeper, michewir, of the local shrine is a feqir.

Figure 4.2 The Melekadi Shrine in Qibare. Source: Gundi Ersqibar — Qibar/قرية قيبار by Eng. Luqman Alkhdo, 15 May 2014. https://ciyaye-kurmenc.com/doc/?p=1464.

Locals would visit the shrine on a Wednesday hoping to get their wishes come true or to be cured from sickness, infertility, or other psychological problems. The first Wednesday in April (according to the Julian calendar), also called the Red Wednesday, Charshemasor in Kurdish, is the most important and popular of those visitation days. It coincides with the Yezidi New Year celebrations.

The Melekadi shrine has another important feature, a tower called Birche Jindo, which is a little hill, built by Jindo, one of the Yezidi ancestors. It is said that this hill was built with dirt and milk collected from the neighboring villages. Milk was used instead of water because of its perceived purity over water. The hill was used to store the retired kherqe and perhaps even as a burial place.

In Qestel Jindo two shrines are located: the shrines for Sheikh Hamid and the shrine for Parse Khatune. Parse Khatune is a small building located on top of Mount Parse. In front of the building stands an old oak tree. The gate is to the East, while an old cemetery is connected to the western side. Next to the cemetery is a large cistern which belongs to an ancient fortress called Junblat. The name of the shrine refers to a Lady Parse, and it was told that Parse was a hermit. Some continue the story by saying the Parse was in fact the wife of Sheikh Barakat, the main Yezidi saint in the area, who also lived a hermit life on the nearby Mount Barakat. The second shrine, Sheikh Hamid, is about two kilometers south-west of the village. The gate also points to the east, and to the west is an old Yezidi cemetery. On the inside is a carved-out niche, similar to a *mihrab* or alter space. The surrounding ruins and pillars indicate a pre-Islamic sanctuary.

Some twenty kilometers south of Efrin is another concentration of Yezidi shrines near the village of Basufan and Mount Barakat. The main sanctuary devoted to Sheikh Barakat is on top of the mountain overlooking the plains of Guma and Ghumq. The shrine is a small square building with some inscriptions that sit on the remnants of old sacred structures. According to Yezidi lore, the shrine is connected to Ibrahim Adham bin Darwish, a legendary Yezidi leader, and the name goes back to Sheikh Abu al-Barakat Sakhr bin Sakhr bin Musafir, the nephew of Sheikh Adi bin Musafir, the great reformer. Sheikh Barakat was allegedly killed at this location and people built the shrine in his honor.[46] A second shrine also dedicated to Sheikh Barakat is located in the Sinjar Mountains in Iraq. The one in Syria is frequented for the Yezidi New Year's celebrations. Muslims and Druzes visit the shrine as well; however, they trace the origin of the shrine back to one of the early Muslims, Muhammad Nufal Barakat, who died here. Another shrine dedicated to Sheikh Ali is located inside the village of Basufan.

There are also a few other shrines in the third Yezidi enclave, like the Hanan Shrine located to the south of the village of Mash'ala near Qatme on the road between Aleppo and Efrin. It is believed to be the resting place of one of David's brothers. Like many other shrines, a special power has been associated with the place, the power of healing, and thus, during the celebrations hundreds of locals come to the shrine to pray for cure from illnesses. It was also considered a special blessing to be buried near the shrine, and today the area has transformed into one of the largest cemeteries in the region. One grave inside the shrine holds the remains of Dr. Nuri Dersimi, a Kurd from Turki, who lived in the area with his wife. The shrine was renovated and expanded in 1964 on his costs. A Yezidi informant told me that the place used to be a Yezidi shrine, but now has been turned into a Muslim shrine with a mosque.

About one hundred meters northwest of the shrine is another smaller sanctuary, the Shrine of Pir Ja'far, which is devoted to the Yezidi community; however, it was more or less abandoned, and the Yezidis visit the Hanan Shrine instead. On top of the nearby Mount Kefer Jenne is another small shrine, Mazar Manan, the sister shrine of Mazar Hanan. The patrons Manan and Hanan were actually brothers.[47] In the nearby village of Baflun is another smaller shrine dedicated to Sheikh Sherfedin.

In Feqiran (formerly Karabash or Qerebaş), which is an isolated Yezidi village near Jindris, two local shrines are located: Pir Sayid and Sheikh Junayd which are frequented not only during the main religious holidays, like Charshemasor (Yezidi New Year), but every Friday evening when people light candles and worship in these shrines. Generally, the shrines in this village used to be in bad condition, but the Pir Sayid shrine has been renovated recently. The shrine for Sheikh Junayd, who lived in the area from 1845 to 1934, was dedicated during the 2011 Charshemasor celebrations in Feqiran.[48]

A shrine dedicated to Sheikh Abd al-Qadir Gilani is located in the small village of Turunde, which has a mixed Muslim-Yezidi population. His shrine is frequented by both groups. As mentioned before, Gilani was a famous Sufi-sheikh, founder of the Qadiriya brotherhood, and a good friend of Sheikh Adi bin Musafir.

Finally, the Shrine of Sheikh Rakkab in the village of Shadere is another example of a small building with a dome at the local cemetery that serves the Yezidi communities of Basufan, Ghezewiye, Iskan, and Kefer Zeyt. Naturally, some ancient ruins and hills are also found nearby. The famous Yezidi community leader Sheikh Huseyn Brimo, who died at the age of 79 in 2013, was buried here.

4.5.4. Religious Leadership among the Yezidis in the Kurdagh

As mentioned earlier, Yezidism knows of two main socioreligious groups, laymen and clergy. Among the clergy two distinct subgroups coexist, the sheikhs and the pir. Specific rules of interaction between the three groups apply and are strongly enforced. Furthermore, the sheikhs belong to three lines of descents, Shemsani, Adani, and Qatani. The forefather of the Shemsani group, according to the Yezidi interpretation from Efrin, was an important religious source, who left behind four children: Sheshams, Fakhredin, Nasredin, and Sijadin. Sheshams is considered a symbol of the light of God and savior of the Yezidis. He had ten sons: Shekhasan, Sheikh Babek, Sheikh Amadin, Sheikh Bababin, Sheikh Havand, Sheikh Tokal, Sheikh Khidr, Sheikh Ali Shamsa, Sheikh Avdal, and Sheikh Ali Rash, as well as three pious daughters: Balqun, Eys, and Nasret. Fakhredin was also a religious leader and protector of Yezidi unity. He had three children: Sheikh Mend, Sheikh Bahdin, and Sheikh Aqub.

Each Yezidi must have a sheikh and a pir. This means that even members of the sheikh caste need a pir and vice versa, pir families need to have a sheikh who performs certain rituals and has other responsibilities for his or her mentees. The pir family in charge of the Sheshams sheikhs is Pirefat. The Najjar family (Sheshams) lives in Eyndare. Fakhredin's pir family is represented by Pire Eslanek. Fakhredin has a family Evdali Shemo in Birche Abdallo. Sheikh Nasredin is served by the Pire Hechali Memon family. Members of the Nasredin family live in Turunde and over two hundred families in Basufan. Among the leading Nasredin sheikhs was the late Sheikh Ali bin Sheikh Barakat. The Sheikh Mend family lives in Basufan and

Ghezewiye (Hemgul family), Turunde (Sheikh His Hese family), as well as a family in Iskan. However, most members of the Sheikh Mend family live in Qestel Jindo. The Pir of Sheikh Mend is Pire Eslanek. All Shemsani sheikhs belong to the Dina tribe.

The Adani sheikhs trace their origin back to Sheikh Adi himself, the legendary reformer through his nephew Abu al-Barakat Sakhr. The main lineages in this Sheikh clan are Sheikhisn, Sherefedin, Zeynedin, Sheikh Ibrahim al-Khatmi, and Sheikh Mus. Two of those Adani Sheikhs clans live in the Kurdagh. There is Sheikhisn in Ghezewiye with the families of Sheikh Brim, Sheikh Mele, and Hassan Besroki. In Feqiran live the families of Sheikh Humayd and Miro. Sherefedin has families in Birche Abdallo and Ghezewiye, among them the Zeyndo family. All Adani sheikhs belong to the Khalta tribe.

The third sheikh lineage is the Qatani branch that goes back to Darwish Adam al-Qatani. Their Pir is Pire Siva. The main clans are Sheikh Muhammad al-Arabli, Sheikh Ismail al-Anzali, Sheikh Abd al-Qadir, and Sheikhobakr. The latter is arguably the most famous branch, because the forefather Sheikhobakr was the first to wear the kherqe. Sheikhobakr/Qatani families live in Qibare (families Bekire Qedi, Sheikh Nasr, Shero), in Qestel Jindo (families Seyde Evdeko, Deli Beko, Sheikh Hannan), and in Basufan (family Menane Feqir). All Qatanis belong to the Reshwan tribe.[49]

Well-Known Religious Figures from Efrin

Yezidis from Efrin remember a religious man from the nineteenth century called Sifri from the village of Feqiran who memorized some five hundred qewls and other religious texts. He gathered some students around them who would be the next generation of Yezidi religious leaders among them—Rasho Hanan from Abu Ka'aba and Sheikh Mele from Ghezewiye. Sheikh Hasso Khalo, also from Ghezewiye, was a student of Sheikh Mele. All of them belong to the lineage of Sheikhisn.

Sheikh Hasso Sheikh Brim was a student of Sheikh Hasso Khalo. He also studied with Shamo bin Kalo, another Sheikhisn from Iskan, and Naser Evdike from Qibare, who belonged to Sheikhobakr.

In recent times other religious men including Sheikh Ali bin Sheikh Barakat, the brothers Sheikh Huseyn and Sheikh Brim from Ghezewiye, Sheikh His Hese Hemushe, as well as Muhammad Khelil Kalo from Birche Abdallo, were prominent in the Kurdagh. Sheikh Ali bin Sheikh Barakat was born in 1930 in Basufan. He was a Shemsani-Nasredin sheikh from the Dina tribe who traveled to Sinjar in 1949 and stayed there until 1955 when he returned to Syria. In Sinjar, he stayed and studied with a feqir who wore the kherqe and was from the mirids of Sheikhobakr. After his return he was invited by Naser Shamo, the brother of Darwish Agha Shamo, to settle in Qibare where he stayed until he died in 1994. It is said that Sheikh Ali knew about one hundred qewls as well as a number of religious hymns and stories. In the 1980s he contributed to the works of Celile Celil, the Armenian Yezidi anthropologist, who collected and published religious texts.

Sheikh His Hese Hemushe is from the Shemsani branch. He grew up in Qatma, but later settled in Turunde. His family descends from Sheikha Khatune, whose shrine, Parse Khatune, is located near Qestel Jindo. Sheikh His was well respected among the Yezidis and Muslims for his power to heal snake bites. He died in 1993 when his son Heyder followed to take his position.

Sheikh Huseyn bin Sheikh Hassan Sheikh Brim belonged to the Adani lineage and Sheikhisn and his family to the Khalta tribe. He received his religious training from his uncle Sheikh Hasso Brim as well as from Sheikh Ali bin Sheikh Barakat. He was born in 1936 in Ghezewiye. Throughout his life he was known for his knowledge and wisdom with the help of which he preached religious tolerance and coexistence. He did participate in the big Yezidi conference in Germany in the year 2000 and returned to his homeland where he died in 2014. His funeral possession was one of the largest in Yezidi history.

Finally, Sheikh Muhammad Khelil Kalo was born in 1938 and lives in Birche Abdallo. He belongs to the Shekhisn branch and studied under both Sheikh Ali and Sheikh Huseyn.

4.5.5. Religious Leadership among the Yezidis in the Jezira

Yezidi settlement in the Jezira started at a much later time around the end of World War I when families and clans from Tur Abdin and Sinjar were forced to migrate to the French Mandate territories fleeing persecution and violence. Among the migrants were individual families of clerics who used to perform their duties in the old homeland and continued doing this in Syria. However, those migrant families were cut off from their original homeland and communities and struggled to build a strong, coherent community. The lack of this cohesion left the Jezira Yezidis vulnerable, and quickly they found themselves at the bottom of the social, political, and economic hierarchy. Another factor that contributed to the general ambiguity of their situation was the loss of contact with the Yezidi religious authorities in Iraq. Although Yezidi cleric families congregated in a few villages, such as Khirbet Khwe and Otelje, they were unable to reach out to the mirid families spread over many small villages and hamlets in four separated enclaves. The important work and functions of the clerics were thus performed by a few motivated individual sheikhs, pirs, and peshimams, like Peshiman Sileman

Omar, who often took great risks and privations to reach their constituencies. Furthermore, they and their families endured reprisal from government authorities and the security apparatus. Once the door for immigration was opened, many cleric families left the Jezira and moved to Germany. Only with the installation of the self-administration and concurrent stabilization of the security situation have some clerics such as Sheikh Bedi Memo and Peshimam Sheikh Meqbul Sheikh Nasr started to emerge as community leaders. Open borders with Iraq allowed for qewals to visit the Jezira and for Jezira Yezidis to perform the pilgrimage to Lalish, rebuilding the old relations between the two regions.

NOTES

1. Spät (2002): 28.
2. Omarkhali (2009): 13.
3. Asatrian and Arakelova (2014): 6.
4. In Muslim tradition, the peacock is often viewed as the assistant of the devil, who was expelled from paradise.
5. The other angels include Azrail, Dardail, Israfil, Mikail, Jibrail, Shamnail, and Turail.
6. There were Kurds among his ancestors. See Zourab Aloian, Sheikh 'Adi, Sufism and the Kurds (n.d.).
7. Sheikh Adi allegedly arrived in Lalish in the year 1111, which coincided with the year when the most influential Sufi al-Ghazali died. See Issa (2007): 61 and Aloian (n.d.).
8. The miracle story is narrated in the qewl Sheikh Adi u Mera, The Hymn of Sheikh Adi and the Holy Men, see Kreyenbroek (1995): 291–299.
9. Another lineage includes several more generations and the possible link to the Umayyad ancestry: 'Adi b. Musafir b. Ibrahim b. al-Walid b. 'Abd al-Malik b. Marwan b. al-Hakm b. al-'As b. 'Uthman b. 'Affan b. Rabi'a b. 'Abd ash-Shams b. Zuhra b. 'Abd Manaf. See Aloian (n.d.).
10. Ortac (2005).
11. Omarkhali (2008): 105.
12. Issa (2007): 75.
13. See interview with Idris Zozani at http://edrishasso.blogspot.com/2013/09/140.html
14. Issa (2007): 87.
15. Eszter Spät directed a documentary on the journey of the sinjaq through the Sinjar communities in 2012, see *Following the Peacock*.
16. It seems that during the Ottoman Empire the clergy in the Kurdagh was represented only by the feqir.
17. Kreyenbroek reports of competition among Sheikhs in Sheikhan who is the one who has the most "Brother of the Hereafter relationships and would receive the most offerings." See Kreyenbroek (2009): 76.

18. Kreyenbroek 2009, 18; Asatrian and Arakelova 2014, 122.

19. On the tribal affiliation and character of Yezidi society, see Mark Sykes, "The Kurdish Tribes of the Ottoman Empire," *Journal of the Anthropological Institute* 38 (1908): 451–486; Lescot, *Enquête* (1938): 251–268; Ahmad Wasfi Zakariya, *'Asha'ir al-Sham* (Damascus, 2007): 657–674, and Omarkhali (2008): 104–119.

20. Muhammad Abdu Ali (2008): 165.

21. See Hajo Agha's story in Chapter 2.5.

22. Usually the morning and the evening prayer are recited. In addition, there is a ritual prayer at sunrise, noon, and one before going to sleep.

23. Kreyenbroek (2009: f19) notes that the Yezidi year is actually based on the Seleucid calendar, which runs two weeks (or 13 days) behind the Western calendar. The first month of this calendar is called Nisan, and the Yezidi New Year is celebrated on the 1st of April (Nisan).

24. Sultan Ezid is a divine figure or incarnation and part of the triad that also includes Tawsi Melek and Sheikh Adi.

25. Issa (2007): 108.

26. Schulz (2009): 71–73 provides a detailed summary of current divorce rules.

27. Allison (2012) observed and described the various forms or laments and mourning among Yezidi women from Iraq.

28. Rüdiger Benninghaus analyzed the different funeral and cemetery practices in Germany and Turkey. See Rüdiger Benninghaus, *Friedhöfe als Quellen für Fragen des Kulturwandels* (2005): 247–288.

29. See Victoria Arakelova's thorough attempt to sieve through the few available, mostly oral, data in Victoria Arakelova, "The Hereafter in the Yezidi Beliefs," *Iran and the Caucasus* 16 (2012): 309–318.

30. Kreyenbroek and Jindi (2005): 158.

31. Kreyenbroek and Jindi (2005): 397.

32. Although other informants from Efrin insisted on the nine days of fasting, they also mentioned a three-day fasting during Khidr Elias.

33. The festival is also celebrated among the Sinjar Yezidis and in a slightly different version as Belinde in Sheikhan.

34. Some Yezidis in Tur Abdin, those belonging to the Khalta tribe, do not recognize this holiday because Pirali never made to their villages.

35. Detailed description of Batizmi celebrations can be found with Salo (2015) and Issa (2007).

36. Cited in Kreyenbroek (2009): 83.

37. Ibid., 149.

38. Ibid., 117.

39. Ibid., 103.

40. See the documentary film Following the Peacock (2014) by Eszter Spät.

41. In Sinjar, the Tawaf to the many local shrines follows a stricter regiment and starts with the harvest season.

42. Muhammad Abdo Ali (2009): 55–58.

43. For more on the Yezidi cosmology and the role of the seven angels, see Asatrian and Arakelova (2014).

44. A detailed description of the seven pieces is given by Nidal Yusuf (2013).

45. Hawarnews, October 16, 2013. http://www.hawarnews.com/2013-02-14-17-53-15/7069-2013-10-16-12-09-01.

46. Interview with Sheikh Huseyn (1998).

47. See the notes of Dakhil Shamo (n.a.): 124–127.

48. Among the presents offered during the dedication service was a wooden placard with the image of Zarathustra. The placard was given by Luqman Efrin, one of the most active and popular cultural centers/websites in the area. See www.lokmanEfrin.com/ezdieen.htm.

49. For more on the genesis of the Reshwan federation and its history in northern Syria, see Winter (2008): 228–231.

Chapter 5

Historical Developments

5.1. THE YEZIDIS BEFORE SHEIKH ADI

Due to the lack of written sources and documents, the origin and early developments of the Yezidi community cloudy. It is commonplace nowadays to call Yezidism an ancient religion; some go as far as calling it 4,000 years old, citing evidence and similarities with the language and practices of Zoroastrianism and other Mesopotamian religions such as Mithraism. Scholars of Yezidism are unanimous in their opinion that it is a syncretistic religion that emerged in northern Mesopotamia. But then the speculation starts. Perhaps it has been the original religion of all Kurds; perhaps it used to be a cult of sun worship; perhaps Muslim historic figures like Yazid bin Muawiya, Hassan al-Basri, and al-Hallaj were indeed proto-Yezidis. While it seems largely impossible to proof or refute these claims, the important question is how these claims translate into the issue of identity building in our time. Among the fundamental questions in this matter are those related to the Zoroastrian or Muslim origin of Yezidism.

The former is vehemently discussed among the Yezidis, with some groups strongly opposing the idea, while others supporting it by wearing amulets with a Zarathustra pendant or even erecting statues in his honor as was done in 2014 in Efrin.

The Baba Sheikh was compelled to issue an official statement about his non approval of the statue:[1]

> *Clarification to whom it may concern:*
> *The statue of Zarathustra, which was erected in the Efrin region in Syria does not represent Yezidi religion nor does it have any connection with it. Yezidism*

has their own obvious symbols, but it also respects the symbols of other religions such as Zoroastrianism. There are influences on the Yezidi traditions from neighboring religions such as Zoroastrianism, Judaism, Christianity, Islam, Sabism, Kakais and others.

The office of his Excellency BabaSheikh Xeto Haji Ismail, Religious Source for all Yezidis in the World.

No consensus has been reached on this issue, and while it is not the job of the observer to instruct the target community; however, linguistic evidence suggests that there is no direct connection between Yezidism and Zoroastrianism.[2] On the other hand, some influential Yezidis interpret the nonwritten, oral history and support the following thesis: the Zoroastrians at one time split into two groups, the Kurds and the Iranians. And so did the Zoroastrian religion: the eastern believers kept the old name, while those in the west, what was known as Kurdistan, became Yazdanis. This western Zoroastrian group evolved as an independent religion with separate customs and beliefs. They became known as the Yezidis.[3]

To call Yezidism an Islamic sect is nowadays almost completely rejected by Yezidi and non-Yezidi scholars. This call must rather be seen as an attempt to justify the age-old persecution by Muslims. As a syncretistic religion, Yezidism do include elements and rituals similar to other religions, such as baptism (Christianity), circumcision (Judaism, Islam), and pilgrimage

Figure 5.1 Zarathustra Statue in Efrin. *Source*: With permission from Basufan Rangin.

(Islam). Since the majority of Yezidi neighbors were Muslims, it should not surprise us that other Muslim customs found their way into Yezidi religious tradition. Even Sheikh Adi, the legendary reformer, has a solid Sunni and/or Sufi pedigree. However, the defining element of Yezidism, as it emerged in the twelfth century, was the rejection of orthodox Islamic law and the incorporation of pre-Islamic aspects.[4]

5.2. YEZIDI HISTORY FROM SHEIKH ADI UNTIL THE END OF THE OTTOMAN EMPIRE

The Yezidi community becomes first noticeable in the twelfth century with the reformist works of Sheikh Adi. It can be best understood when comparing the group to one of the many Sufi brotherhoods that existed in Kurdistan around that time. The mystical Sufi beliefs combined with ancient dualistic and sun-worshiping elements represented the world view of the Yezidis in northern Mesopotamia around Mosul at that time.

Sheikh Adi was in born 1077 in Beyt Far (present-day Khirbat Qanafir) in the Beqaa Valley in Lebanon and sought religious instruction in Baghdad. Here, he met the famous Sufi Sheikh Abd al-Qadir al-Gilani, and the two developed a strong bond. Sheikh Adi went on to preach among the Kurds in the Hakkari plains where he quickly became well known among the local tribes for his mystical and magical abilities. A group of devoted disciples was formed around him, and they started teaching the locals. Sheikh Adi took over the shrine in Lalish[5] and soon expanded his influence over neighboring territories. However, it was only under his successor, Sheikh Hassan, that the community was recognized as a group independent from the regional authorities under Badr al-Din Lulu, the Atabeg of Mosul. The two clashed, and Hassan was killed in 1246. During the subsequent Mongol invasion, the community was dispersed as far as Egypt and Syria.

For over two hundred years, news about the community disappeared; the community, however, continued to exist and prospered according to Ottoman court records from the fifteenth century. The community retook possession of the Hakkari territory as well as areas in the vicinity of Aleppo and Kilis.

5.3. YEZIDI HISTORY IN SYRIA

5.3.1 Yezidis in Greater Syria

A variety of often contradictory opinions regarding the origin of the Yezidi community can in general be found among Yezidi and non-Yezidi scholars.

Often, a connection with ancient Mesopotamian cultures and religions is suggested. Others still support the idea of an Islamic faction. However, the latter argument has finally disappeared in Western publications, giving room to a general consensus that views Yezidism as a system of pre-Islamic Kurdish traditions,[6] which was reformed by the Sufi Sheikh Adi bin Musafir. Under his successor al-Hassan bin Adi the transformation continued, integrating additional pre-Islamic elements and rituals.

According to some, Yezidism is also a religion based on sacred books, drawing parallels to the People of the Book, and their status of protection under Islamic law. One of the two holy scriptures of the Yezidis, the Meshaf Resh, allegedly mentioned a Yezidi community near Aleppo. However, since their publication, the appearance and the authenticity of the books have come under question, and therefore, the issue needs to be treated with caution. Also, the main source of religious tradition was the oral transmission of hymns, psalms, and other religious texts.[7]

The documented history of the Yezidis in Syria began around the year 1070 with the birth of Sheikh Adi bin Musafir in Beyt Far, a small village in the Beqaa Valley. Today located in Lebanon, it was then part of Greater Syria (Bilad ash-Sham). His parents and nephew also came from this region, giving the area some religious significance. A shrine in the predominantly Christian village is dedicated to Sheikh Adi. However, people in the area do not associate Sheikh Adi bin Musafir with Yezidism, but remember him as a Sufi saint.

In another sacred text it is mentioned that Sheikh Adi's family originally came from the Hakkari Mountains and that his grandfather was the first to move to Beyt Far. Sheikh Adi later moved to Baghdad and then back to the Hakkari Mountains, where he founded the Sufi order of the Adawiya, which merged with local religious traditions of sun worshiping.[8]

The first written accounts on the Yezidis and their most important historical and religious figure, Sheikh Adi bin Musafir can be located in sources from the twelfth century.[9] The main reason for dealing with this then relatively small and unimportant group is the accusation of heresy which Islamic orthodoxy brought against them. Therefore, many prominent Islamic historians, jurists, and geographers wrote about the "strange" beliefs of the Yezidis.

Most likely the first reference to the Yezidis can be found in Sharastani's (d. 1153) *kitab al-milal wa'n-nihal* (The Book of Religious and Philosophical Sects). A contemporary of Sheikh Adi, he mentioned a sect of Kharijites[10] originating from one Yazid bin Unayza. Sam'ani (d. 1167) in his *kitab al-ansab* (The Book of Pedigrees) described the same group as descendants of Yazid bin Muawiya, that is, belonging to the Umayyad dynasty. He mentioned Hulwan and Sinjar as places where they lived.[11] The notion that the Yezidis descended from the generally unpopular Caliph Yazid, who was not elected but appointed caliph and whose armies killed Husayn bin Ali, is often given as a reason for the persecution of Yezidis in Syria.

Sufism was and still is very popular in Kurdistan and adjacent areas, with the Naqshbandiya and Qadiriya as the two most important orders. Sufis represented a symbiosis between traditional religious forms and Islam in recently converted areas. Thus, it is not surprising to find similarities with a Sufi order in the early history of Yezidism. Sheikh Adi, who apparently founded his own order, the Adawiya, was a contemporary of Sheikh Abd al-Qadir al-Gilani (d. 1166), the founder of the Qadiriya Order. Gilani, as well as other famous Sufis such as Mansur al-Hallaj and Hassan al-Basri, are still very popular among the Yezidis.[12]

With the establishment of the Adawiya as a separate Sufi order in the eleventh century, the number of references to the Yezidis in Islamic sources increased quickly. Another explanation for this is the positive attitude of some Muslim Kurdish rulers in Damascus, Aleppo, and Mosul toward the community, which, however, changed drastically when Badr ad-Din Lu'lu became the Atabeg of Mosul in 1234 and started to fight the Adawiya and persecute the Yezidis. After the death of their leaders Sheikh Adi and Sheikh Hassan, the community split into two factions. One moved to Egypt and Syria under the leadership of Zeynedin and later Izzedin, both descendants of Sheikh Adi, where they continued following the Sufi tradition.[13] On the basis of the description of Febvre, Fuccaro argues that the community in Syria maintained its typical Sufi character until the seventeenth century, that is, the master-disciple relationship outweighed the caste structure of Yezidi society.[14]

Other descendants of Sheikh Adi remained in the Mosul area and established the new Yezidi character of the community, who was later taught by Sheikh Hassan. However, it is necessary to highlight the relationship by blood of both leaders, which connects the origin of the Syrian community with the one in Mosul.

Only in the works of Bar Hebraeus (d. 1286), the famous Syrian-Jacobean bishop, do we find a note on the survival of the community after the two devastating blows dealt to them by the Mongols and Badr ad-Din Lu'lu. For the first time the Yezidis in Jebel Sim'an are now mentioned, which is part of present-day Kurdagh, and whose origins Bar Hebraeus connected to the Kurdish troops of Saladin al-Ayubi, the sultan, general, and liberator of Jerusalem of Kurdish origin.[15]

Ibn Taymiya (d. 1328) commented on the Yezidis too, in his *risalat al-'adawiya* (The Adawiya Epistles).[16] Given his authority in Islamic orthodoxy it is noteworthy that he did not criticize the Yezidis for being unbelievers, but for being deviant and extremist in their veneration for Yazid and Sheikh *Adi*. This is an accusation, however, which has been widely used to condemn Sufis in general.[17]

The next evidence of medieval Yezidi existence in Syria can be found in Ottoman archival files from Raqqa[18] as well as in the Kurdish chronicle *Sharafname*. It was written by Sharaf ad-Din Khan, the Emir of Bitlis, between 1588 and 1596 and describes in detail the history of seven major Yezidi tribes. The *Sharafname* also provides information about the number of Yezidis and their settlement areas. For example, it reports on Yezidis whose origins are said to go back to the Hakkari regiments of Salah ad-Din who had granted one Hakkari sheikh and descendant of Shemsadin named Mend the region around the castle of Qusayr west of Aleppo, where many Yezidis lived. It is also reported that Mend was the ruler over Yezidi communities in the valley between Efrin and Kilis. During the fifteenth century, the original ruler of Kilis was dismissed by the Mamluks and replaced by the Yezidi Sheikh Izzedin.[19] His descendants in the socio religious caste of Sheikh Mend are to this day very prominent in the region.[20]

The next chapter of Yezidi history in Syria began in the middle of the seventeenth century, when for the first time, European scholars, namely French clerics, dealt with the Yezidis in the vicinity of Aleppo. The Yezidis in western Syria came under the influence of French missionaries of the Order of the Capuchins, who, protected by powerful consuls, originally aimed to proselytize Nestorian and Jacobean Christians. Contact with the Yezidis was established by Armenian Christians, which quickly led to the baptism of several Yezidis. From the Yezidi perspective, this seemed to be the perfect opportunity to abandon the status of an unprotected minority and to become an officially recognized *millet*. In order to obtain this status, they proactively contacted representatives of different Christian groups in the area. These were aside from the Catholic Capuchins and the Armenians, as also English Protestants. They proposed that they would convert to the denomination that provided the best protection. The various contacts created a close relationship between the monks and the Yezidis as described in Febvre's detailed account. However, internal disputes among the different orders of the Capuchins, Jesuits, and Carmelites aborted the efforts of strengthening the Christian-Yezidi relationship.

From now on news about the Yezidi community found its way to Europe more frequently. In 1674 the first book on the Yezidis was published in Rome.[21] The author Michel Febvre described social relations and conventions including many ethnological and geographical details. He described, for example, how the Yezidis were living as nomads between the Efrin River and Jebel Sim'an. Further, he mentioned how one of their important religious doctrines was not to pronounce the name of the devil. He also mentioned the unique Yezidi caste system with laymen and clerics. The Whites (laymen) or *mirid* as well as the Blacks (clergy) or *feqir* were distinguished by their dress code, with the *feqir* wearing the kherqe, the traditional black shirt.[22] However, he recognized the *feqir* only as a member of the clergy and did not mention *sheikh* or *pir*, the other two religious castes in Yezidism. It seems that the *feqir* caste initially was not separated, but remained open to all qualified Yezidis. Hence, this might be the reason why marriage restrictions among Yezidis in western Syria are less rigid and not enforced as in communities. To break with the tradition of endogamy is still considered a major sin in the eyes of most other Yezidi groups.

In the following years, more European missionaries, explorers, and merchants traveled through the area and brought with them additional news about the Yezidis to Europe. For example, a Russian traveler reported on the Yezidis in the Efrin Valley that they lived as a nomadic group and had two leaders, one secular leader called *amir* and the other a religious leader.[23] These reports contained information about the ways of life, material culture, and difficult relations of the Yezidis with their Muslim neighbors. Since many of the informants of the Europeans were Muslims, much prejudice and negative stereotyping of the Yezidis were introduced into Western sources and scholarship.

The German traveler Ulrich von Seetzen stayed for a year in Aleppo to learn Arabic and visited some of the neighboring villages in 1803. While he reported the usual stereotypes, he also mentioned their exclusion from the People of the Book and subsequent difficulties for their community.[24]

The eighteenth and nineteenth centuries, however, found the Yezidis in the Syrian Jezira at the bottom end of the local political, social, and moral order. They did not belong to the People of the Book, like Christians and Jews, who enjoyed degrees of autonomy regarding their religious and administrative affairs within the Ottoman millet system. As ethnic Kurds they faced Ottoman taxation and conscription. The Yezidis in Jebel Sim'an (as the area was commonly known then) did not suffer from Ottoman persecution in the same way as their fellow Yezidis in the Jezira (or neighboring Tur Abdin area); but many of them were conscripted and some of them were sent to distant places, like Yemen, from where they never returned. Apparently, the Yemen episode is still prominent in Yezidi memory. It was narrated to me several times, when I asked about the distribution of Yezidi communities.[25]

According to Siouffi, at the end of the nineteenth century a representative of the *feqir* caste lived in Aleppo, who was addressed as *kak* (brother).[26] Jullien mentioned between 10,000 and 15,000 Yezidis in northern Syria until Aleppo,[27] a relatively high number which should include the Yezidis west of Aleppo. A large Yezidi community was also found in Damascus, which faced hostility from the Arab Sunni population because of its involvement in the massacres of 1860 and the Syrian Revolution of 1925.[28] In 1905, the region of Jebel Sim'an was visited by Gertrude Bell, a British traveler and politician, who was accompanied by Yezidi guards and leaders. They conveyed basic information to her, in particular about the issue of sun worship.[29]

5.3.2. The Yezidis during the French Mandate

After the end of the Ottoman Empire and the establishment of British and French mandates in the area, the political borders of Syria were redefined at subsequent conferences in San Remo, London, and Lausanne. The result was an official split-up of the Kurdish territories which ended in the separation of the Western Yezidi community from their main homeland. The border between Syria and Turkey followed the tracks of the Baghdad Railway, which led to the creation of three Kurdish enclaves around Aleppo, Ayn al-Arab, and the Jezira. These enclaves were separated from each other by hundreds of kilometers, which made personal and economic interaction communication increasingly difficult. From now on it was almost impossible to maintain regular contacts with the sanctuaries and leaders in newly established Iraq. In some cases, for example in the village of Sere Kaniye (Ras al-Ayn) or Dirbesiya (Darbasiyah), the new borderline was drawn directly through existing settlements by cutting them in half and placing them under two different political and legal authorities.

French rule in Syria brought two new political concepts to the Kurds and Yezidis: autonomy and decentralization. These played a major role in the development of a Kurdish national identity, which was further strengthened by the immigration of Turkish and Iraqi Kurds after failed revolts against the new political leadership. Yezidis in the Jezira were drawn into these events and started to develop their own identity, both religiously and politically. However, they were mainly influenced by events and encounters of the Yezidis in the Sinjar Mountain with British authorities in Iraq.

French rule gave previously disadvantaged groups the opportunity for participation and self-organization. Like other religious minorities (Druzes, Alawites, Maronites), the Kurds/Yezidis were ready to serve in special Mandate troops. This offered a unique chance to escape from economic misery and a rare opportunity to advance within the social hierarchy. Yezidis took advantage of this opportunity and were overrepresented with regard to the total population. In 1930, they measured with 0.06 percent of the total Syrian population, but they counted for 0.2 percent of the Special Forces.[30]

However, because most Yezidis were illiterate, only a few were actually acquitted. It was a custom that only members of the ruling Sheikh lineage were permitted to attend school. Community leaders feared that attending school would lead to further Islamization or Christianization of their children. It took Yezidi activists many years to overcome this age-old tradition. The logical consequence was to establish their own schools, which they did in the village of Qibare. However, since no official permit was issued and anti-Yezidi resentments grew, the school was closed a few years later. But it was regarded as a first step toward a distinct Yezidi approach toward religious education, a struggle that would last for several decades.

Henri Lammens(1907) came up with the number of 3,000 Yezidis in the Kurdagh area at the beginning of the twentieth century, which he said was confirmed by his informants.[31] Fuccaro cited an unofficial census from 1937 which listed 1,082 Yezidis in the Jebel Akrad, 87 in the Hasake region, and 797 in Qamishli.[32] Zakariya in 1945 mentioned 700 families with an estimated family size of five members, which adds up to 3,500 individuals.[33] The French Mandate administration then conducted a census, in which the Yezidis made up 10 percent of the Kurdish population of 200,000.[34]

During the first years of the mandate, Syria became a safe haven for Kurdish refugees from Turkey and Iraq, who had to flee their homelands after failed nationalist uprisings. Among them were Yezidis from Sinjar who found refuge with their Syrian brothers. Similar to the situation in neighboring countries, Syrian Kurdish intellectuals as well as aghas and tribal leaders from the Jezira established a well-organized autonomy movement.[35] However, their movement and agenda were not supported by Yezidi Kurds, mainly due to the lack of an educated class among them. Only some individuals both from the Kurdagh and the Jezira supported the national movement and thus contributed to the development of Kurdish nationalism in the region. They were members and subscribers of *Hawar*,[36] a journal devoted to the Kurdish cause published between 1932 and 1943 by Jalalat Bedrkhan. The journal used the Latin script, which widened the cultural gap between the Yezidis in Syria and Iraq, the latter using the Arabic script. However, during this time, the Kurdish areas in Syria witnessed a period of cultural enlightenment through the publishing of Kurdish newspapers, airing of radio programs in Kurdish, and the maintaining of specific customs and traditions in everyday life (clothing) as well as artistic expression. Leading Kurdish intellectuals and writers, such as Bedrkhan and Cigerxwin, used this freedom of expression to publish articles and poems related to the Yezidis.

Influences from Turkey and Iraq

Despite the newly drawn political borders, limited contacts between the Yezidis in the Jezira and Sinjar continued; however, this happened mostly in the form of a one-way-movement into French territory. After gaining nominal independence in 1932, the national government in Iraq immediately began to enforce the conscription law on religious minority groups like the Yezidis. In addition, Yezidi sanctuaries had to be registered as Islamic endowments, *waqf*. In response, the Yezidis in Sinjar under Dawud al-Dawud[37] rebelled against the central government. During the military skirmishes, many villages were destroyed, Yezidis killed, and others sentenced to long prison terms, some even executed. A larger group including leader Dawud al-Dawud managed to escape to Syria, where their descendants can still be found near the city of Amuda.[38] Others followed their example and voluntarily moved to Syria, thus using the creation of the new states to their advantage. Syrian Yezidi leaders, such as Jamil Shamo from Efrin and Sheikh Khidr from the Qiran tribe, lobbied and negotiated with the French authorities in order to allow other Iraqi Yezidis to follow. Up to 10,000 Yezidis wanted to move to Syrian territory to escape the conflict with the Iraqi government.[39]

In April 1939, Sheikh Khalaf, supreme leader of the Haskan tribes, led some of his tribal groups into Qamishli, with French permission. However, three years later, large contingents of refugees had to return to Iraq after the political tensions between the mandate powers had eased up. Hence, it is noteworthy that the border at this time was relatively open and the migration of entire groups and communities was still possible. It was in the interest of the French, who had their headquarters in Hasake, to encourage large-scale resettlement of Yezidi groups. This would create another small and decentralized minority canton, but also offered economic stimulus to the area, because Sinjar Yezidis were well-known skilled farmers. Otherwise, the region between Hasake and Qamishli was dominated by nomadic groups.

In contrast to earlier practices, the new refugees were not granted land allocations, but had to rely on tribal and religious support. Even Dawud al-Dawud had to ask for permission to settle with his relatives in Amuda.[40] High taxation and custom fees prevented the Sinjar Yezidis from bringing their herds. French Mandate authorities were worried that the Yezidis would become too influential, especially considering the possible introduction of a Syrian recruitment law.

The Yezidis in the Sheikhan district in Iraq remained quiet during the rebellions. And after the defeat of the Sinjari Yezidis, the Sheikhan leaders, in particular Mayan Khatun, mother of Mir Said Beg, were ready to take control of the Sinjar Yezidis. After the death of their charismatic leaders Ismail Beg and Hamo Shiro and the expulsion of Dawud al-Dawud, no one remained to oppose these challenges. Only Ismail's son Yazid Khan rose against Mir Said Beg in 1937/38. However, the death sentence, which he was given for his rebellion against the Yezidi authorities, could not be carried out because Mir Said Beg was shot down by his wife Wansa, the sister of Yazid Khan. Eventually, she fled to Syria, to the Yezidi communities in Efrin. French authorities granted her asylum to stay in Aleppo. Only two years later, during World War II, she was deported back to Baghdad because as a refugee she could provide no proper paperwork and documentation.[41] She later married an Egyptian and settled in Cairo.[42]

Other Kurds came to Syria from Turkey after several nationalist revolts there were crushed, such as the Sheikh Said rebellion 1925–28, the rebellion at Ararat in 1930, or in Dersim in 1937–38. In Syria they continued their political and military activities. The largest political organization Khoybun had for many years its headquarters in Damascus and branches in Aleppo and Hasake. Khoybun was the first pan-Kurdish association that tried to combine nationalist ideas with the heterogeneous tribal society of Kurds and Yezidis. The association also idealized Yezidism as the only true religion of the Kurds, without however including prominent Yezidi members.[43]

Hajo Agha, the leader of the Heverkan tribal confederation that included many Yezidi clans, organized Khoybun activities in Hasake. He was in close contact with Ismail Beg Col, the Sinjar Yezidi leader, who tried several times to become the overall leader of the Yezidis in the name of Khoybun. After Hajo returned from Turkey in 1926, he settled with his Yezidi fellow tribesmen and with French support in Syria and built the city of Tirbespi (Qahtaniya). Other Yezidi families from both sides of the border followed suit and added to the demographic, but not economic, growth of the community during this time. Issa provides a lively account of the quarrels among the various Yezidi, Kurdish, Turkish, and Arab groups in the 1920s:

> Disputes occurred mainly between the Heverkan and other Kurdish tribes that collaborated with Turkish authorities. The cause of the conflict was the age-old enmity between the Yezidi Shamdin Coli from the Dasikan tribe and the Muslim Kurd Ali Hassa, who was a land owner in Tall Sagan. Ali Hassa approached the local Turkish authorities in Nusaybin with the request to expel the Yezidis from the Tur Abdin region. For this, he would provide the soldiers and supplies. The Heverkan, which included many Yezidi families, placed their fighters under the command of Hajo and his oldest son Hassan and sent their women, children and elderly to Merbab. Then they took position around Bagok Mountain. Initially, the Turkish army did not take the Yezidis seriously and sent only a small unit to break the resistance. However, the Yezidis killed the commander of the troops. After this incident, the Turkish authorities pressured other Kurdish Muslim tribes into joining the Turkish troops against the Heverkan. These tribes included the Saliha, Domanah, Dorlah, Seyde Memolanah and others. Those, who supported Hajo and the Heverkan, were the Yezidi tribes of Afsi, Bahminman, Mihokan, Dasikan and Kiwekhan. They also featured several women, for example, Halima and Adule from Hajo's family, who encouraged their fighters. The battle started at dawn and lasted the entire day. Over hundred Turkish soldiers were killed in the attempt to conquer Merbab and take the women and children there hostage. The governor of Nusaybin, Qudur Beg had to intervene in order to reach a cease fire. Sometimes later in 1926, the Yezidis were again attacked by Turkish troops and their Kurdish allies. This time however, they were outgunned and had to surrender after a long siege of their stronghold on Mount Bagok near the town of Nuseybin. Of the 250 prisoners,

only two children survived the massacre. Fighters, such as Hajo and his sons, Shamdin Coli, Meke Shamo, Omar Khalid and other Yezidi tribal leaders were able to flee across the border to the Syrian village of Tirbespi, where they sought asylum with the French authorities.[44]

They also obtained identity cards and in some cases land allocations. With the support of the mandate power, Hajo and his Muslim and Yezidi followers rebuilt the city of Tirbespi. Later, more Yezidi families settled here. Among them were many Yezidi families from the Turkish border region, for example from the village of Kiwekh, who then settled on the Syrian side of the border. They kept their tribal names and identity and were known as the Kiwekhis.

It was an official policy of the mandate powers to settle religious/ethnic groups in separate villages. Public land[45] was granted for free or cheap loans and the settlements allotted to homogenous groups such as the Christians, Yezidis, Arab tribes and Kurdish Muslims. Altug gives a detailed description of the land distribution policies along ethnic-confessional lines:

> Ibrahim Pasha Milli, the leader of the Kurdish Milli tribe, took possession of the lands to the west of Ras al-'Ayn. The Chechens who were settled to the south of Ras al-'Ayn at the end of 19th century appropriated vast plots of land on the banks of the Khabur River, between Ras al-Ayn and Hassaka. The Kurdish tribe Heverkan became the landholder to the south of Qamishli. The Kurdish tribes of Alian and Hasanan ... possessed the land in the east of the Djagh Djagh River towards the Tigris. As for the nomadic Arab tribes, it was especially the lands of the Arab tribe Tayy which were opened to agriculture thanks to the Armenian peasants working on their lands. The leader of the Tayy, Abd al-Mohsen, owned the villages in the west of the river Djgah Djagh. Daham al-Hadi of Shammar owned Chill agha, close to Demir Qapu and several other villages in the eastern part of Qamishli.[46]

Mixed villages with two dominant groups were also established in which case two mukhtars were appointed, one for each community. The land was usually given to the two or three leading families of the interest group, many of which had served in the paramilitary forces. Also, refugee communities were granted lots, in particular the Armenians and the Assyrians, but also Yezidi groups from Urfa, Tur Abdin, and Viranshehir. Those were often located on the banks of the rivers (Euphrates, Khabur, Ja'ja, and Tigris) and the outskirts of the new urban centers (Hasake, Qamishli, and Ras al-Ayn). This is how many of the Yezidi villages in the Jezira were founded.

On the Yezidi Community in Kurdagh

As mentioned earlier, the Yezidi community in the Kurdagh has a much longer recorded history than the Jezira Yezidis. However, only little is recorded about the situation of the Yezidis in Efrin during the French Mandate. We thus have to consult reports and sources that describe the general cultural, political, and economic situation in the region with regard to the Kurd. It is necessary to mention that the region retained its character as a closed socieconomic unit, whose inhabitants had settled there for centuries. The Yezidis were part of this region; however without a strong, unified leadership. Kurds in Efrin regarded the new French rulers differently; some supported them, while others rejected the French Mandate. Some Yezidis fought actively against French authorities and promoted Kurdish national interests, such as Darwish Shamo, leader of the village Qibare.

Darwish Shamo was not one of the rich landowners or Aghas like most of the Kurdish-Muslim community leaders; however, through his actions and with a little help from the French he became the undisputed leader of the Yezidis in the area. His family originally was from Aleppo where they worked as carpenters and later moved to Qibare. During World War I, Darwish made a good fortune as a wood trader with the Ottoman army which needed a continual supply of wood for its train system. Because of his important business he was also exempted from military service. As a successful businessman he gained some reputation among his Yezidi followers. Thus, after the war, he was selected to represent the community at a meeting with King Faysal, along with his brother Nasr, during which they expressed their allegiance to the new ruler.[47]

In the aftermath of the war and the ensuing chaos, Turkish paratroopers scuffled with Yezidi fighters near Qibare. During the fighting Darwish was wounded. The French troops ended the clashes and demanded a meeting with the Yezidis. Darwish and Ali Jindo, his father-in-law and family head[48] in

Figure 5.2 Stone Plate at Former Yezidi School in Qibare. *Source*: With permission from eSyria.

the villages of Qestel Jindo and Qatme, were chosen as their representatives. Although Darwish was still young, he already made a name among his folks. In the meeting he asked for permission to open a special school for their children, and the request was granted.

While education for the masses was still frowned upon by the local elite, Darwish opened the first Yezidi school in the Kurdagh inside his house in 1926. He received official permit from the Mandate authorities and donated the building and school supplies. A teacher was brought from Iraq. His name was Khidr Jum'a Effendi from Bahzani who married a local Yezidi girl and started a family. After the killing of Darwish Shamo and the death of his wife, Khidr left Syria.

The stone marker over the school house had an inscription: *This library was founded by the grace of God for the Yezidi community in the Kurdagh Region and the efforts of Darwish Agha bin Shamo 1927/1344.*

The children were taught reading, general science, Arabic language, and Yezidi religion, the latter, of course in Kurdish. Teaching continued until 1931 when Darwish Agha died and the teacher moved back to Iraq.[49]

The French authorities also granted Darwish the right to form a local militia, which was put under the leadership of Umar Effendi, the brother of Darwish, and became known as the Kurdish Cavalry. So well received were his actions and accomplishments that the entire Yezidi community in the Kurdagh accepted him as their leader. The Qaimaqam approved this selection and Darwish became known as the Agha of the Yezidi tribes in the District of Azaz and Kurdagh. Two years later on June 2, 1927, he received an official appointment letter from Mir Said Beg, the Mir and supreme Yezidi leader in Iraq, entrusting him with the administration of Yezidi affairs in the Kurdagh:[50]

> According to my general authorization as Amir of Sheikhan, Said Beg bin Ali bin Huseyn Beg, who lives in the village of Ba'adhre in the Sheikhan District in the Mosul Province, I grant him with the power according to my wishes. This happens according to the Book of Certified Authorization by the Justice Secretary in Mosul, dated February 10, 1923, and numbered # 461/217 when I decided to grant Darwish Agha bin Shamo from the village of Qibare in the district of Azaz and Kurdagh, part of the city of Aleppo in Syria the general authorization for all lawsuits and quarrels, which occur to my clients and him on my behalf. Accordingly he is inaugurated to the endowments of Sheikh Adi mentioned in the book of authorization for all legal civil courts, legal trade courts, criminal and reconciliation courts and for all other institutions, official councils as prosecutor and defendant and third person for complaints that are happening. I, with my general authority mentioned above, refer my own position and the position of the Sheikh Adi endowment to Darwish Agha Bin Shamo hoping that he will do well and protects the rights of my people and the rights of

the above mentioned endowment. He has to deal with everything that is directed at him. This authority is given to him for two full years. This statement is given to the secretary of the agency for approval. The general representative of Said Beg bin Ali Beg, Amir of Sheikhan, according to the authorization mentioned above, date and number.

The Lawyer Abd al-Ahad bin Eliasi

Apparently, some local Yezidi families resisted his appointment which goes along with the concurrent power struggle within the Mir's family in Sheikhan and in Sinjar between Mir Said and his rival cousin Ismail Beg.

When the city of Efrin was founded in 1925, Darwish like other Kurdish Aghas built himself a house there. From here he continued his political activities, which included his membership in *Khoybun* as well as his relationship with the Syrian National Movement and Ibrahim Hanano and the Kurdish National Movement and the Bedirkhan family. Both Jaladat and Kamiran Bedirkhan traveled several times to the Kurdagh and met their close friend Darwish. It was speculated a lot about this seemingly overstated interest of the Bedirkhan brothers in the Yezidis. Possibly they looked at the community as the most cohesive and distinct Kurdish group, which was also hostile to the Islamists for religious reasons, but maintained friendly relations with the French. However, it appears that Darwish, although being a friend of the Bedirkhans, remained somewhat independent and did not provide them with any material or even military support.[51] However, he did join Khoybun after all. After his death, the communication with the Bedirkhans intensified through his son, Jamil Agha.

During these times, British and French plans were revealed that discussed the possible creation of a Yezidi territory in Sinjar and Sheikhan. Some Yezidi communities were supposed to move there. Darwish, in favor of this plan, sent his brother Naser to discuss the details of the plan with the Mir in Sheikhan, Said Beg. But, because of the resistance of the Sinjar Yezidis the plan was never implemented. Darwish kept his position and good relationship with the French, the Syrian nationalists, and the Kurds, and in 1926 he was even awarded a French honor medal. On the other hand, he also created many enemies among the Kurdish Aghas, and he was killed in 1931, some say in blood revenge.[52]

Jamil Agha

After Darwish' death, his son Jamil Agha was chosen as the new leader of the Efrin community. This was confirmed officially from the governor in Aleppo who appointed him a chief and judge of the Yezidi tribes in Azaz and Kurdagh according to this authorization letter:

Aleppo Province
Kurdagh District
Department of Letters
To HE the Qaimaqam in Kurdagh,

HE the deputy high commissioner informed me that the person called Jamil bin Darwish Shamo requested on February 27, 1932 the recognition of the administrative and legal authorities as religious chief of the Yezidis. In support of his request I send a copy of the transcript to support his followers in the district of Azaz and Kurdagh. HE the Deputy High Commissioner added that he saw no wrong in answering his request. Please issue the necessary instructions in this regard to the authorities in the two mentioned districts. With this, HE sends his regards and answer to his request for recognition in the same way as for his late father.

Accept my respect
March 9, 1932
Regent of Aleppo Muhammad Nabih

In recognition of Jamil Bin Darwish Shamo as religious chief of the Yezidi sect this letter was filed for the department heads.

Qaimaqam Kurdagh, Ahmad Hamdi Abd al-Nur,

Like his father, Jamil also received an authorization letter from Mir Said Beg on May 14, 1934 entrusting him with the legal and religious affairs of the Yezidis in the Aleppo region. After Mir Said's death, Jamil received a renewed authorization from Mayan Khatun, mother of Said and interim ruler of the Yezidis until Mir Tahsin Beg reached legal age.

Jamil Agha continued the legacy of his father by maintaining good relations with the French, the Syrian nationalist leaders, and the Kurdish Bedirkhan brothers. The latter introduced him to Bayard Dodge[53], then president of the American University in Beirut, with whom he exchanged letters about their friendship and the progress of the few Yezidi students in Beirut.[54] In addition, Jamil Agha was one of the participants/subscribers to *Hewar*, the first Kurdish-speaking journal in Syria published by Bedirkhan. Jamil Agha resided in Qatma, then the administrative center and largest settlement with a railway connection, but he was also involved in the development of the city of Efrin.

The first census and registration of Yezidis in the Kurdagh was conducted during Jamil's reign in 1932, and they were given ID cards, which mentioned Yezidi as the religious affiliation of the card holder. Some cards said Syrian—Yezidi, while other cards wrote Syrian—Yezidi—Kurd.

Some evidence was found that linked the Murid Movement, an active military Sufi movement in the Kurdagh under the leadership of Ibrahim Khalil to the Yezidis.[55] The local tribe of the Shikak, which included both Muslim and Yezidi groups, was opposed to the movement, and the Yezidi village of Qestel Jindo was attacked and besieged as a result. During another encounter, Jamil Agha traveled together with Sheikh Isa of the Shikak tribe, and they were attacked by the Murids. Only Jamil survived the assassination attack, while the sheikh was killed.[56][57] During this time, the entire area witnessed an increasing Islamization, where individuals, families, and sometimes entire villages were forced to convert. Many Yezidis superficially converted as well, but maintained their true religious identity. Others gave up their religion, because they saw an economic and social advantage, something Yezidism was unable to offer. Religious ceremonies and instruction were difficult to maintain due to the lack of trained clerics. In addition, the qewals who were supposed to visit the Yezidi communities annually during the tawaf rarely traveled as far as the Kurdagh. As mentioned earlier, this led to misunderstandings about the religiosity of the community, and these resentments were expressed among Yezidis from the Jezira and Iraq. Even the young Mir Tahsin Beg doubted the seriousness of religious practice in the Kurdagh.[58] On the other hand, Yezidis from Kurdagh continuously tried to revive contacts with the Yezidis in the mainland. Jamil Agha, for example, had close relations with Ismail Beg Col until the latter's death. Mir Said Beg spent a few days in 1933 in Qibare, and Dawud al-Dawud paraded through the village in 1936.[59]

After Syria gained her independence, most of Jamil's activities had to cease because of his close ties with the French authorities. He was forced to withdraw from public life and into reclusion until his death on December 11, 1972. Jamil's brother Masto briefly reappeared in public life when he participated in a large gathering of tribal chiefs from Syria, Iraq, and Jordan held in Amman in the 1950s.

Until the end of the Mandate period, both Syrian Yezidi communities were able to maintain their position within the regional minority context. This was possible due to the growing Kurdish nationalist movement and its temporary support by the French authorities. However, as a result, the Yezidis drifted into a clash of loyalties between nationalist (Kurdish and Arabic), colonial (French and British), and Islamic movements. The growth of the Kurdish national movement in Syria and neighboring countries, the often militarist response of their governments, as well as the increasing Islamization of the entire society, led to a permanent weakening of the traditional structure of the community and brought them to the verge of extinction.

By that time, however, the Syrian Yezidis developed a unique identity among the other minority groups. As ethnic Kurds they had similar experiences with Ottoman, French, and Arab ruling elites, who tried to extend their hegemony over Kurdish territories. Hence, Yezidis were treated like other Kurdish groups. However, their status as a heterodox religious minority contributed significantly to their persecution and their subsequent relegation to the bottom end of the social hierarchy. Very little outside support was noted, as well as very little Kurdish solidarity.

However, because of the physical separation of the settlement area, two different developments unfolded, with long-lasting consequences with regard to the formation of Yezidi religious and social identity in Syria: Yezidis from the Kurdagh consider themselves and are considered by others as different from their brothers and sisters in the Syrian Jezira. The proximity or distance to the religious centers of the group in northern Iraq fostered this dichotomy as did the lack of interaction between the groups. With Syrian Yezidis generally being stigmatized as heretics by the society at large, Yezidis from the Jezira were also (mis)-treated as such outcasts. Yezidis from the Kurdagh experienced this much less. The self-perceptions of the two groups reflect this dual approach. While Yezidis from the Jezira incorporated the issue of victimization in their identity building, Yezidis from the Kurdagh drew on their partial integration into society in order to create a more assertive and proud Yezidi identity.

5.3.3. Short Account of Modern Yezidi History in Iraq

After the end of World War II, the Yezidi territories in Iraq remain in the spotlight. Mayan Khatun served as the regent for her minor grandson Tahsin, who inherited the office from his father Said who died in 1944. When Mayan Khatun died in 1957, she left a community that was cohesive, consolidated, and isolationist. The Grand Dame of the Yezidis stood for a period of peaceful developments, which was based on her skillful political and organizational maneuvering between the nationalist and religious forces in Iraq. In 1947 she was able to install a Yezidi member of parliament.

The July revolution of 1958 and subsequent abolishment of the monarchy brought an end to this era and saw the beginning of renewed clashes with "progressive nationalistic" Iraqi Arab forces. The Yezidis sided with Mulla Mustafa Barzani during his rebellion in 1961, which led to a new campaign of repression. The Yezidis participated only partly in the rebellion when an antigovernment revolt broke out in Sinjar in 1965 that required several Iraqi brigades to contain. The government's response was much harsher and brutal and usually included the exemplary punishment of selected villages: in 1969 Dokian in the Sheikhan region and in 1973, Cesivan in Sinjar were raided. In the following years, however, forced relocation of entire regions became a favorite tool of oppression in the hands of the government. First in Sheikhan and since 1975 also in Sinjar, the government started to remove the village population and resettled them in so-called *mujammas* or collective towns in the plains of Nineveh near the main road. This allowed for better control and separation from other Kurdish/Yezidi groups.[60]

Another tactic used by the Iraqi government was to separate the Yezidis from the Kurdish block and to Arabize them. Because of the unclear connection with the Umayyad caliph Yazid bin Muawiya, they were declared ethnic Arabs. This would not have happened without the support of some elements from within the community; those who trace their descant back to Arab origin (and even to Yazid), and those who thought it would be a perfect opportunity to challenge the authority of the Mir's family. In particular Ismail Beg children and grandchildren, Bayazid and Muawiya, played a decisive role in the power struggle. However, the majority of the population had little knowledge about or interest in these dirty political games. Their priority was to cope with the ongoing displacement and discrimination. For many, the only solution was to escape; some went to Syria, while many others, including the Mir and members of his household, went to Germany.

The Iraqi government created a new agency to be in charge of the administration and issues regarding the Yezidis. The Yezidi Committee was to educate the underdeveloped and primitive Yezidi villages about the achievement of central planning and agrarian reform and to make the Yezidi complete Iraqi citizens.[61] What sounded progressive in theory and on paper, and brought to the collective towns running water, electricity, paved roads, schools, and health centers, was in reality a clever attempt to concentrate the population of different regions in a camp where old traditions were abandoned and state control was exercised. The Mir and his family were labeled as feudal oppressors and their properties confiscated (but not redistributed).

In addition to the official Yezidi committee, a subcommittee of notables and clerics was founded "who support the state policies."[62] The committee was tasked for a transitional period to collect the religious fees and use them to preserve the shrines. They served as a temporary link between the Yezidis and the government.

The period between 1975 and 1991 was characterized by a profound change within the Yezidi community in Iraq. They not only lost their leadership, but were concurrently uprooted, dispossessed, and evicted from their villages and lands. At the same time, the previously rural, mostly uneducated, community was exposed to new political, social, and religious influences. Not surprisingly, the ensuing internal conflict led to a split within the group: on the one hand were those who profited from the changed and made arrangements with the regime. This group was led by members from the Adani sheikh family, who was previously secondary in rank and power to the Mir family. Those Adani sheikhs used the power vacuum created by the departure of the Mir and his family and occupied the worldly leadership position. Their relatives were appointed as directors of the collective towns, which required the membership in the Ba'th party and recognition of the Arab identity for the Yezidis.

The other group was comprised of mainly communists who collaborated with non-Yezidi Kurdish communists and stressed the ethnic bonds between Yezidis and Kurds in contrast to the mandatory Arabic nature of Yezidis. This group actively participated in the Kurdish resistance movement, while the Yezidi population at large was sympathizing with them.

The religious leaders maintained a mostly neutral position insofar as they were not collaborating with the Yezidi committee. Only the institution of the Baba Sheikh provided some religious stability and was considered a guarantor for the continual existence of Yezidi religious tradition during these troubled times. However, he too had to deal with the new political and religious elites.

Mir Tahsin Beg had to go into exile in 1974 first to Germany and later to Great Britain. However, he tried to win back the position and influence of his family. For this, he accepted the amnesty offer by the Iraqi government and returned to Iraq in 1981. He moved to Baghdad where he was given an office and a house. The other members of his extended family who usurped the power, for example, Bayazid Ismail Beg and Muawiya Bayazid Beg, remained in charge with the official approval of the government. The meddling in the Yezidi political affairs continued when the government tried to install yet another candidate as the Mir; for example, Kheyri Beg, brother of Tahsin, was groomed to curb the influence of the Ismail clan. At the same time and especially among the Yezidis abroad, Tahsin Beg remained the undisputed and widely recognized leader of the community. However, his political influence diminished significantly.

After the Gulf War a large-scale Kurdish rebellion broke out against the Iraqi regime. Due to the passivity of the West, this rebellion was brutally crushed and more than 1.5 million Kurds fled to Turkey and Iran, among them many Yezidis, including Kheyri Beg. Only after the establishment of the no-fly zone and the Kurdish safe haven did the security situation improve. Within the newly established Kurdish Autonomy Zone, a government was elected and civil society prospered with the recognition of minority rights. Some Yezidi territories were located within the zone, such as Lalish and the Sheikhan region, while Sinjar remained under Iraqi control.

For the first time in the history of the Yezidis started an era free from religious or ethnic persecution inside the Kurdish autonomy zone. Even though they did not participate in the electoral process, they were widely recognized as a separate Kurdish-Yezidi community. Among the highlights of this evolutional process was that the community was able to celebrate its annual pilgrimage to Lalish and build or renovate some shrines. It founded a center in Dohuk, which coordinated the cultural and religious activities and was given the name Lalish Center.

The separation of the Sinjar community and their isolation from the religious centers and ceremonies remained a heavy burden and subsequently fostered the development of two different identities. Thus, a third identity group emerged from among the many Iraqi Yezidis who left the country and settled in the diaspora. The connections, contacts, and material support remained an important factor for the individual families and villages. However, the community now has to accommodate three groups struggling over the political leadership.

The community's traditional leadership is located in Sheikhan and so are the main sanctuaries as well as the main pilgrimage destination in Lalish near Mosul.[63] With roughly half a million followers, Yezidism is now the second largest religious community in Iraq after Islam. Previously, Christianity held this position, but many Iraqi Christians left the country out of fear over increased sectarian attacks by radical Muslims.

After the fall of Saddam Hussein's regime, the political and religious leaders of the Yezidi community in Iraq and in the diaspora initiated an informal meeting between the leader of the community, Mir Tahsin Beg and Paul Bremer, the head of the Coalition Provisional Authority and the then president of Iraq, Ghazi Yawar, with the objective to sanction the Yezidis in the draft constitution as a protected, recognized minority. The earlier misspelling of the group name that resembled a Shiite group from Yemen has now been corrected. But, apart from the temporary appointment of Pir Mamo Othman as minister without portfolio, no other significant political gains have been made. Local Yezidi representatives are ignored and often barred from attending important meetings. Local city and village councils rarely include Yezidi members. Requests for a quota of representatives have not been recognized, while during the elections in January of 2005, Yezidi voters faced significant interference and discrimination, and many of them were locked out from the election process.

Since the liberation from the Ba'ath regime, the Iraqi Yezidis made many efforts to build a stable and functioning community within the Kurdish territories. They enjoyed much financial support and military protection from the Kurdish Democratic Party (KDP) (Kurdish: Partiya Demokrat a Kurdistane—PDK) of Mas'ud Barzani and the Peshmerga militia. For some Yezidis from Sinjar, who feared that they would lose their newly gained autonomy, the support provided by the KDP went too far. However, cultural centers were opened throughout the Yezidi villages, seats for Yezidi representatives were finally reserved in the regional parliament, and religious sites and shrines were renovated with public funds. All this speaks for the reasonably well-established relationship between the Kurds of different religions.

On the other hand, Arab Muslims still hold many grudges against the Yezidis and show their antipathy through various means of hate speech, discrimination, and violence. During the height of the insurgency in 2007, leaflets were distributed in Mosul and preachers at local mosques called Yezidis infidels and outlaws. The presence of radical militant groups such as al-Qaida and IS contributed to the growing tensions between mostly Arab Muslims and the Yezidis. When news about the stoning of a Yezidi girl by her family spread because she wanted to convert to Islam and marry a Sunni, violence erupted again, and the number of deadly attacks against the Yezidis community increased rapidly. The execution of twenty-four Yezidi workers who traveled by bus from Mosul to Bashiqa is just one example. Sometimes one or two persons and at other times several Yezidis have been shot, kidnaped, and executed during this period. But the most horrific one was the coordinated suicide bomb attack on the Sinjar villages of Qahtaniya (Kurdish: Giru Izer) and Jazira (Kurdish: Siba Sheikh Khidr) on August 14, 2007. During the deadliest attack in the entire Iraq war, more than 500 people were killed and over 1,500 wounded. Although no one claimed responsibility, it was believed to be carried out by al-Qaida operatives.

After the American and coalition troops' withdrawal from Iraq, the situation in northern Iraq remained stable; however, attacks on Yezidis outside the Kurdish zone continue. On May 14, 2013, ten Yezidi shopkeepers were killed during an armed attack on alcohol vendors in Baghdad. It is worth mentioning that only non-Muslims are permitted to sell alcohol and that the security forces do little to protect them. The Muslim-dominated public opinion looks down upon the trade and those who work it, which adds to the general anti-Yezidi resentments. In an ever highly segregated Iraqi society, Yezidis have not found acceptance or safety outside their traditional realm.

5.3.3.1. The Shingal Massacre

In early August of 2014, the fighters of the Islamic State in Iraq and Syria (ISIS) carried out a surprise attack on the Sinjar Mountain, home to approximately 250,000 Iraqi Yezidis. A small Peshmerga unit was stationed in Sinjar in order to protect the Yezidis; however, in a surprise move, they abandoned their posts in the night before the attack leaving the Yezidis unprotected and vulnerable. Within a few days ISIS troops conquered all Yezidi villages located around the mountain and started killing, enslaving, and expelling the Yezidis. Some 80,000 Yezidis fled to seek refuge on the mountain where they ended up stuck for days without shelter, food, or supplies. Those who could not flee and had to remain in the villages were subjugated to brutal treatments that included mass executions, rape, destruction of their homes and properties, looting, and kidnaping of women and children. A week later the US-led international coalition started airstrikes against ISIS positions and with the help of Kurdish militias a corridor was created to allow the refugees on the mountain escape the siege. Although in safety now, the huge number of refugees created another humanitarian crisis. Estimates speak of 200,000 Yezidi refugees in addition to those 250,000 Iraqis who fled from the ISIS advance and earlier conquest of Mosul. During the month of September, ISIS expanded their activities and started attacking Yezidi villages within the Kurdish Region. They managed to conquer Bashiqa and Bahzani, but were stopped by PKK fighters before they reached Lalish. With an intensified airstrike campaign, a fierce resistance operation by Yezidi units, and a ground offensive by the Peshmerga it was possible to liberate most of Sinjar from ISIS occupation. However, at the time of writing, this campaign is not finished; fighting continues in the foothills of the mountain and the refugees still cannot return home.

Many Yezidis from Sinjar blamed the Kurdish regional government for betraying the Yezidis and failing to protect them. Thus, they call for an autonomous region in Sinjar and the arming of the community to defend them in the future. Other voices call for abandoning Sinjar for good and moving to a safe place, possibly Germany. Going back to Sinjar is not a viable alternative because the situation on the ground is very unsafe and the relationship with their Arab/Muslim neighbors is poisoned.

5.3.4. Yezidis in the Syrian Arabic Republic

After the declaration of independence in 1946 and subsequent French withdrawal, Syria became a republic with an unstable political system defined by growing Arab nationalism. Political rights gained by minority groups during the mandate system were gradually displaced, for example, the representation of minority groups in the parliament dropped Christians, Alawites, and Druzes, while Kurdish and Jewish representatives were left out completely. Frequent military coups illustrate the political instability and deep resentments between the various ethnic, religious, and political factions. A national Syrian identity did not emerge or perhaps wasn't encouraged to emerge. Instead the national discourse was captured by Arab nationalists with slight sectarian undertones. The three-year-long union with Egypt enforced the political centralization and Arabization of Syria.

The Ba'th party was founded in 1947 on the principles of unity, freedom, and socialism by the Christian Michel Aflaq, the Sunni Salahudin Beytar, and the Alawite Zaki Arzuzi. They focused primarily on pan-Arab nationalism with a lesser emphasis on Islam. After a failed coup, Ba'th with the help of the military took over the government in 1963, eliminating political rivals and representatives from other identity groups. From now on, Arab nationalist policies were the maxims of the Syrian government, with state institutions actively suppressing other ideologies such as sectarian, communist, or Kurdish groups.

In 1962, Muhammad Talib Hilal, former security chief of Hasake province, published a study about the national, social, and political situation in the province, in which he made recommendations to improve the security situation and strengthen the Arab character of the region.[64] These recommendations were hostile and discriminative against the majority Kurdish population of the Jezira province, which included and affected the Yezidi community as well. Among the main issues raised by Hilal were the displacement of the Kurdish population, the gradual reduction of service provision, especially in the education sector, and the stripping of Syrian citizenship for many Kurds who were believed to have Turkish citizenship originally. This was accompanied by a media and propaganda campaign that focused on the positive aspects of the Arabs and the negative sides of the Kurds. Furthermore, a military security zone along the border with Turkey was planned as well as agricultural cooperatives on the Kurdish land for Arab farmers.[65]

In order to facilitate these recommendations, the notorious law no. 93 was passed, which stipulated a population census in the Hasake governorate, which resulted in the stripping of citizenship for approximately 120,000 Kurds. All of those were unable to prove to the authorities that they have been living in Syria before 1945. Overnight they lost all of their constitutional rights and livelihood, and so did their children and offspring. The issue was further complicated by the fact that a legal differentiation was made between those affected by the decision. Some were now considered foreigners, *ajanib*, and were issued a red ID card, others weren't given any papers, leaving them unregistered or *maktum*. In some rare cases, local village headmen wrote them a white paper stating their personal information, which was rarely recognized by government authorities.

In 1965, the Syrian government decided to establish a security belt along the Turkish border, 10–15 kilometers deep and stretching some 300 kilometers from the border with Iraq to the city of Ras al-Ayn. Although never fully completed, it brought renewed clashes between the Kurdish and Arab ethnic groups, especially on the local level and in the villages. As a result, many Yezidi villages, especially those in the Wadi al-Jarrah and near Ras al-Ayn, got new Arab/Muslim neighbors, with whom they struggled over the already meager resources. The new arrivals, landless Arab families from Aleppo and Raqqa provinces,[66] clearly had the advantage and state support on their side. Some forty villages for those 4,000 families belonging to the Welde tribe were constructed and approximately two million hectares of Kurdish farmland expropriated. According to the plan, another 140,000 Kurds were supposed to be deported to the southern Syrian provinces. Although many Kurdish families were dispossessed of their lands, they often refused to leave their homes and farms. In some cases families were forcefully evicted and in other cases they actively resisted the expulsion, like in the Yezidi village of Tell Khatun. While the refusal to leave was tacitly accepted by the authorities, those Kurds who lost their citizenship were not allowed to own any property or to build new houses.[67]

Other disadvantages of being stateless or unregistered included severe restrictions in domestic and international travel, limited access to the labor market, denial of access to higher education[68] and health care, and the overall feelings of depression, frustration, and humiliation as unwanted citizens.[69]

Between 60 and 75 percent of the Syrian Yezidis in the Jezira were *maktum* (stateless, no citizenship).[70] As shown earlier, this is a subtle form of discrimination by the authorities with far-reaching social, political, and economic consequences. It denied the maktumin their constitutional rights, such as the right to own property, the right to change the place of residence, the right to exit the country, the right to vote, and the right to be employed in the public sector. Some maktum and ajanib even had to serve their mandatory time in the army, while others were to pay taxes for property they weren't allowed to own.

But generally, as Kurds and Yezidis were conscripted to the Syrian army, some were killed in action. For example, in the Six-Day War in 1967 about a dozen Kurds from Efrin died, and during the 1973 war with Israel, Corporal Hassan Kur Abdo from Qestel Jindo was killed in action alongside sixty other (Muslim) Kurds from Efrin.[71]

Authority in all Syrian villages and towns was in the hand of the mukhtar or village head. Most of the headmen in villages with Yezidi population were Arabs, in some instances they had to be Ba'th party members. But in some villages with a larger Yezidi presence, the mukhtar was appointed from their ranks. For example in Wadi al-Jarah, the two largest Yezidi villages Tell Khatun and Drechik both had Yezidi headman, while the other Yezidi villages were too small to have their own mukhtar or the headman was selected from the Muslim or Christian majority. In the Kurdagh, the villages of Qestel Jindo, Qibare, and Basufan had Yezidi headmen. Some other Yezidi villages near Amuda and Ras al-Ayn had Yezidi headmen too.

As mentioned earlier, this was a position that combined trust, reputation, and the ability to maneuver and balance between the different sectors. For example, the mukhtar was permitted to issue the white ID paper for the maktum. With the overall population growth, most Yezidi settlements grew in number, but usually not in size. They lost many *donums* to Arab farmers, who were resettled among the Yezidi villages. The land was confiscated by the Syrian government when it built the Arab Belt and the Euphrates Dam and given to the Arab newcomers. The mukhtar was helpless against these efforts.

The Uprising in Tell Khatun in 1967

Tell Khatun is one of the Yezidi villages in the Wadi al-Jarrah northeast of the city of Tirbespi (Qahtaniya). On May 15, 1967 the villagers openly resisted the order of the government to turn over their land to Arab settlers during the so-called Arab Belt campaign. A military escort under the leadership of the assistant director of Qamishli province Muhsin Ghabra came to the village to enforce the decision; however, the local families (most of the Yezidis) gathered under the leadership of Osman Sabri, who was a member of the left wing of the Kurdish Democratic Party in Syria (Partiya Demokrat a Kurdi li Suriye PDK-S), and they pushed them back. This was one example how Yezidi Kurds resisted the authorities and avoided expulsion. At the end, many donums were still confiscated; however, the villagers did not have to vacate the village.[72]

Although generally described as nonpolitical, some Yezidi individuals and communities were involved in the political struggle against the Ba'th-dominated state institutions. The Yezidi village of Barzan[73] near Hasake, for example, was known for its strong support of the Syrian Communist Party (SCP), especially in the 1960s. University students from the village, who studied at the University of Aleppo, organized meetings and conferences for the party in the village. The SCP was attractive to Yezidis because it was led by a Kurd, but did not promote Kurdish rights or supported the nationalist/Arabist ideology.[74] Among the first activists from the village were Hanna Ajam, Pir Ahmad Ibrahim, and Ismail Daud. Initially, the SCP was the most popular party among the Syrian Kurds. Unlike the other older political organization, Khoybun, the SCP promoted the integration of the Kurds into Syrian society. But in the 1970s and 1980s, when the party was streamlined into the National Front, the activities ceased.

The main political representation of the Kurds in Syria, the Partiya Demokrat A Kurdistane li Suriye or Kurdish Democratic Party of Syria (PDK-S), was established in 1957. The political events in Iraq clearly affected this decision as well as future decisions to break away from the mother party and to found smaller political factions and divisions.[75] Individual Yezidis from the Jezira region were actively involved in these party politics, but neither the PDK-S nor any other of the many emerging and disappearing parties took a specific stand toward the Yezidis. Instead, those individuals were embedded into the national Kurdish struggle, while the general Yezidi population remained marginalized and underrepresented, lacking any form of political clout to improve their lot.

It came as no surprise that with the worsening of the economic and social situation many Yezidi villagers turned their backs on the Kurdish national struggle and left their villages. Especially, in the 1980s, a large-scale migration from the Yezidi villages to the cities and abroad was noted. While the city of Tirbespi in 1974 did not have any Yezidi family, a decade later, many villagers had left their homes in the Wadi al-Jarrah and moved to the county seat, often abandoning their fields and farms. Equally large numbers of Yezidis continued the move to the provincial centers in Qamishli and Hasake or further to Aleppo and Damascus or even further to Germany. Emigration was a problem and required large efforts and bribes to facilitate it, especially for those without proper documents. However, it was equally rewarding for those who remained at home because they started to receive money and other items from those family members who succeeded abroad.

Many families went to leave to Germany, which ultimately led to a depopulation of many villages in the Jezira and the Kurdagh. For example, the above-mentioned village of Barzan had over 150 families in the 1960s. In 1992 there were some eighty families in the village, and today only a handful has stayed. What made the move more appealing was a decision by the German high court in Lüneburg on June 17, 1997 to grant the Yezidis from small villages in the east Syrian district of Hasake the asylum status of a persecuted group.[76]

Other tragic and dramatic events shaped the general Yezidi opinion regarding the state authorities. For example, the 1960 fire at the Amuda cinema which killed several hundred children[77] or the 1993 fire at the Hasake prison were events that affected the Syrian Kurds at large. Although they were also part of the Yezidi discourse and historical memory, and have been brought up regularly in discussions about Yezidi identity in Syria, I was unable to find evidence of immediate Yezidi casualties in these two tragedies.

The state policies regarding citizens, (and noncitizens) however, affected the Yezidi communities more drastically. For example, in order to register a marriage with the local authorities, a Syrian citizen needed a copy of his civil registry. However, this was not available for foreigners, stateless persons, or nonregistered persons (*maktum*), which is why their marriages could not be registered and documented. As stated before, many, or as much as 70 percent of the Syrian Yezidis in the Jezira were either *ajanib* or *maktum*. At least one spouse must be a Syrian citizen in order to register the marriage. The local mukhtar can issue only a white recognition permit in which he confirms that he knows the person. Occasionally this worked as a substitute for a marriage license when the mukhtar (and the witnesses) was willing to testify that he knows the petitioners personally. Those Yezidis who had citizenship and thus were able to obtain the registry's copy had to go to the municipal court for registration. These courts were located only in the big cities and administrative centers; and it required patience, bribes, and luck to get the desired results.

Table 5.1   Maktum—Ajanib—National Legal Relations

Wife	Husband	Can their marriage be legally registered?	Can their children be legally registered?
Maktum	National	No	Yes—under father
Maktum	Ajanib	No	Yes—under father
Maktum	Maktum	No	No
Ajanib	National	Yes	Yes
Ajanib	Ajanib	No	Yes—under faher
Ajanib	Maktum	No	No
National	National	Yes	Yes
National	Ajanib	No	Yes—under father
National	Maktum	No	No

But yet, ultimately, it was possible to register as a Yezidi couple. The nearby local Sharia court would have willingly registered their marriage too, but on the condition that it was an Islamic marriage. Table 5.1[78] summarizes the legal options for Yezidi couples and parents affected by the citizenship law.

That there was a legal gray zone was admitted by a sharia court judge in 1993, who sought clarification on the matter of registering a marriage or birth as "Yezidi." Apparently, some of his colleagues decided one way or the other. His recommendations about how to deal with the problem were remarkable: Should we force them to change their religion from Yezidi to Muslim, which would violate the Islamic principle of "There is no compulsion in religion"? Or should we advise them to file a lawsuit at the courts demanding the correction of their affiliation from Muslim to Yezidi?[79] In response to his query, another judge and colleague summarized the ministry's official position about the Yezidis: they were considered a deviant, polytheistic sect founded by the heretic Adi bin Musafir. At no time were they associated with Islam. Thus, there was no need for a sharia court to accept complaints or lawsuit with one of the parties being Yezidi.[80] Unfortunately, no other official documents pertaining to the debate were found; thus, we had to rely on the personal testimony of Yezidis who tried registering their marriages or birth as Yezidi. The standard reply was no, but with bribes it sometimes worked.

The political situation in the Kurdagh during this time period was different from the Jezira regarding the notable absence of Kurdish political parties until the state-sponsored arrival of the PKK in the 1980s. This coincided with the government's move to tactically support the PKK against Turkey. The party was allowed to operate more freely and quickly expanded their sphere of influence among the inhabitants of the Kurdagh. Yezidis in the area were lacking any sort of political or religious leadership and were thus easily attracted and incorporated into the party apparatus. The PKK also competed with local Muslim religious elites, in this case the Sufi sheikhs and brotherhoods over material and ideological resources. Ultimately, they reached a consensus and status quo of mutual tolerance and accommodation. The resulting Sufi/Kurdish identity alienated and confused the local Yezidi community. First they had to accommodate those families who converted earlier to Islam. And furthermore, they were exposed to the PKK propagated idea of a joint Yezidi-Zoroastrian identity. But the idea gained momentum and became a well-established fact in the new millennium. It took another two decades until the PKK reversed its position on the idea of Sufism as the representation of Kurdish Islam and its adoption of Yezidism as the true Kurdish religion appropriating a new sense of Kurdish unity under its banner.

The semiofficial ban on education among the Yezidi masses was mentioned earlier. It should be noted here that this was a prewar position and mostly enforced in the Jezira and more so among the Yezidis from Efrin.

In the Kurdagh, Yezidis had their own school in the early 1930s, and they contributed to the cultural and intellectual movement in the area. Among the intellectuals and writers in the Efrin area were some prominent Yezidis, for example, Walid Hassan Hasso. He was born in 1955 in Qibare and later worked as a French teacher in Aleppo. In 1998 he published his collection of stories "Ice and Sun."[81] There is also Nayruz Malik, born in 1946 also in Qibare. Although he received only primary education, he later enrolled at the Arts Institute in Aleppo and worked as a high-school teacher. He published several collections of short stories.[82] Dr. Muhammad Abdo Ali from the Yezidi village of Turunde is not Yezidi, but a Muslim Kurd and historian who researched local history and wrote a book about the Kurdagh area and one on the Yezidis and Yezidism in northwestern Syria.[83]

When Hafiz al-Asad died in 2000, he left behind a Kurdish society that was too weak to pose a threat to the regime and a Yezidi community too weak to survive. During his tenure, he was more worried about and engaged in the Kurdish activities in the neighboring countries of Turkey and Iraq. For this, he allowed the opening of bureaus of the PKK, the KDP, and Patriot Union of Kurdistan (PUK)[84] (*Yekitia Nishtimani ya Kurdistane*—YNK) in Damascus and Qamishli. But the true opportunistic nature of these policies became apparent with the signing of the Adana Agreement in 1999, which paved the way for a short-lived rapprochement between Syria and Turkey and ultimately led to the arrest of Abdullah Ocalan, the charismatic and widely popular leader of the PKK.[85] As much as 20 percent of the PKK fighters came from Syria,[86] among them were some Yezidis.[87] Their struggle now became illegal, and the state cracked down heavily on them. Kurdish political parties were banned. PKK sympathizers were arrested from Yezidi villages, and sometimes their families were punished as well. Random arrests, travel restrictions, and banning from professions were reported.

In the following paragraph, the two representative life stories of Peshiman Sileman Omar[88] (1893–1958) and Shemo Meke Shemo Isa[89] (1940–2006) are recounted.

Peshimam Sileman, son of Peshimam Omar and grandson of Peshimam Mosik, is a descendant of Sheikh Adi II, son of Sakhr Abu al-Barakat, and is thus related directly to the great reformer Sheikh Adi bin Musafir. Peshimam Sileman was born in 1893 in the Khalta region of Batman near Diyarbakir in present-day Turkey. The Khalta region is known for its battles between Yezidis and Muslims, which was the reason why his family left and moved the to Daska plain, an area dominated by the Yezidi tribe of the same name. In 1913 another conflict broke out between the Turks and the Daska tribe and its leader Shemdin. The tribe and the peshimam's family moved again, but this time to Sinjar where they encountered hostile Arab tribes. His family traveled back to Syria and settled in the French mandate region in the village of Mizgeft near Tirbespi. Here another dispute erupted with the landowners who belonged to the Hajo family of the Heverkan tribe. This forced the family to move again, this time to the nearby village of Zorava, which belonged to Hajo's rivals, the Abbas family. Apparently, the Yezidi families weren't content there and wanted to go back to the Mizgeft area, which they did and where Peshimam Sileman spent the reminder of his life until his death in 1958. He was buried at the famous Yezidi cemetery Diyare Feleke.

Peshimam Sileman was married and had four children, three sons, and one daughter. The sons continued serving as peshimams. Peshimam Shekhmus, the oldest son, lived in Tolko in the Hasake region. Peshimam Hassan, born in 1933, lived in Tell Khatun until he immigrated to Germany; and Peshimam Ismail, born in 1938, lived in Bachina in Turkey. He later moved to Germany too, but after his death in 2005 was interned at the Hassan Beg Shrine in Turkey.[90]

Peshimam Sileman is described as a righteous, fearless, and compassionate leader who always helped the poor and mediated conflicts. He was able to resolve local disputes because of his close relations with the religious and societal leaders in the region. But he also intervened directly to protect the oppressed, deprived, and disadvantaged Yezidis. One day, Muhammd Sharif Hajo, the local agha, insulted and pressured an old Yezidi man, Ramo Bisi. When the Peshimam heard about the incident, he took his cane, jumped on his horse, and rode to Hajo's house in Tirbespi, where he confronted the agha and warned him never to attack a Yezidi again. When a similar incident happened between Shukri Ismail, the agha of the village of Tell Hasanat,[91] who threatened the Yezidi Ali Sileman Broka, Peshimam Sileman beat up the agha. Shukri complained about the Peshimam to Jajan Hajo, the agha of Mizgeft, who sent some men to punish Peshimam; however, Peshimam Sileman stood his ground and did not let them take anything from him.

Another story about the uncompromising attitude of Peshimam Sileman talks about the kidnaping of a Yezidi girl by one of the Muslim servants of Jajan Hajo. Peshimam got involved by demanding the return of the girl from Jajan Hajo; however, the culprit fled with her. So, Peshimam went to the local government authorities, but they too refused to help. Then, he and some of his Yezidi followers surrounded the house of the governor, who finally had to intervene and sent the girl back.[92]

As the most prominent Yezidi leader in the Wadi al-Jarrah, Peshimam Sileman worked with other Yezidi activists to protect the Yezidi community and improve their conditions. One of those nonclerical activists was Shemo Meke Shemo Issa.

Shemo was born as the youngest of five children in the village of Chelhumiye. Most people in the village were Aramaic Christians, but some Yezidi families live there too. His father was a local healer and participated in the Tur Abdin revolt with Hajo Agha. During the Christian massacres in World War I, he helped and protected many of the persecuted Christians, often facing personal dangers and attacks. Eventually, his family had to flee from Tur Abdin and settled among the Christians of Chelhumiye in Syria. Shemo was born into this family. When he reached age seven, his father and the local Yezidi cleric Peshimam Sileman decided to send him to a private Christian school in the nearby city of Tirbespi from where he graduated in 1950. He also received a teacher diploma and was hired at the same school to teach until 1955. The following year he visited the neighboring Yezidi village of Tell Khatun where he found that the people were completely isolated and had no school. After the Peshimam granted him permission, he built a small school there, but without state support. Some local elders and tribal leaders were strongly opposed to the

Figure 5.3 First Yezidi School in Tell Khatun (1958). *Source*: Telim Tolan and Chaukedin Issa, Yezidisches Forum e.V., Oldenburg.

idea because they feared it would expose their children to the Muslim world, and they would lose their faith. Shemo Issa, however, assured them that he would collect the traditional Yezidi psalms and hymns with the help of Feqir[93] Hissi and teach them to the children. A stable was turned into a classroom, and the women and men of the village helped restoring the school building. Shemo bought the teaching material and taught for three years, when he registered the school at the provincial school board in Hasake. He received the approval and funds to finance a new school building. The local families also contributed by providing the mud brick stones. Peshimam Sileman dedicated the building in the name of God and Tawsi Melek in 1958.

Shemo was also a founding member of the Kurdish Democratic Party in Syria, which was established in 1957. During the three-year union between Syria and Egypt, when many Kurdish activists were persecuted and arrested, Shemo went into hiding. His family supported him during these times, although they too were harassed by the secret service and the local police. After he was pardoned, Shemo had to serve in the army again, but continued his engagement with the Kurdish party. The Syrian government banned him from his teaching profession. The following year, the government held the infamous population census with the aim to confiscate land and expel the Kurdish population. Shemo participated in the Tell Khatun revolt where over seventy Yezidi farmers were arrested, and he organized the support movement for the prisoners.

In 1969, he learned about the visit of Mir Tahsin Beg to the area and organized a welcome reception for the group. He wanted to show to the people of the region that Yezidism was still alive and had a strong leadership. During the visit of Mir Tahsin, Shemo had him sign a petition to drastically limit the amount of dowry. Many young Yezidis were so poor that they had no chance of ever getting married.

The early 1070s saw Shemo intensifying his efforts for the Kurdish struggle both in Syria and Iraq, which brought him reprisals from the authorities but also more respect and higher reputation among the Yezidis and Kurds. He mediated conflicts between Arab and Kurdish tribes and Syrian and Iraqi officials. However, in 1973, he quit membership of the KDP-S due to disputes with the party's leadership. After the signing of the Algiers Accord between Iraq and Iran and the subsequent collapse of the Kurdish struggle in Iraq in 1975, he supported refugees coming to Syria and was again arrested by the Syrian secret service. He then joined the Patriotic Union of Kurdistan (PUK) and fought for improving the infrastructure in the Wadi al-Jarrah where his village was located. During this time, he also started his support of the PKK-led Kurdish uprising in Turkey. Shemo Issa died on August 30, 2006 and is remembered among the Syrian Yezidis and Kurds as a generous, peace-loving, and pious leader who led his life according to the following motto: I will finish the mission Tawsi Melek has tasked me to do and help other people regardless of their religion.

5.3.5. Yezidis under Bashar al-Asad

Hopes were high among the Syrian Yezidis and Kurds that Bashar al-Asad, the young, Westernized son of Hafiz al-Asad would eventually bring change and improvements to the Kurdish situation. But their hopes were quickly dashed and after a decade of Bashar in power things were even worse in many areas, such as the economy, the legal sector, as well as the cultural sphere. Bashar al-Asad continued the successful "divide-and-rule" policy of his father by supporting those Kurds who distanced themselves from political activities, while the Kurdish political activists were still persecuted. Cracking down with an iron fist on any signs of open protest and paying political lip service to cultural and political demands were other markers of his early legacy.

This was particularly true in the aftermath of the Qamishli revolt in March and April of 2004.[94] The large-scale and wide spread uprising of the Kurdish population was a turning point in the relationship of the Kurdish national movement with the central government. What was different this time was the number of participants, the geographical extent, and the transnational support from Kurds from Iraq and Turkey. The clashes erupted after scuffles following a soccer game between the local (Kurdish) team *al-Jihad* and the visiting (Arab) team from Deyr al-Zor, *al-Futuwwa*. The situation escalated quickly and became overtly political. Government institutions in various cities, among them Hasake, Amuda, Tirbespi, Aleppo, and Efrin, were attacked and destroyed. The following brutal crackdown of the protest led by the Syrian security apparatus and secret service saw thirty-two people killed and over 2,000 arrested. An indirect victim of the fighting was Kheyri Jindo, a 21 year-old Yezidi from Qizlacuq. He did his mandatory service time in the army and was constantly abused, beaten, and attacked. While the conflict in Qamishli escalated, the attacks by his superior Arab/Muslim officers became more frequent, which eventually led to his killing on March 24, 2004.[95]

The demonstrations were used as a vehicle to express other Kurdish grievances; however, the uprising should not be viewed as an Arab-Kurdish conflict. Instead Kurdish political parties conferred with Arab tribes to conclude that it was an antigovernment, anti-Ba'th protest. Obviously, the development of events in neighboring Iraq where a Kurd (Jalal Talabani) became the country's new president and where the Kurdish Region under Masud Barzani enjoyed autonomy and prosperity encouraged the protesters. The government at the same time was alarmed that things may go in the same direction in Syria. Although the protest ebbed down in the following weeks, it led to an increased awareness and politization of the Syrian Kurds.

One year later the prominent Sufi Sheikh Khaznawi was killed, some say by the secret service because he became too popular among the opposition groups and rallied the Muslim Brotherhood and the Kurds behind him. Others accuse terrorist elements for the killing. Regardless, his funeral led to another Kurdish mass rally and protest. Yezidis from Hasake condemned the killing as an act of aggression against the religious and ethnic minorities of the country.

Unlike the uprising in the previous year, however, this time the Kurdish political parties were not unified in their response, but presented conflicting agendas and action plans. Both events, however, were important identity markers for the Syrian Kurds in general, but not so much for the Kurdish parties who, in subsequent years, struggled to build a larger base and expand their influence.

On the other hand, the state managed to recover from the loss of authority and responded with increased repressions against the Kurdish national movement. Savelsberg and Hajo summarized the difficult situation that Kurdish activists faced in the courts. They recorded 283 cases of political arrests predominantly with charges under Article 288 for joining a political organization without approval.[96] No Yezidi cases were confirmed. Additional restrictions on travel, employments, and/or expression were recorded too. The economy of the Jezira suffered and the standard of living declined, unlike other Syrian areas, which saw an economic liberalization and subsequent rise in living standards. And these developments affected the living conditions in the Yezidi villages of the Jezira significantly, and ultimately led to an increase in migration.

After the 2004 Qamishli football massacre and the assassination of Sheikh Muhammad Mashuq Khaznawi in 2005, the secret service became omnipresent in public life and political opposition retreated into the private homes.[97] Both Arabs and Kurds used the demographic argument of minority versus majority. The Arabs in the Jezira felt that they were a minority in their own country, while the Kurds complained about drastic and violent Arabization practices. The number of Kurds was growing faster, however, due to a higher birth rate and immigration from Turkey and Iraq, where the situation for the Kurds was even worse than in Syria. As we learned, the government reacted to this demographic threat by relocating Arab families to the Kurdish lands, building new villages for them, and Arabizing the names of the existing Kurdish villages. Now for example, New-Tanuriya (Arab village) is located next to Tanuriya (Kurdish village). The school and other services were located in the Arab village, and the

Kurdish children had to go to this hostile place in order to attend school. And for the Yezidi children this meant attending mandatory Islam classes.

The Kurdish movement was split into two major groups, one that saw itself as the leading opposition group and key in the fight for democracy. Democracy can be obtained only when the Kurds are granted their rights, according to Hassan Saleh, the secretary general of the Yekiti Party. The other group works closer with the Arab opposition and does not support unilateral Kurdish approaches. Democracy must be fought for together and only then the Kurdish question will be solved automatically, says Abdulhamid Darwish, secretary general of the Kurdish Democratic Progress Party in Syria (*Partiya Dimoqrati Peshveru Kurdi li Suria*—PDPKS). However, Damascus is continuing its repressive policies by inciting the different ethnic and religious groups against each other. In order to remain in power, the regime might provoke a civil war, according to Mishal Tammo, the speaker of the Future Movement. In the past, they arrested the Kurds at the demonstrations, today they send the Arab neighbors to beat them up.[98]

Many Kurds still lived in mud houses in their villages and on the outskirts of the larger cities. They were excluded not only spatially, but also legally, because they did not have any citizenship, neither the Syrian nor any other. In a typical family the father would have lost his passport in 1962, while the mother was able to retain it. However, their children would be considered stateless. Instead of a passport, they had a red identity card, which allowed them to travel domestically, but not internationally. They were not allowed to study, or to get a hotel room, to work for the government in the public sector or to register a house or business under their name. The fathers and the sons might work as day laborers, making a very meager income. This was a fate they shared with 150,000 other Kurds in Syria, a situation that threatened to become dangerous if not addressed by the authorities. Thus, from time to time, the government promised to fix the problem[99]; however, it wasn't until 2010 when facing a civil war, that the government passed legislation to recall the decision and to grant citizenship to selected individuals. The reaction to this slow process was a slow radicalization among the Syrian Kurds and their turning away from the government.

Anti-Kurdish and to a lesser extent anti-Yezidi sentiments remained high, and violent acts and crimes against were reported. On October 25, the body of a Yezidi man was found. Anad Haydar, age 25 from Tell Tewil, was abducted, tortured, and killed. However, no one claimed responsibility and the killers were not found, nor did the authorities in Hasake do anything to find them. The Yezidi Forum in Oldenburg documented thirty-one additional cases of land dispossession between 2000 and 2008, among these were occupation of farmland, theft of equipment and livestock, cutting off water supply, or burning of harvest.[100]

In order to restore normalcy, the governor of Hasake, Muhammad al-Namur, on December 15, 2006, visited some Yezidi villages in his precinct officially to join the celebration of religious holidays. Informally, he came close to lowering the tensions between the Yezidi and Arab villages. However, the larger political scene intensified the conflict. In continuation of applying the land redistribution act, several Arab villages, whose lands were flooded by dam building projects in the Jabal Abd al-Aziz area and south of Hasake, were re-located and their inhabitants granted land plots of 37 donum each. A total of 5,560 donums were confiscated from Kurdish villages around Hasake and among these was the Yezidi village of Kar Rash.[101]

How little the Yezidis meant to the central authorities was shown in the lack of official recognition and ignorance about their status and background. President Asad never mentioned the community in his speeches, and a high-ranking member of the Ba'th Party and minister in the regional leadership referred to them as devil worshipers who were against education. At the same time, he insisted that many Yezidis were members of the Ba'th Party.[102]

On September 10, 2008, the presidential decree number forty-nine was passed, which expanded the restriction on landownership in the border areas. It modified the older decree no. 41 from October 2004, which provided the legal framework to restrict property rights in the border area. According to the new text, property registration of land deeds would no longer be allowed. If fully implemented, it would be illegal to buy, sell, or inherit land property.[103] The population in the border area with Turkey and Iraq is predominantly Kurdish, and many Yezidi villages are located within this zone, especially those near Tirbespi, Amuda, and Ras al-Ayn. However, the outbreak of the civil war has prevented the implementation of the decree. According to observations by Savelsberg and Hajo, by June 2009, the building activities in Qamishli, the largest city in the border area, had declined by two-thirds.[104] The damage to the economy of the region was severe and complicated the situation for a population that already suffered from earlier restrictions as well as a lengthy drought period.

The number of physical attacks against Yezidis increased significantly over the last decade. The Oldenburg-based Yezidisches Forum listed forty-four cases of assaults against Yezidis, including killings, kidnapings, rape, and severe beatings.[105] The general lack of security and widespread anti-Yezidi feelings led to further depopulation of their villages. Most decided to follow their relatives to Germany, which was known for its more liberal interpretation of the asylum law. However, the German Federal Administrative Court in 2005 refused to grant family asylum to stateless Syrian Yezidis who were married according to Yezidi customs but not to the Syrian civil status, that is, those who did not have a registration number for their marriage. As stateless Kurds they were not allowed to get married officially in Syria. In this particular legal case, the husband was a legal refugee, but his wife was stateless. They were married in Syria according to Yezidi customs and have three children. The court stated that the woman, like all other stateless Kurds who left Syria "illegally," can no longer return to Syria. However, this ban is not politically based; thus, Syria is no longer the residence of the woman and also no longer the persecutor.[106]

On April 5, 2011, a delegation of citizens from the Hasake Province presented the president with a document[107] with thirty-four suggestions for economic, social, and, to a lesser extent, political reforms. Many of the grievances and complaints applied to the local Yezidi community too, especially those demands for reforming the personal and legal status, property rights, and the ineffective and discriminative bureaucracy. For example, they demanded:

- national reconciliation after the Qamishli uprising
- increased efforts to legalize the status of the maktum
- issuing of agricultural property deeds
- remitting agricultural debts
- preferential treatment of locals in public employment
- reconsidering certain fees, taxes, and tariffs

No official response or recognition of the demands was heard; however, it was now apparent that Yezidis and other marginalized groups in the Jezira started to raise their voice and demanded their rights. The timing of the publication is important because it coincided with the first large antigovernment demonstrations in Qamishli and Hasake. And two days later came the president's surprising announcement about granting many of the stateless Kurds Syrian citizenship.[108]

The first decade of Bashar al-Asad's rule brought no improvement for the Yezidi community. Concurrently, the relationship between the state and Kurds deteriorated and left the two camps more polarized and divided. And since the Yezidis were not invested in the political struggle, they easily fell through the grid and off the radar. The main actors in this struggle had other priorities than to be concerned about a mini minority which did not see a future for themselves in this country. Those who could afford it, landowners, intellectuals, and clerics, left the country and those who remained dug in in order not to expose themselves and become scapegoats in the proxy war between the security apparatus and the Kurdish political movement.

NOTES

1. Letter from Baba Sheikh Kheto Haji Ismail, 28 April, 2014, published at Aranews.

2. Kreyenbroek gave a lively demonstration of the non existing link between the two religious groups at the Second Conference for Ezidi Academics, October 4, 2014.

3. Al-Jarrad (1996): 16.

4. Kreyenbroek (1995): 17.

5. Different theories on the nature of the takeover are discussed. Among them are claims that the temple used to be a Christian monastery and the inhabitants were evicted by Sheikh Adi. However, most convincingly, Pir Khidr Sileman (in Issa 2007: 45–52) argued that it used to be the site of a Mithra temple for sun worshipers. The connection between sun worshipers and early Yezidism is explained elsewhere (Kreyenbroek 1995; Othman, 1997).

6. Philip Kreyenbroek & Khalil Jindy Rashow, *God and Sheikh Adi are Perfect: Sacred Poems and Religious Narratives from the Yezidi Tradition* (Wiesbaden: Harrasowitz, 2005), 3.

7. On the Yezidi sacred books, see Maximilian Bittner, *Die heiligen Bücher der Jeziden oder Teufelsanbeter* (Vienna: Denkschriften der kaiserlichen Akademie der Wissenschaften, 1913), Celile Celil, "Mythologie, Kult und zwei heilige Bücher der Yazidi," in *Yazidi: Gottes auserwähltes Volk oder die "Teufelsanbeter" vom Djabal Sinjar (Irak)*, eds. Axel Steinmann and Karin Kren (Wien: 1998) and Kreyenbroek (1995).

8. Jasim E. Murad, *The Sacred Poems of the Yazidis: an Anthropological Approach* (PhD diss., University of California, Los Angeles, 1993).

9. Rudolf Frank, *Scheich 'Adi, der große Heilige der Jezidis* (Berlin, 1911) summarized the early Islamic sources.

10. This refers to the Kharijites, an early Islamic opposition movement that was also considered heretic.

11. Anis Frayha, "New Yezidi Texts from Beled Sinjar, 'Iraq,'" *Journal of the American Oriental Society* 66 (1949): 20.

12. Victoria Arakelova, "Sufi Saints in the Yezidi Tradition I: Qawlē Husēyīnī Halāj," *Iran and the Caucasus* 5 (2001): 183–192.

13. Lescot, *Enquête* (1938), 112 reported on a Yezidi community in Qusayr in the early thirteenth century. This leads Kreyenbroek (1995: 42) to argue that the tribes living closer to the religious center in Hakkari/Lalish converted earlier.

14. Nelida Fuccaro, "A 17th Century Travel Account on the Yazidis," *Annali* 53, no. 3 (1993): 241–253.

15. Bar Hebraeus, *Chronology*. Ed. Paul Bedjan, translated by E. Budge, 2 vols. (Oxford, 1932); John S. Guest, *Survival among the Kurds: a History of the Yezidis* (London, New York: Kegan Paul, 1993), 45.

16. Ibn Taymiyya, "Risalat al-'Adawiya," in *Majmu'at al-rasa'il al-kubra*, vol. 1, (Cairo, 1906/1323) after Michael Leezenberg, *Political Islam among the Kurds*. Paper originally prepared for the International Conference "Kurdistan: The unwanted state," March 29–31, 2001, (Jagiellonian University, Cracow, Poland, 2001), 21.

17. Leezenberg, *Political Islam* (2001), 3–4.

18. Stefan Winter, "The Province of Raqqa under Ottoman Rule, 1535-1800," Paper presented at the Great Lakes Ottomanist Workshop, Toronto, March 18, 2006. Seven of the Ottoman court files contain a reference to Yezidi rebels in the Raqqa region.

19. Acikyildiz (2010): 63–64.

20. John S. Guest, *Survival* (1993), 45; Lescot, *Enquête* (1938), 206.

21. It took until 1681 when an expanded edition under the title of Teatro della Turcia was distributed across Europe. The author, the same Michel Febvre, received his information mainly from two monks working in the area, Père Jean-Baptiste de Saint Aignan and Père Justinien de Neury. See Fucarro, *Travel Account* (1993).

22. On clothes and other sacred objects among the Yezidis, see Eszter Spät, *Images and objects of the supernatural and sacred objects among the Kurdish Yezidis*. http://www.personal.ceu.hu/students/09/Eszter_Spat/index.htm, 2009.

23. Paul Perdrizet, "Documents du XVIIe siècle relatifs de Yezidis," *Bulletin de la Société de Géographie de l'Est* (1903): 433, after Fucarro, *Travel Account* (1993): 246.

24. Seetzen (2012): 120, 245, 246.

25. See also Henri Lammens, "Le massif du Gabal Sim'an et les Yézidis de Syrie," *Mélange de la Faculté Orientale*, 2 (1907): 366–96.

26. Siouffi, *Notice* (1885): 93. after Kreyenbroek, *Yezidism* (1995): 134.

27. R.P.M. Jullien, *Sinaï et Syrie. Souvenirs bibliques et chretiens* (Lille: Desclee de Brouwer, 1893): 17.

28. Al-Hasibi (1982): 493 and New York Times, June 2, 1926.

29. See the Gertrude Bell Archive at www.gerty.ncl.ac.uk.

30. N.E. Bou-Nacklie, "Les Troupes Speciales: Relgious and Ethnic Recruitment, 1916–1946," *International Journal of Middle East Studies* 25 (1993): 651; Lescot, *Enquete*, 209–210.

31. Lammens, *Le massif*, 386.

32. Nelida Fuccaro, "Ethnicity, State Formation, and Conscription in Postcolonial Iraq: The Case of the Yazidi Kurds of Jabal Sinjar," *International Journal of Middle East Studies*, 29/4 (1997): 579–580.

33. Zakariya, Ahmad Wasfi, *Asha'ir*, 673.

34. Cited after Fuccaro, *Nationalism*, 194.

35. See Fuccaro, *Nationalism* (2002); Vahe Tachijan, *La France en Cilicie*, and Jordie Tejel, *Syria's Kurds: History, Politics, and Society* (London: Routledge, 2009).

36. See Zengi at www.yekiti.nl/htmal/erebi/dilawer1.htm

37. Dawud Dawud Isa was the tribal leader of the Mihirkan tribe in Sinjar. He was born in 1882 and rose to prominence in the armed struggle with the Iraqi government over conscription in the 1930s. Afterward, he moved to Syria to live among the Yezidis in the Wadi al-Jarrah.

38. Lescot, *Enquete*, 190–195.

39. Fuccaro, *Ethnicity*, 569.

40. Ibid. 573.

41. John S. Guest, Survival, 190–191; E. S. Drower, *Peacock Angel: Being Some Account of Votaries of a Secret Cult and their Sanctuaries* (London: J. Murray's, 1941), 106–107.

42. She married the Egyptian businessman Wasil Raslan and became a socialite in the upper class of Cairo. She died on June 26, 2015. See https://elwafeyat.com/mushatra/18814.

43. Martin Van Bruinessen, "Nationalisme kurde et ethnicities intra-kurdes," Peuples Mediterraneens, 68–69 (1994): 36, mentioned informants who claimed that

Hajo Agha, the leader of the Heverkan tribe and member of Khoybun, was himself a Yezidi.

44. Issa (2007: 172–174). His account is based on oral narratives that only partly comply with the information from written sources and archival material. According to them, it was Hajo who started a revolt against the Turks in 1926 and immigrated to Syria after the defeat.

45. Usually the land for distribution was considered *matruk* (abandoned) or *mahlul* (uncultivated for three years).

46. In his dissertation, Altug gives a very detailed description of the sectarian land distribution in the Jezira; see Altug (2011): 188–196.

47. Muhammad Abdu Ali (2008): 107–108.

48. The Ali Jindo from Qestel Jindo, the Ma'juni from Qatma and the Shamo family from Qibare were all related.

49. Nidal Yusuf, "Darwish Shamo and the First School," http://www.esyria.sy/ealeppo/index.php?p=stories&category=face&filename=201404221322334, published April 22, 2014, accessed Sept. 21, 2015.

50. The letter was published in Muhammad Abdu Ali (2008): 133.

51. Rozad Ali, "Bidayat al-yaqzha al-qawmiya wa bawadir nashat siyasi al-murafiq fi mintaqat Jabal al-Kurd Efrin 1919–1957," [The Beginning of National Awareness and Sign of Political Activism in the Jabal al-Kurd Region, Efrin (1919–1957)], *Hiwar* 64 (October 2011): 22–35.

52. Tirejefrin. "Afrin al-Madina." Tirejefrin.blogspot.com. http://tirejEfrin.blogspot.com/2014/06/blog-post_4579.html (accessed June 5, 2016).

53. Dodge was instrumental in getting the earliest account written by a Yezidi (Ismail Beg Col) published. Apparently he had an interest in the community; however, no files or letters were found at the AUB archive.

54. Among them was Wansa, daughter of Ismail Beg Col, who would later be granted refuge in the Kurdagh after seriously wounding her husband, Mir Said in 1938.

55. See Lescot, *Mouvement Mouroud*, 1988, 101–126.

56. Khalid Issa, "Dirasa tarikhiya al-akrad taht al-intidab al-firansi – 2; rabi'an: intifadat al-thalathinat," Kurdistanabinxete.com. http://www.kurdistanabinxete.com/Tarix_Kurdistan/TarixaSuri_Tevlihev/XwendinekDiroki_kurdilisuri.htm (accessed June 5, 2016).

57. Mohamed Abdo Ali. "Ashira Shikak al-Kurdiya," Lokmanafrin.com. http://www.lokmanafrin.com/images/3sher/shikak.htm (accessed June 5, 2016).

58. Sadiq Damluji, al-Yazidiya (Mosul): Matba'at al-Ittihad (1949), 251.

59. Lescot, *Enquete* (1938), 216.

60. Savelsberg, Hajo and Dulz (2010): 101–116.

61. al-Jabiri 1981: 218.

62. Ibid., 215.

63. In Sinjar Mountain, many other local shrines remained important to the local population.

64. محمد طلب هلال: دراسة عن محتفظة الجزيرة من الناحية القومية والاجتماعية والسياسية. 1963 [Muhammad Talab Hilal: A Study about the al-Jazeera Province with regards to the national, social and political situation, 1963]

65. Hassan Biro, The Arabic Belt, 2012, published at http://all4syria.info/Archive/53030, accessed 10/10/2012.

66. A tragic-ironic footnote is the fact that these Arab families were also dispossessed of their land earlier with the building of the Tabqa dam on the Euphrates.

67. Emin Liebscher, *Flucht aus dem Wilden Syrien* (Verlag Kern, 2013).

68. Although many Yezidis were ajanib and maktum, there is also a significant number of Yezidis attending university and obtaining final degrees in their field. Others managed to study abroad and graduate from international universities, especially in Russia (Soviet Union), Egypt, Czechoslovakia, and of course Germany, where the number of academics is very high for a small migrant community.

69. For some details and examples of how statelessness affects the Kurdish population in Syria, see Lynch & Ali, Buried Alive (2006). For a discussion of the larger impact of the census on the Kurdish population, see Peter Fragiskatos, The Stateless Kurds in Syria: Problems and Prospect for the Ajanib and Maktumin Kurds (2007).

70. Interview with Serhan Issa, Oct 15, 2013. The number seems too high for me. He probably meant 65–70 percent of the Jezira Yezidis.

71. Abd al-Rahman Haji Othman, "The Martyrs are the builders of the Nation," published March 16, 2008, http://www.tirejEfrin.com/site/sh-1973.htm, accessed Sept. 21, 2015.

72. Interview with Chaukedin Issa, Jan 15, 2015.

73. The village was first settled by Yezidi families from the tribes of Dinna, Khawalta, and Dawadiya some two hundred years ago. The government later changed the name of the village to Tishreen.

74. Tejel (2009): 48.

75. The PDK-S saw many divisions and reunions and even today is represented by two factions under the same name.

76. Decision # 9 B 492.97, cited in Weber (1997): 126.

77. For details on the incident and a discussion of the possible perpetrators, see Kurdwatch Report No. 2, 2009.

78. Lynch and Perveen (2006): 6.

79. Letter by Nuri al-Jum'a (1993).

80. Letter by Abdullah Urfi (1993).

81. Walid Hassan Hasso, al-Jalid wa'l-shams, [Ice and Sun]. Dar al-Hassanayn lil-nashr wal-tawsi', Damascus, 1998.

82. Nayruz Malik, al-Sudfa wa al-Bahr, [The Coincidence and the Sea], Itihad Kuttab al-Arab, Damascus, 1977; Harb saghira, [A small War], Wizarat al-Thaqafa, Damascus, 1979.

83. Muhammad Abdo Ali, Jabal al-Kurd "Efrin": Dirasa tarikhiya, ijtimaiya thaqafiya; al-Ezidiya wal-Ezidiyiun fi shamal gharb Suria, Sulaymania, Mudiriyat al-Tab' wa'n-nashr, 2009.

84. Both the KDP and the PUK are known to the Western audience by their English acronym.

85. The text of the agreement is available on http://www.mafhoum.com/press/50P2.htm

86. Sinclair and Kajjo (2011) at http://www.merip.org/mero/mero083111#_3_

87. Interview with Yezidi activist from Syria, Oct. 14, 2014.

88. Narrated by Fermaz Gharibo on April 11, 2010.

89. Abbreviated version of the oral obituary read by Chaukedin Issa at Shamo Issa's funeral.

90. See his obituary at http://www.kurdistanabinxete.com/Daxweyani/Tevlihev/Peshimam_Mir.htm

91. Tell Hasanat is another mixed village in the Wadi al-Jarrah near the Turkish border. The large majority are, however, Sunni Kurds with only a few Yezidi families.

92. While the Gharibo's account ended here, another chapter was revealed in an interview: after the girl was returned, her father, uncle, and brother killed her to protect their honor. When Hajo confronted Peshimam Sileman about the killing and did not want to be responsible for it, he replied: "I wasn't thinking about you! You're not worth it! But if Jelila went that road, tomorrow Zelila [i.e. some other girl] might follow. Stay in your own place, Hajo. This is not a cattle shed. A Yezidi woman is not for Moslems!" See Kreyenbroek (2009: 55–56).

93. See the description of feqirs in the religious hierarchy in Chapter 4.2.4.

94. For a detailed review of the facts and consequences, see Kurdwatch Report No. 4, (2009).

95. See this detailed report about his case as well as the commemoration of his death in 2014 at http://www.kurdistanabinxete.com/Gotar/Suri/Kushtina_Cindo.htm

96. Savelsberg and Hajo (2011): 6.

97. Tejel (2009): 126–128.

98. Interviews with Saleh, Darwish, and Tammo conducted by Helberg (2005).

99. At other times, they expand the restrictions and limitations. For example, on September 17, 2008, the Directorate of Education in Hasake circulated a letter among the principals of primary and secondary schools in the district requesting them not to issue any grade report or official school documents to maktum students. See Directorate of Education in Hasake, letter, 2008.

100. Yezidisches Forum (2009): 29–33.

101. Al-Dimuqrati, no. 404, July 2007, 2.

102. Interview with A.N., June 15, 2006.

103. The fully translated version of Decree 49 is available at http://supportkurds.org/reports/decree-49-ethnic-cleansing-of-kurds-in-syria/, accessed September 2, 2015.

104. Savelsberg and Hajo (2011): 32.

105. Yezidisches Forum (2009): 33–42.

106. Decision # (Az.: 1 C 17.03), cited in Integration in Deutschland 1/2005, 21.Jg., 31. März 2005.

107. Petition (2011).

108. See "Stateless Kurds in Syria granted citizenship," CNN, April 8, 2011, available at http://www.cnn.com/2011/WORLD/meast/04/07/syria.kurdish.citizenship/, accessed 9/3/2015.

Chapter 6

Yezidis in the new Syria

6.1. THE EVOLUTION AND MOBILIZATION OF YEZIDI IDENTITY IN SYRIA

It is no surprise that Syria like most other states in the Middle East is still working on forming a national identity that would reflect and represent the ethnic and religious diversity of its citizens. As a young nation-state, the overarching layer of national identity needs time to evolve and gain acceptance. But because of ongoing conflicts, war, and insecurity, other layers of identity take precedence and provide a stronger and more realistic mode of identification.

In the process of finding a common denominator acceptable to most groups it is very natural that some groups resort to opposition, rejection, and even discrimination because of their anxieties and fears of political and/or social change. External threats, of which Syria saw plenty, intensified the pressure on the majority to shape a cohesive, yet not necessarily all-inclusive, form of identification. In the Syrian case, Arabism dominated the discourse, which left little room for non-Arab stakeholders such as the Kurds. Islam too was a majority, identity label, although in a much more diverse way due to the prominence of Alawites in the country's elite, the general appeasement of the Sunni majority and the special position of the Druze in the religious landscape. Non-Muslim groups, however, were not specifically targeted or discriminated against; they were rather tolerated except for the Jews and the Yezidis.

Yezidi identity is shaped by these negative experiences as well as specific concepts and beliefs that express the inferior self-image vis-à-vis neighboring groups of different identities. The concepts represent something unique about the Yezidis as a group and to a lesser extent as an individual. Uniqueness is however, in the eyes of the beholder and thus the two angles of looking at the Yezidi uniqueness must be taken into consideration, the internal view, that is, how Yezidis describe themselves as unique, and the external view, that is, what others think about these unique features.

A good starting point to look at these concepts is the beginning of all concepts, creation. Like other religious groups, the Yezidis believe that they represent the only true religion, and that all other religions came after them. The Yezidi creation story, however, includes an intriguing twist that helps to make them stand out: while the dominant religions in the Middle East assert that they descended from Adam and Eve, Yezidis claim their distinct descent from Adam alone.[1] Spät calls this story the basis or cornerstone of Yezidi identity.[2] It is also important to note that Yezidis do not allow for proselytizing or conversion. Instead, they protect their unique purity and promote this as a symbol of their group identity. This represents one of the few positive images in the self-described Yezidi identity.

The desire for positive experiences, which helps build self-esteem and group esteem among the Yezidis, is equally high among other groups in the region. Being proud and feeling good about yourself and your identity group may boost your overall standing in the social hierarchy. People with high group esteem are more likely to build a strong identity. But in order to do this, they must compare their standing and perceptions with others, thus affirming the group's superiority. However, minorities, especially when living under stress, often lack high group esteem. Comparing their situation to others does not make them feel good. On the contrary, it creates frustrations, grievances, and anxieties.

These comparisons may occur within the identity group or by comparisons with other external groups; however, for the building of group esteem and identity, comparisons with outsiders are more common. If the identity group feels superior to the external group, then they may build a positive identity. However, when external groups create a hierarchical system on the basis of status differences, our identity group becomes insecure and weak. As described in the history chapter, it was impossible for the various Yezidi communities to take a lead in the building of strong identities due to their small number, scattered living areas, continual state of war, and overall vulnerable position. Since the destruction of the Yezidi community in Lalish by the Mongols, their adversaries always had the upper-hand.

It was only for a short period of time that the Yezidis enjoyed high groupesteem. Sheikh Adi bin Musafir, the great reformer of the twelfth century, gave the Yezidi community a new religious order and identity. He cemented the caste system, which is the fundamental social structure of the community, and he called it Sed u Hed or limits and rules. The following are the main components of the system that are deeply engrained into the Yezidi consciousness:[3]

1. Every person has a particular place within the social hierarchy.
2. Every community member is extremely loyal toward the members of his own group as well as the religious leadership.
3. The family of the Mir is the undisputed, legitimate ruler. The relationship with each caste is clearly outlined.
4. Mobility within the community's caste system is strictly defined.
5. Yezidis are born as Yezidis. Conversion to Yezidism is unacceptable.
6. Switching to another caste is impossible.
7. The duties and responsibilities for each individual member are clearly defined.
8. Every Yezidi must have a sheikh and a pir who looks after him. If a region does not have any sheikh or pir, it is permissible to join a different sheikh or pir group until it is possible to return to the originally assigned sheikh or pir family.
9. Members of a group, family, and caste should support each other.

Generations of Yezidis in near and distant places have internalized these rules and made them part of their self-perception. When one asks Yezidis about the essence of their religion, they frequently refer to sed u hed.[4] In the diaspora, however, a growing trend must be noted that calls for the reform of these regulations. Yezidi Identity Inventory (EZI) recorded a 40 percent approval rate for an at least partial reform with the largest group of supporters coming from Syria.[5]

Yezidis see themselves as members of an exclusive group, which despite constant persecution, managed to preserve their religious and ethnic characteristics. The ethnic affiliation with the Kurds (and sometimes as ethnic Yezidis) is just another component of the complex, unique Yezidi identity, which includes other aspects too, such as family, clan, tribe, region, gender, language, citizenship, and caste. But especially the religious identity with its distinct classification of laymen and clerics includes unmodified social collective norms of interaction and marriage. These norms are enforced through a rigid self-imposed system of isolation and distancing from other groups.

Unlike other religious groups in Syria, the Yezidis until recently were not able or allowed to build their own religious institutions. The Sunni community was able, since the early days of the Syrian independence, to develop a working relationship with the (Alawite dominated) government, with ups and downs. At times the government tended to formally regulate the process of institution building, while at other times, they allowed private initiatives to strengthen the religious sphere.⁶ The Christian community enjoyed a high degree of autonomy in their religious, legal, social, and even economic affairs, and so did the Druze, all with the blessing of the government. While the state was not interested in officially recognizing the Yezidis as an autonomous entity, the community too was not in the position to openly promote their religious beliefs and create a formal network of structures, regulations, or institutions. No schools taught Yezidism, no training was provided for the clerics, no authority was appointed or elected to make necessary religious decisions, no directorate was in charge of the religious buildings, shrines, and sanctuaries, no personal status law was codified, no literature was published, and no formal relationship with the government was ever formed. Lacking these resources and institutions, the community had only very limited capabilities to develop a strong, coherent, and cohesive religious identity. Furthermore, the few existing mechanisms and aspects of religious identity building that existed among the Iraqi Yezidis were largely off-limits to the Syrian groups. We heard about the rare visits of the qewals and the notable absence of visits by the Mir's family. Even the pilgrimage to Lalish was a religious duty, the Syrian Yezidis could hardly ever observe. Only in 2012, however, when Syrian state power and authority already declined, a delegation of 140 Yezidis managed to go to Lalish with the administrative help of the people's council in West Kurdistan and safety assurances by the YPG.

Thus, any initiative for religious instruction, preservation, or application depended solely on the courage, goodwill, efforts, and reputation of individual clerics, some of whom were living abroad. With the creation of semiautonomous cantons under a Yezidi-friendly administration, however, things started to change. Yezidi communities in Syria are in the process of redefining their identity. Recent developments in the area as well as internal decisions and actions contributed to the formation of two separate identity groups. A look at five areas of contentions, which include spatial, ethnic, religious, economic, and political features, will illustrate the current ideological, religious, and political struggles within the community.

Analyzing the historical situation, social status, and identity of Yezidis in Syria means to highlight the territorial differences between the two major groups. The position of the Yezidis in the Syrian Jezira is, indeed, significantly different from the Yezidis in the Kurdagh region of western Syria. I have argued that the latter suffer discrimination due to their religious origin and thus primarily define their identity along those lines.⁷ Yezidis in the Jezira, however, consider both religion and ethnicity the base of their identity because they are persecuted for both reasons. Through an analysis of the history and a comparison of the doctrines we can show how the two groups evolved, developed, and found their current space within the Syrian context of minorities.

As mentioned above, Yezidis in the Kurdagh lived in the area for several centuries and thus were better integrated into the society at large. The distance to the religious centers in northern Iraq has always been far, which led to the development of unique customs and traditions. However, as for the Yezidis in the Jezira, this was not the case. Although they settled in the villages about a century ago, they were constantly confronted with new political borders and population exchanges with the local communities, which overall contributed to the weakening of their position in the social context of the region. On one hand they were cut off from other Yezidi areas in Sinjar and Tur Abdin due to the arbitrary drawing of political borders after World War I. On the other hand, their area was systematically Arabized and Islamized through the displacement of Kurdish families and the resettlement of Arab-Muslim peasants in the so-called Arab Belt in the Jezira. In addition, this region has been the destination of various waves of refugees from Turkey and Iraq.

Until the end of the Mandate period, both Syrian Yezidi communities were able to maintain their position within the regional minority context. This was possible because the Syrian Kurds did not constitute a homogenous ethnic group at this time. White argues that the category 'minority' was not even fully evolved and merely used as a political tool.[8] Tejel goes further asserting that geographical, kinship, or religious factors superseded the ethnic component in the process of identity building.[9] However, the Kurdish nationalist movement kept growing with temporary support by the French authorities.[10] As a result, the Yezidis drifted into a clash of loyalties between nationalist (Kurdish and Arabic), colonial (French and British), and Islamic movements. The growth of the Kurdish national movement in Syria and neighboring countries, the often militarist response of their governments, as well as the increasing Islamization of the entire society, led to a permanent weakening of the traditional structure of the community and brought them to the verge of extinction.

Syrian Yezidis were well aware of the plight and difficult situation of their fellow Yezidis in neighboring Turkey and Iraq, a fact that added some consolation to their own negative image. They base this on the better relationships with other religious groups, where Syrian Yezidis often lived together with Muslims and/or Christians in the same village, while in Turkey and Iraq Yezidi villages were mostly segregated.

Until the outbreak of the Syrian revolution and civil war, Yezidis were deprived the right of practicing their religion. Yezidism is defined as a religion of orthopraxy, that is, not the correct belief is the main characteristic, but the correct practice of rituals, customs, and taboos. The main Yezidi practice is the public celebration of certain holidays, such as New Year, Cemaye Sheikh Adi, Tawaf, Eida Ezid and Batizmi. An orthopractical religion such as Yezidism cannot spiritually grow or even survive without them. In Syria, for most of their recorded history, but especially under the Ba'th rule, these celebrations were illegal and impossible to conduct due to the lack of official recognition or protection. As soon as Yezidis were permitted to gather for these events, the local communities emerged more cohesive and began asserting a stronger position in the public sphere. This process started around 2008 in Efrin when Yezidis celebrated their holidays publicly. Initially, images and symbols of the Syrian authorities were displayed; this had gradually faded away to be replaced by Kurdish national and political symbols. Under the new self-administration, the Yezidi community tries to use every opportunity to publicly display its rituals, provided the security situation permits.

Generally, Syrian Yezidis developed a unique identity among the other minority groups. As ethnic Kurds they had similar experiences with Ottoman, French, and Arab ruling elites, who tried to extend their hegemony over Kurdish territories. Hence, Yezidis were treated like other Kurdish groups. However, their status as a heterodox religious minority contributed significantly to their persecution, often caused by (Muslim) Kurds, and their subsequent relegation to the bottom end of the social hierarchy. Very little outside support was noted, as well as very little Kurdish solidarity.

However, because of the physical separation of the settlement area, two different developments unfolded, with long-lasting consequences with regard to the formation of Yezidi religious and social identity in Syria: Yezidis from the Kurdagh consider themselves and are considered by others as different from their brothers and sisters in the Syrian Jezira. The proximity or distance to the religious centers of the group in northern Iraq fostered this dichotomy as did the lack of interaction between the groups. With Syrian Yezidis generally being stigmatized as heretics by the society at large, Yezidis from the Jezira were also (mis)-treated as such outcasts. Yezidis from the Kurdagh experienced this to a lesser degree. The self-perceptions of the two groups reflect this dual approach. While Yezidis from the Jezira incorporate the issue of victimization in their identity building, Yezidis from the Kurdagh draw on their partial integration into society in order to create a more assertive Yezidi identity. This new identity is strengthened in the ongoing process of identity building in areas under the self-administration.

6.2. SHIFTING IDENTITIES

A particular group of Yezidis, those residing in Armenia, recently underwent a dramatic shift in their identity. They renounced their Kurdish ethnicity in place of a separate and unique Yezidi ethnicity. Yezidis in Armenia are called a dual minority[11], a label that describes their continual struggle to define their position in the ethno-religious spectrum of the country. However, their problem was related to the question of which nationality they had. Most Yezidis called themselves Yezidis instead of Kurds, which referred to Muslim Kurds. In fact, Armenian Yezidis still get very irritated when they are called Kurds. But it is extremely difficult to clearly distinguish between the two groups, because identity is a complex thing and not confined to one expression or factor. While language is often used as a way to differentiate between groups, it does not work in the Yezidi case: although many Armenian Yezidis maintain that they speak Yezidi as their native language, it does not differ from the Kurmanji language that the Muslim Kurds speak. Thus, they speak the same language, but call it differently. Furthermore, Yezidis use the Cyrillic alphabet, while the Kurds prefer the Latin alphabet. How deep the rift between the communities is, can be seen by the strong resistance to the introduction of a Yezidi language textbook. Both sides insist on their rights to have their own language.[12] The author asserts that the division and boundary between the two groups are primarily based on a different educational level.[13]

These observations raise the question about shifting identities among the Syrian Yezidis. Both groups settled on the periphery of the Yezidi realm and both previously highlighted their religious identity layer over the ethnic one. While Armenian Yezidis shifted from Kurdish to Yezidi ethnicity, the Syrian Yezidis adopted the Kurdish ethnicity as their own in order contrast the dominating Arabness. By joining the Kurdish national movement their status was elevated, and they immediately gained powerful allies (and enemies). The rise of the Kurdish national movement in Syria brought the most obvious changes to the Yezidi group identity. While Yezidis in the past saw themselves as Yezidis first and to a lesser degree as Kurds and even less as Syrians, they started focusing on the ethnic component of their identity since the 1960s and even more so in the new millennium. This has been a mutually beneficial process, whereas the Kurdish movement was able to expand into the Yezidi villages and earn legitimacy by collaborating with the original Kurdish religion. For the Yezidis, Kurdish nationalism meant a shift in their comparison factors. By joining a more or less successful external group, they were able to improve their group esteem and overall ranking in the hierarchy. They were no longer the outcasts; now they had powerful allies. This new reality came of course with a price tag. In order to be accepted into the new group, they had to give up or adjust some of their unique characteristics. And as we will see, not all members of the in-group participated in the identity shift and refused to raise the ethnic component over the religious one.

The Kurdish national movement in Syria and its political representatives willingly and gladly accepted the Yezidis in their ranks while benefitting from their religious reputation as the original Kurdish religion. This certainly added legitimacy to the claims of hegemony and political power. The PKK and her sister organization in Syria, the PYD, both took advantage of this move and extended their sphere of influence deep into the Yezidi community. Eventually, this led to the severing of ties and relations with the Yezidi leadership in Iraq, who disregard the PKK/PYD claims. The siege of Kobani and the Sinjar massacre created a short momentum where these claims and accusations were put aside. But in the aftermath, during the liberation of Kobani and Sinjar, it became apparent that the Yezidis are still trapped between competing self-proclaimed protectors and their own incohesive group identity. What further complicated this dilemma are attempts by outside groups to weigh in and influence the decision-making and identity-building process.

6.3. THE DIASPORA COMMUNITY

Due to the permanent persecution as a double minority, Syrian Yezidis have long considered the option of leaving their homeland in search of better living conditions. Since they don't feel welcome in their own country, leaving it behind did not seem to be a difficult step. However, although they may not been attached to the country, they feel closely connected to the land, that is, the land of their ancestors. This counts for the Yezidis from Kurdagh even more so, because of long presence in the area. Yezidis in the Jezira did not settle there until a century ago. They also did not engage in physical building of identity, for example through shrines, cemeteries, or other sacred communal places as the Kurdagh Yezidis.

As it was shown from the data about population growth, Syria's Yezidi community experienced a sharp increase in migration. Some villages lost over 80 percent of their population over the past few years. The issue became a great concern for community leaders, village elders, and party representatives, who all pleaded with the public begging them to stay. In the Efrin canton, the local administration even placed a temporary travel ban on all citizens.[14] As shown in the diagrams depicting population growth/decline among the Yezidi villages in the Jezira, a mass exodus of Yezidis from that region to Germany occurred for the following reasons: many complained about the uncertain future for their family and community, the looming threat of possible Muslim attacks, the dire economic situation, and of course the ongoing Syrian crisis with the revolution and civil war. Although considered the original people of the land, they have no choice but to emigrate. To some extent it is the economic situation, but most of them are looking for a life of dignity and safety. The fear from yet another *ferman*,[15] the 73rd (or 74th depending on the counting), drove many away to Europe where they found safety and security. Muslim pressure, in combination with government neglect, made most Yezidis see their future somewhere else where they don't have to attend Islamic religious classes, where they can register their marriages and children under their religion and not as Muslim, and where they don't have to face a possible genocide.

At times, especially during the 1990s, it was considered popular to emigrate, mostly because those who left were economically better off and thus would set the standard for the other to follow. It seemed that everyone who left back then now owns a large house, a car, send money, gets an education, opens businesses and files for the immigration of family members.[16] And with the increasing institutionalization of the diaspora community, they were able to spread the message of successful integration and prosperity among the followers at home. The image of the well-off relative in Germany who has a good job, status, educated children, and does not fear persecution was duly noted among those who stayed in Syria, waiting for their chance or turn to leave. The warnings of some community elders about the possible loss of identity in Germany or possible extinction of Yezidism in Syria fell on deaf ears.

Syrian Yezidis from all areas seriously contemplate to immigrate to Germany. Most of them already have relatives living there, who are calling on their family members to join them. Especially the events in Sinjar have exaggerated these feelings, and now more than ever do the Syrian Yezidis want to leave their villages, homes, and properties. The fear that this attack might be repeated runs deep. While in the past it was mostly the poor families who left to find better living conditions, today even the rich and well-connected families have started selling furniture and other belongings or finding trustworthy friends who can take care of their properties while they are gone.

The current mass migration to central Europe, either across the Mediterranean Sea or across the Balkan land route, is dominated by Syrians. Consequently, among the victims of the passage are also many Syrians. And so are Syrian Yezidis, who have been caught in the boats to the coast of Italy. A common escape route is from Syria to Lebanon where they board planes to Libya from where they go on boats to cross to Italy, Malta, or Greece. On July 23, 2013 the Greek coast guard found the bodies of 12 people (three men, four women, and five children) who tried crossing from Turkey to Greece. According to their papers they belonged to two families from Basufan.[17]

Sabriya Khalaf, a Yezidi woman from Otelje, earned media attention because she was the oldest refugee in the world. One hundred and seven years old, she fled her village with her son to Turkey and later got stranded in Athens, Greece. Too old to travel the land route, she finally made it to Germany where some of her relatives live.[18]

6.3.1. Yezidi Organizations in the Diaspora

A mentioned above, the Yezidi community in the German diaspora is well organized and highly institutionalized, two characteristics the Syrian community is lacking. However, it took the community some forty years to establish themselves in this foreign culture and environment while they concurrently made efforts to preserve their heritage and religion. Ultimately, this led to the creation of a new diaspora identity. Yezidis in Germany emerged as a homogenous group in the eyes of the general public where no distinction was made regarding the country of origin. Furthermore, this new identity promoted a distinction to the Kurdish diaspora group. In essence, religion topped ethnicity and tried to overlook regional differences. The new Yezidi was proud of his unifying religion and worked on integrating into German society, a strong, devout, and law-abiding resident/citizen who left behind the internal quarrels.[19]

Yezidi communities in the diaspora followed their own path of identity building based on the conditions, challenges, and laws of the host country. In addition to the quest for unification of the different regional groups, two major trends can be observed, one that favors a return to traditional values, and the other that strives to develop a modern form of Yezidism. The two approaches are supported by different age groups, where the older generation upholds conservative views and the younger generation is more likely to adopt a modernized version of their creed.

This can also be seen among the various generations of immigrants. The first group of Yezidis, those from Turkey, came in the 1980s often with the hope of going back to the homeland. Their children who accompanied them and who were born in the homeland experienced a different way of growing up and socializing and becoming Yezidis. And for those Yezidis who were born in the diaspora it becomes even more difficult to relate to the old customs and traditions, because all they know was life in the Westernized and modernized society.

Generally, one must describe the exile community as conservative in comparison with the majority population of the host country. People revert to conservative and preservative values in order to respond to the pressures of integration and assimilation into the host country's society. Among some extremely conservative families this had led to acts of honor crimes.

Yezidi psychotherapists Shefik Tagay and Ibrahim Kus developed a scientific method to measure Yezidi identity in the diaspora from multiple dimensions aiming at the trajectory of identity, migration, and health. For this study, they surveyed Yezidi immigrants in Germany and developed the Yezidi Identity Inventory (EZI). This questionnaire asked about attitudes, opinions, and assessments regarding the influence of Yezidism in the life of the interviewees. Almost four hundred respondents participated in the survey[20] and the results can be analyzed according to variables, such as age, gender, geographic origin, and education. For this chapter, EZI data were analyzed according to their relation to religion and tradition, and they focused on the entries submitted by Syrian Yezidis. Then they were compared to the answers given by Yezidis from Turkey, Iraq, and German-born. The number before the country of origins indicates that ranking with the highest approval rate of the question-statement.

Q1: I am aware of the five basic pillars.
1 Iraq, 2 Turkey, 3 Syria, 4 Germany
Q2: I consider myself a pious and faithful Yezidi.
1 Iraq, 2 Germany, 3 Syria, 4 Turkey
Q3: Yezidi traditions are important to me.
1 Iraq, 2 Germany, 3 Syria, 4 Turkey
Q4: I feel empowered by my Yezidi religion.
1 Iraq, 2 Germany, 3 Syria, 4 Turkey
Q5: Lalish is an important place of pilgrimage for me.
1 Iraq, 2 Syria, 3 Germany, 4 Turkey
Q6: I based my attitude of life on Yezidism.
1 Iraq, 2 Syria, 3 Germany, 4 Turkey
Q7: Yezidism helps me to explain this world.
1 Iraq, 2 Germany, 3 Syria, 4 Turkey
Q8: Yezidism helps me to find the meaning of life.
1 Iraq, 2 Germany, 3 Syria, 4 Turkey
Q9: Hed u Sed, the Yezidi caste system should be reformed.
1 Syria, 2 Turkey, 3 Germany, 4 Iraq
Q10: I am Yezidi, but not religious.
1 Turkey, 2 Syria, 3 Germany, 4 Iraq

From these ten sample questions it becomes apparent that Yezidis of Syrian origin have a different attitude toward important religious questions than those from Iraq and those who were born in Germany. It also appears that the Syrian responses are similar to those from Turkey, and both groups represent the least conservative part of the diaspora community.

The Yezidi community in Germany is diverse in their geographical background and origin. As we learned, almost the entire Yezidi community from Turkey came to Germany, and they are considered the largest subgroup, only next to the Iraqi Yezidis. The Syrian community is much smaller; however, because of the housing practices of the Germany refugee authority, they are equally distributed among the other Yezidi groups.

Until recently, they have not pursued the formation of regional representations such as a Syrian Yezidi House or Association. Instead, they participated in the country's two largest Yezidi lobby groups as well as in the many local branches.

The landscape of Yezidi institutions and organization in Germany is multifaceted and includes local Yezidi houses, regional centers, intellectual gatherings, and national councils.[21] Two groups emerged as the leaders and aspired to form a central or umbrella council representing all Yezidis living in Germany. The Federation of Ezidi Kurds (Föderation Ezidischer

Kurden—FEK) and the General Council of the Yezidis in Germany (Zentralrat der Yeziden in Deutschland—ZYD), however, differ on political and religious grounds. Especially the FEK is criticized for its position toward the Zoroastrian nature of Yezidism. Although it was attempted several times to create a unity council with representatives from both groups, this never materialized. The main reason for the failure can be found in the leadership claim by Yezidis from Northern Kurdistan (Turkey) and Yezidis from Southern Kurdistan (Iraq) and the respective affiliation with a political party (PKK and KDP). The Yezidis from Western Kurdistan (Syria) have little influence over this debate.

The diaspora community and its many institutions organize seminars, workshops, and conferences to bring together scholars, experts, and other interested parties, Yezidis and non-Yezidis, to educate about Yezidi religion, history, and sociology. These meetings are a great opportunity for Yezidi representatives from the different regions to get together, exchange opinions, and perhaps find common denominators. Certainly, party affiliations, the multiple interpretations of religious doctrines, as well as the regional background, led to factions and conflict among the community.

6.3.2. Legal Status of Syrian Yezidis in Germany

While Yezidis from Turkey were granted group asylum in the 1990s, those from Syria did not. Instead on a case-by-case basis, they had to go through the court system and experienced inconsistent rulings. At times, Yezidis from the Jezira did receive group asylum status, only to have taken it away shortly after. Yezidi lobby groups and experts testified before the courts and occasionally saw positive rulings. However, more often these decisions were overturned in the higher courts, and only a few Syrian Yezidis enjoyed permanent residence or asylum status in Germany.

In July 2008, the governments of Germany and Syria signed an agreement (*Abkommen*) to repatriate citizens without official status. This repatriation act, which targeted Syrians living in Germany, threatened the expulsion of Syrian Yezidis living in Germany.[22] While family members had different residence status, it occurred that families were separated; sometimes the mother, the father, or siblings were deported to Syria. Many of those deported to Syria were immediately arrested by the Syrian authorities, interrogated, imprisoned, and tortured. With the outbreak of the Syrian civil war, German authorities suspended the program and dangerous practice; however, they have yet to cancel the agreement.[23] Several Syrian Yezidi refugees were deported as late as February 2011.

One of the first deportation cases was that of Ms. Abde Houran, a then 25-year-old pregnant Syrian Yezidi woman. She was born in Barzan and came with her husband Daham in the year 2000 to Germany seeking asylum. Her temporary refugee status was regularly renewed until after the signature of the repatriation agreement when she was immediately arrested and brought to the airport where she collapsed and had to be hospitalized. She married her husband, a lawful refugee, according to Yezidi custom; however, since both spouses were stateless, they were unable to register their marriage officially. The German authorities had no issue with deporting a single, pregnant woman to Syria, a country known for its cruel practices of persecuting Yezidis. Ms. Houran was indeed arrested after her arrival to Damascus and held for several days until a hefty bribe was paid for her release.[24]

The case of the Naso family also received media attention where police with a canine squad surrounded the family's home in Hildesheim and arrested the 62-year-old father Badir Naso, his wife Bashe Hasso, and the 15-year-old son Anwar. Only the 18-year-old daughter Shanas was not taken into custody. The wife collapsed and had to be hospitalized, while her husband and son were immediately deported to Syria. According to the family, they were arrested upon arrival.[25]

6.4. RELIGIOUS IDENTITIES

Syrian Yezidi religious identity evolved significantly since the sixteenth century, especially in the Aleppo area, and reached a high point during the Mandate time. The process of identity formation can be traced to four important stages: the formative years during their emergence in the Kurdagh, the consolidation stage during the Mandate years, the decline under the Ba'th rule, and the final stage of reemergence under the self-administration. Each stage was defined by certain social and historical conditions, which influenced the development of identity. Foreign influences have been dominant with the Christian missionaries, the Ottoman administrators, French mandate authorities, secular Kurdish policies, and radical Muslim militants. But domestic factors, such as local Muslim resentments and Arab nationalism, contributed most to its recent demise. And ultimately, it was the political advance of the Syrian Kurds that enabled the Yezidi communities to redefine themselves.

Throughout history, the Syrian Yezidis have been generally recognized as a religious minority by the neighboring groups. However, recognition never meant acceptance or tolerance. Because the Yezidis usually did not practice their faith in public, and they did not have religious assembly halls and other religious gatherings, they were marginalized, often overlooked, sometimes forgotten, and always pushed to the periphery. Misconceptions about their faith prevailed, such as the issue of devil worship, the descant from Yazid bin Muawiya, or their consideration as a heretic Islamic sect.

The debate over the question of religious persecution of Yezidis in Syria is very controversial. While in the past there were periods of calm and indifference about them, there were also those times of constant pressure and even open hostility and persecution. Since the main concern of this study is the recent situation, the inquiry seeks to find out whether the article in the Syrian constitution about religious freedom applied to the Yezidis? Or did the Syrian state persecute Yezidis because of their faith? What is the view of the self-administration regarding the Yezidis? Can they practice their faith in public? What does the non-Yezidi population have to say about this? And how is the community regarded in the areas outside government control?

Due to their small size, the Syrian government did not deal with the Yezidis except on a local level. And it is here where the problems for both Yezidi communities began. The biggest concern was not the restriction to practice the faith, but how to register and recognize it officially. Because Yezidis were never a *millet* in the traditional sense nor were they considered *Ahl al-Kitab*, they did not have their own religious legal system or personal status law like the Christians, Druze, or other religious minorities under Islamic rule. Instead, they had to register at Sharia or state courts, which often objected to writing the label Yezidi and wrote Muslim instead. Birth records, marriage licenses, and death certificates thus became major areas of contention. And so did cemeteries. Would a Yezidi grave be permitted on Muslim cemetery? Some argued that since Yezidis were perhaps a Muslim sect, they should be allowed to bury their dead here; while others did not want to be associated with devil worshiping infidels in this life or the next. However, the local administration rarely allowed Yezidis to have separate cemeteries. Mixed Christian-Yezidi cemeteries existed in the Wadi Jarrah area and in the case of Derek Falak, an exclusive Yezidi cemetery was located near the village of Otelje. Usually, it depended on the local bilateral relations whether Yezidi families were allowed to have unique Yezidi grave structures and tombs or not. In case of the Kurdagh, where Yezidis settled among the majority Kurdish-Muslim population and where they had their own shrines and sanctuaries, they were permitted to bury their dead here. But this must not be seen as an act of generosity or tolerance, but rather a convenient decision, since Muslims had their own cemeteries, and they did not want to share the sacred space with Yezidis.

Other divisions among the two Yezidi communities existed too, for example in the case of marriage taboos. Yezidis society consists of clerics and laymen with strict endogamous marriage rules. Laymen cannot marry clerics, and the various cleric groups cannot marry each other. These rules were arguably the most visible distinction of Yezidism and became some sort of the brand name of the religion. As said earlier, Yezidis from the Jezira disregarded their fellow Yezidis from Efrin as deviators because marriage rules were not strictly enforced over there. Subsequently, marriage ties between the two groups were very rare and usually resulted in outrage and sometimes the expulsion of the couple from the community.

Both communities suffered from the official enforcement of attending (and succeeding) Islam courses in schools and university. Unlike Christian students who were exempted and had their own religious classes, Yezidi students had to go through the entire Islamic curriculum, which included many lessons denigrating and offending Yezidism. Students who rebelled against this system were expelled or not allowed to graduate. In the rural setting of most Yezidi villages, where everybody knew everyone, it was also impossible to hide or deny Yezidi identity. This strategy may have worked later in life during the military service or at university. However, it still had negative effects on the formation of a strong religious identity.

Local attempts have been made both in the Kurdagh and the Jezira to offer Yezidi religious classes; however, authorities quickly dismissed them and insisted on the Islamic instruction. This has been recently revoked under the self-administration when Yezidi religious courses and schools opened with official permission. Generally, after the liberation of the areas of Efrin, Jezira and Kobani from the Syrian regime on 19 July 2012, the social, religious, and political Yezidi movement started to grow stronger every day.

But for the longest time, the two communities were isolated from their neighbors and more importantly from their fellow Yezidis in Iraq. There were some concerns that the religious leadership with the Mir and the Spiritual Council was not active enough in promoting Yezidism among the more distant communities. They would like to see initiatives to codify Yezidi dogma and rituals and distribute this among the groups; however, the initiative should come from the religious leaders in Iraq.[26]

The continual physical separation of the three cantons effected and hindered the development of a united Yezidi identity. Instead we must note the emergence of separate trends and unilateral decisions as well as a lack of coordination between the three areas.

6.4.1. The Kurdagh/Efrin Region

The Kurdagh with its long history of Yezidi settlement always had a few learned men and clerics who were regarded as religious authorities among the villages. This also means that not every member of the sheikh or pir caste was able to attain this status. In fact, only a handful of religious leaders were known and active over the last half century. During the time of recent transformation, some of those religious leaders passed away. In August 2009, the well-known Sheikh Nasr Jafar bin Manan Sheikh Sheikhobakr died in Basufan. He was approximately 80 years old and the head of the Jafar family in Basufan. Suleyman Jafar, the current minister of foreign affairs in the Efrin Canton, is from this family. On August 26, 2013 Sheikh Husayn Sheikh Hassan Sheikh Brim from Ghezewiye died, who was arguably the most respected religious leader of the Kurdagh. While they were able to connect with the earlier generations of clerics and scholars and received training from them, a new generation is nowhere in sight. Due to the lack of religious instruction and training for clerics, it was almost impossible to recognize the next religious authority. Some well-known, but older, sheikhs still perform their duties, but it takes time until the first cohort of new religious teachers graduates from Yezidi seminaries.

For this purpose, the Yezidi Association in Efrin was founded and tasked with organizing Yezidi affairs in this canton. On October 6, 2013, the association's official headquarter was opened in Efrin. Several committees were found to deal with specific issues such as mediation, training, information, culture, sports, and women. Members of the administrative board include: Suleyman Jafar, Abd al-Rahman Shamo, Mustafa Ali Nabo, Abdo Jamil, Nuri Najjar, Nisrin Jafar, Imad Marko, and Gule Jafar. For example, they discussed ways to revive Zoroastrian (!) traditions and customs, because they saw that Yezidi religion had been vanishing due to the pressures and discriminations. This clearly indicated to a great amount of uncertainty about where to go from here. It was Suleyman Jafar himself who talked about the importance to revive and preserve these Zoroastrian rituals arguably not really knowing which rituals he referred to. However, because of their special circumstances and standing among other Yezidi communities, those Yezidis from Kurdagh show a closer affiliation with the idea of Yezidi and Zoroastrian overlaps. Another reason goes back to the PKK/PYD dogma of a Zoroastrian origin of the Yezidis. Jafar is a PYD member, and as noted before, this party is the most popular party in the region.

The other conclusion for the community was that this revival can only be accomplished through participation in the self-administration project. Because this newly created body was built on the principles of cultural, ethnic and religious diversity[27], they supported Yezidi projects, and the Yezidi institutions collaborated willingly. Seminary schools were opened to first train teachers in Yezidi religious studies. This would be a major step because for the first time in history a teacher training institute and curriculum would be developed, sanctioned by the Spiritual Council in Lalish or not. The other innovation was the fact that most of the teacher candidates were women, when religious instruction had been a male domain in the past. Now qualified teachers can teach all Yezidi children religion and their religious texts regardless of their caste and origin.

On November 25, 2013 another Yezidi House was opened in Basufan to teach the religion and Kurdish language. Suleyman Jafar, who was also one of the teachers at the house, explained the importance of the step of allowing the Yezidis to take care of their own religious affairs. Apparently, the people of Basufan were happy about this opportunity.[28]

The Yezidi Association in Efrin had requested to offer Yezidi religious classes in villages with Yezidi inhabitants, and the educational board of the self-administered Efrin Canton finally agreed to it. The teachers were trained for eight months in the curriculum of the Lalish schools in Iraq. After a graduation ceremony at the association's headquarter in Efrin, the new teachers were sent to the schools in Yezidi villages. This ceremony was one of the first public demonstrations of a newly gained strong and proud Yezidi identity. It started with lighting of the candles and reading of qewls by one of the graduates, Nisrin Iso. Pir Shamo, a local cleric, talked to the graduates about the important role of the religious teacher and the fact that they were able to realize their dreams under the self-administration rule.[29]

Eighteen of them were hired by the board and sent to the villages of Qibare, Ghezewiye, Qatme, Qestel Jindo, and Feqira. Classes were given in the afternoon to elementary students after the regular classes. Mustafa Ali Shan, administrator at the association, stressed the importance of the accomplishment that Yezidism is now taught alongside Islam. Others expressed their hope that this first step will eventually lead to the codification of a Yezidi personal status law in Syria.[30]

In the meantime, Yezidis from Efrin used the newly gained freedoms to further assert their position in the public sphere by celebrating their religious holidays. Since the association had hundreds of members, these events were hugely popular, attracting large crowds of worshipers and supporters.

Over that past decade, Yezidi holidays like Charshemasor were publicly celebrated in villages with a Yezidi majority, such as Qestel Jindo, Basufan, and Otelje.[31] Hundreds of Yezidis gathered at the shrine of Sheikh Hmeyd. Young and old, men and women danced traditional folklore dances and partied for hours. When the government still had some authority in the region, they closely monitored the celebrations and sometimes denied access to locations. The PYD was already present then and issued statements regarding the Yezidis. Thus, the question whether the Yezidis were able to celebrate their holidays always depended on the larger, general relationship between the Kurds and the government. The organizers made sure not to provoke the government, and one must see the display of photographs of Hafiz and Bashar al-Asad and Syrian flags next to Kurdish flags and Ocalan posters in this regard.

Now under the new political circumstances, Yezidis from the Kurdagh were able to attend the annual Cemaya (pilgrimage) Festival in Lalish, Iraq. Among the pilgrims was Abu Nidal, the son of Sheikh Shemo, who swore an oath to his dying father that he would one day perform the pilgrimage. It took him another eleven years before he was able to fulfill his promise. Abu Nidal Sheikh Shemo is a descendant of Sheikh Hassan Abdallo. A village in the Efrin region still carries the name of his ancestor, Birche Abdallo, who was the first to settle here.[32]

In December of the same year, Yezidis also celebrated *Sersala Jiyana Erde* or the New Year of Creation of life. This was one of the ancient traditions that the community revived after enjoying relative freedom and security under the self-administration. Other Yezidi communities dedicated this day to Ezid, but the tenor of the celebrations is the same: three days of fasting precluding the holiday starting on a Tuesday until Thursday and organizing a large feast on Friday. In preparation of the feast, they also visit the cemeteries where they give away fruits, sweats, and treats as offerings of the deceased. This is also the time of forgiveness and reconciliation. Considering the dire situation of the country, Yezidis used this occasion to call for peace and unity.[33]

On April 17, 2013 the Efrin community gathered for a day near the village of Eyndare to celebrate New Year or the Red Wednesday. Organizer Suleyman Jafar spoke about the history of this holiday and stated that it was already celebrated in 612 BC.[34] He also referenced the current situation and the stalemate between the regime and the opposition. His concern was that more people will be killed and many others will emigrate if the conflict lasted longer.[35]

Yezidis in Efrin celebrated Khidr Elyas on February 13, 2014; however in a slightly different way, more like a spring festival: first a three-day fasting before the holiday was held. Then forty different kinds of foods were collected, such as cracked wheat, chick peas, lentils, and grinded wheat. This meal was placed at a special location during the night for Khidr Elyas to descend and bless the offering.[36]

6.4.2. The Jezira Region

The Jezira community too began to build institutions under the self-autonomy administration. The first Syrian Yezidi philanthropic society, The *Shams* (Sun) Organization, was founded on May 5, 2012 in the village of Qizlachuq in front of over three hundred attendees. Several working committees were established, and Ibrahim Sheikh Mlehan was elected at its first director.[37] In preparation for the opening of a Yezidi House in the Amuda region, another meeting of the Shams Philanthropic Society was held in Qizlachuq on September 23, 2012. The board members for the house were elected, and discussions were held about how to facilitate the pilgrimage to Lalish. The speakers included community activists and members of the organization to establish the Yezidi House, among them were Amin Badash, Sheikh Ibrahim, Nuri Ramo, Alo Hassan, and Sa'id Sheikh Hato.[38]

Over a year later, in February 2014, they met again in Qizlachuq for the annual meeting of the Yezidi House with representatives from all over the Jezira in attendance. Looking back to their statement of account for the year

2013, Ilyas Sido recognized the difficulties and hardships that the Yezidi House and the entire community had to go through. He singled out the attacks by the Islamic militants and the unprecedented immigration rate as the two most difficult challenges. On the positive side, it was remembered that the foundation of the Yezidi House was a huge accomplishment and the right step for the community to play a political role in the new Syria. The speakers confirmed their bond with the Kurdish movement by saying that the fate of the Kurds is the fate of the Yezidis and that no foreign institution or organization may speak in the name of the Syrian Yezidis without prior consultation with the Yezidi House. A representative from TEV-DEM[39] highlighted the importance of Yezidi self-organization when he called for a branch of the Yezidi House to be opened in every Yezidi village. This call was incorporated in the final statement of the meeting in addition to an invitation for all immigrants to return to Rojava, especially those from the liberated village of Asadiya. There were also calls for strengthening the role of women in the service of the society and religion.[40]

On May 6, 2014 its second conference was held in Amuda under the motto: Religion for God and the Yezidi House for Kurdish Unity and People's Brotherhood. Aside from discussion of the topic of women's rights, some important decisions were made:

1. Cooperation with all Yezidi organizations and institutions in Kurdistan and in exile.
2. The building of branches of the Yezidi House in Tirbespi, Serekaniye, and Hasake.
3. Cooperation and strong work with the Autonomy Administration to have Yezidi representation in the executive and legal councils as well as in the local councils of the regions.
4. The opening of houses of worship in Yezidi villages to practice their religion.
5. The right to teach Yezidism in the areas with Yezidi population.
6. Travel insurance for Yezidis going to Lalish to perform the Hajj.

As for religious classes and teaching, the celebrations of the holidays, the establishment of religious rites, the observation of pilgrimages and the reception of Yezidi delegations from abroad, all of these fell under the joint responsibility of the Yezidi House in Efrin and the Yezidi House in Jezira. They would cooperate with the canton governments in these affairs. A joint leadership was elected (Ibrahim Keli and Ronaz Bahdin), secretary (Khalil Ibrahim), and financial officer (Ilyas Sido). They also formed a five-member executive committee which would be responsible for carrying out regular work and activities of the Yezidi House.[41]

The Jezira region saw a revival of celebrating Yezidi holidays too, similar to that of the Efrin region, however at a slower pace and after a painful start. On April 21, 2011, the sheikhs of the Yezidi tribes in Syria published a statement calling upon all Yezidis not to celebrate Carshemasor or the Red Wednesday, that is, the Yezidi New Year in public due to security concerns and not to offend the families of the martyrs. Instead prayers should be offered from the homes.

After the establishment of the canton administration, however, it was easier to organize these events, but still some restrictions are observed. On April 17, 2013 Yezidis in the Wadi al-Jarah region celebrated the Yezidi New Year; however, as advised, they cut short the celebrations and did not include the typical large communal gathering because of the concurrent attacks against the Kurdish neighborhood of Sheikh Maqsud in Aleppo. As in previous years, they all participated in the preparations of the holiday with coloring the eggs and baking the *Kleja*, a special sweet bread, to be distributed among the participants. On the Tuesday before the holiday they visited the cemeteries to honor the dead at the cemetery Diyare Feleke in Otelje and the cemetery in Mizgeft and had a communal meal there. On the next day, Wednesday, the actual New Year, the practice was that the families gathered in the natural areas near the Jarah Dam and had dances, speeches, and religious recitations; however, because of the prevailing dangerous situation, they decided to meet at the house of Peshimam Sheikh Maqbul Sheikh Nasr Sheikh Mirza in Otelje. Normally, they would have organized a large communal gathering near the lake or the river with participants coming from other Yezidi areas too and Christian and Muslim families attending as well. There would have been food, music, and lots of dances as well as folkloristic and religious performances. Afterward, they would have been invited to visit the Shams Philanthropic Society in Amuda who put together a larger event for the occasion in the Pilsan Restaurant in the village of Merkeb.[42]

At the same time, the Yezidi community in Amuda celebrated New Year, Charshemasor, in a similar low-key and private way. On the eve of the holiday, they organized a lecture about Yezidism by Hassan Zaza, a well-known writer and journalist. On the Wednesday and Thursday, the Yezidi families in the area visited each other, and on Friday they put together a larger indoor event in Dugerki (Dugar) with many music and dances troops. They refrained from an open, public gathering for security concerns; however, they invited Muslim and Christian families to attend the event. Still, compared to previous years, this celebration was one of the biggest for the local Yezidi community.

Charshemasor 2014 was celebrated widely among the Syrian Yezidis. However, because of security concerns, the different communities celebrated mostly in their own villages and homes. For one day, however, the groups from Tirbespi and Hasake would travel to Dugerki, a Yezidi village near Ras al-Ayn, to hold a larger, joint celebration. This was a large gathering organized by the local Yezidi House and the PYD. The location was decorated with posters of Apo, Kurdish flags and pictures of the martyrs. The speakers included Elias Musa and Barakat Rasho from the local Yezidi House, Hakam Khalo from the Legal Counsel of the Jezira Canton, and Burhan Abdi from the Religious Council. They all referred to the long history of the Yezidi religion and the fact that they now live peacefully with their Muslim and Christian neighbors. They even invited the emigrants to return to Rojava, because the Syrian Yezidis felt they were living in a democratic environment and were protected by the YPG. The celebration was accompanied by musical and theatre performances as well as readings of qewls.[43]

On July 8, 2013, a meeting was organized by the TEV-DEM's religious committee in Khan Tamr to discuss the situation of the Yezidis and their grievances in the past. The other goal was to stop the emigration of young people and families abroad. Farhad Khalti, a member of the religious committee, talked about the ancient religion and strongly encouraged the villagers to preserve it because it is an original part of the Kurdish history. He also called upon them not to leave their villages and to emigrate.

Figure 6.1 The Syrian Yezidi Triumvirate: Lalish, Zarathustra, and Abdulla Ocalan.
Source: Used with permission of ARA News: http://aranews.net/

A banner was shown during the meeting that had all of Ocalan, Zarathustra, and Lalish on it.[44]

6.5. ETHNIC IDENTITIES

Historically, Yezidism has emerged among the Kurds, even though some of the clerics have some Arabic roots. It spread among the Kurds in northern Iraq, Turkey, and Syria. When Yezidis immigrated to Russia, they were considered ethnic Kurds.[45] But growing up among other Kurds and being Kurds caused this identity marker to become secondary and to be pushed back while others took priority, such as religious and tribal identity. Then, they were recognized as Yezidi Kurds. This changed over the past century when Yezidis in all territories became more or less actively involved in the Kurdish national movement. In Syria, this happened as early as the 1930s when both communities (Kurdagh and Jezira) collaborated with the Bedirkhans and Khoybun. During the nationalist rule of the Ba'th party, the various Kurdish parties provided the only viable platform of dissent and attracted many young Yezidis. Ultimately, because of state ignorance, ambivalent Kurdish politics, and Yezidi insignificance, Yezidis during the second half of the last century were largely equated with the Syrian Kurds. Any decision or development regarding the Kurds affected the Yezidis too. Likewise, only a few decisions and developments with specific regard to the Yezidis were noticed. Thus, it was up for them to preserve what little of their unique identity was left. Although in steady decline, the community never disappeared from the religious landscape. And this must be regarded an accomplishment.

Today, and on a more general level, the traditional equation that all Yezidis are Kurds does no longer fully apply. To a very large extent, Yezidis assert their Kurdish roots and bonds, but some groups left the common framework to promote a different ethnic identity. These are the Armenian Yezidis and Sinjaris. The latter, and also some villages in the Sheikhan such as Bashiqa and Bahzani, claim Arabic roots or rather deny an exclusive Kurdish origin. Internal political rivalries might have contributed to this rift within the Iraqi Yezidi community. Attempts by the former Iraqi government under Saddam Hussein to deepen this rift must be noted too, when they used the absence of Mir Tahsin Beg in 1990 to appoint one of his relatives, Muawiya, as the new Mir. Muawiya's side of the family struggled for generations to gain the political supremacy within the Mir's family, and Saddam's offer seemed like the long-awaited opportunity to finally succeed.[46,47]

The recent events in Sinjar with the failure of the Kurdish Pershmerga to protect the defenseless Yezidis contributed to a growing anti-Kurdish sentiment among Iraqi Sinjar Yezidis who no longer want to be recognized as Kurds, but as members of a separate identity group. Even Mir Tahsin Beg stated that in his view the Yezidis are an independent ethnic group with a different religion. Masud Barzani, president of the Kurdish Autonomous Region and the self-declared protector of the Yezidis, vehemently opposed this view saying that "not I nor the Mir nor any other person is able to uncover a Yezidi identity." Mir Tahsin's son Hazim later downplayed his father's comments as the words of an old man who did not feel well.[48]

All these debates do not matter much for the Syrian Yezidis who firmly and strongly demonstrate their Kurdish origin and insist on their rank within the Kurdish national movement. At no time was there ever a hint toward a separate Arabic or even Yezidi identity, especially not after Kurdish nationalistic feelings emerged after World War I. As mentioned before, there is a debate about different religious origins, in particular, the question of whether Yezidis were in fact Zoroastrians, but never was their Kurdishness doubted. On the contrary, from the early days of the Kurdish national movement in Syria during the 1930s, Yezidis were encouraged to join, and they did participate in Khoybun, the main association to promote Kurdish nationalism during the Mandate years.

In a very recent statement, the highest Yezidi authorities (Mir and Baba Sheikh) once and for all declared the Kurdishness of the Yezidis:[49]

> The Yezidis are followers of an old religion from the distant past. Throughout history, this religion and believers were exposed to the worst forms of persecution and surpression and genocide, which led to a decrease of their numbers. However, all of these repressions, and Arabization campaigns which occurred during the era of the Iraqi regime and which aimed to assimilate them with the other religions and ethnicities, did not accomplish that the Yezidis would lose their roots and their religious Yezidi identity and pure Kurdish ethnicity. They preserved this identity and made great sacrifices in this way.
>
> During the various periods of Kurdish fighting, the Yezidis contributed significantly in this field and made great sacrifices for the realization of the national legitimate goals of the Kurdish people. History is witness for their honorable positions in the September and Golan revolutions and the glorious March uprising and Iraq's liberation and in the following political process, like the elections, the drafting of the constitution and the active role in its success and passing.
>
> We are in a time where we need to confirm these realities, at the same time we are reasurring the Yezidi position in the general census project, on October 24, 2010, despite some concerns here and there.
>
> Thus, we emphasize our pride in our Kurdish ethnicity built on linguistic, historic, geographic and traditional facts. We also mention that the Yezidi religion is a unified religion with its texts written in Kurdish.

On this occasion we call on all Yezidis to activly support the coming census because it is a historic chance for all Iraqi groups to determine their real size inside Iraq. And the Yezidis are one of them to verify their Yezidi religion and Kurdish ethnicity and to miss the opportunity for those who only want to split and disperse the Yezidis.

Signed by

His Eminence The Baba Sheikh, member of the Yezidi Supreme Spiritual Council

His Highness the Mir, Tahsin Said Ali Beg, President of the Supreme Spiritual Council

His Eminence Sheikh al-Wazir Barakat, member of the Yezidi Supreme Spiritual Council

His Eminence Peshimam Faruq, member of the Yezidi Supreme Spiritual Council

His Eminence al-Qewal Suleman Safo, member of the Yezidi Supreme Spiritual Council

As noted in the statement above, Yezidis share with fellow Muslim Kurds the same language, culture, history as well as the adherence to traditional practices and customs. This letter also points to a shared belief in the concept of honor and shame, and part of this is the execution of honor crimes. In the Western press, this issue has been dramatized and exaggerated to a degree that has left the entire community with a negative reputation and stigmatized them as frequent perpetrators of honor crimes. However, only a handful of cases with Yezidi complicity have been reported in Germany, while very little information is available from Syria. In 2011, a father and son from Basufan were arrested on charges of killing the daughter because of an illicit relationship and pregnancy. They later confessed to the killing.[50] Another case in Iraq from 2007 received extensive media attention and ultimately led to revenge killings and anti-Yezidi riots. A few days later, ISIS executed twenty-four Yezidi workers in Mosul. Also, the massive bomb attack on two Yezidi villages in Sinjar was said to be reprisal for the honor killing.[51] On the other hand, honor crimes occur frequently among all ethnic and religious groups in the region. It is thus necessary to stress that they are not a specific or unique Yezidi custom or religious dogma. It is solely based on cultural beliefs that are found throughout the region.

The adherence to the Kurdish ethnic identity brings further hardship to the Syrian Yezidis. The political understanding of the Syrian Arab Republic includes the idea of marginalizing non-Arab groups, such as the Kurds. Certainly, after the Ba'th takeover in 1963 with its strong sense for promoting Arabism, public expressions of Kurdishness were suppressed and so were other central elements of Kurdish ethnic identity such as language, music, public holidays, and organizations. In addition, the Syrian government actively sought to change the ethnic status quo by relocating Arabs to the Kurdish region and renaming Kurdish villages, organizations, and shops. At one time, Kurdish parents weren't allowed to register their children with Kurdish names with the overall goal of assimilating the Kurds into the mainstream Syrian Arab society.

In this light, one must see the growing number of Kurdish language courses offered in the self-administered territories. Enrollment is very strong because for the first time in their living memory Kurds can practice and study their own language without interference by the security apparatus. Everywhere from Efrin to Derik in the far northeast of the country are language courses offered. The government-run school board in al-Hasake endorsed, then canceled and finally agreed to Kurdish language classes in the K12 school system. The importance of allowing the Kurds to speak their own language was also recognized by President Asad in his interview with al-Akhbariya station on April 17, 2013; however, the real reason was not a change of heart regarding the Arabic nature of Syria, but rather another attempt to appease the Kurds as they were positioning themselves in the civil war.

For the Yezidis community in Syria, which almost exclusively upholds their Kurdish origin and ethnicity, this meant an important step in the formation of their new identity. Yezidis took advantage of this and attached a religious curriculum to the language courses. Language classes and religious classes have been denied for decades, and the matter became one of the main grievances. Now they can practice their religion more or less freely, speak their own language in public, celebrate and religious holidays, and obtain valid citizenship papers; not thanks to the government, but more so thanks to the efforts of the self-administration and the Kurdish movement and parties to a lesser extent.

The Yezidis like most other Kurds recognize the winds of change, but they were not lured into taking the side of the government. This would be very un-Yezidish. While Yezidis in Efrin live in an almost exclusive Kurdish enclave, their fellows in the Jezira are part of a diverse ethnic and religious framework that includes Kurds, Arabs, Christians, Turkmen, and Circassians. Although the Yezidis stress their Kurdishness, at the same time they want to be recognized as a different group. And so we find their representatives in councils, meetings, and conferences promoting these independent interests.

In the Jezira, a common framework of the local tribes was created at the Conference of the Jezira Tribes, which was held on March 29, 2014 in Amuda. The dominance of the tribal identity in this region was demonstrated by the fact that Kurdish, Arab, Christian, Yezidi, Assyrian, and Circassian tribes participated, that is, a mix of ethnic and religious groups with strong tribal layers in their identity. The framework was to serve as a bulwark against attacks by Islamic militants who wanted to drive a wedge between the united tribes. Yezidi participant Sheikh Ibrahim al-Mlehan, the official speaker of the Yezidi House in Amuda, urged the participants not to let the terrorists to saw dissent between Arabs and Kurds.[52] This organization proofs to be extremely important to the Yezidis: first because they were accepted to be part of it and second because it created a bond with the majority population. Arab and Kurdish tribes in the Jezira are now aware of the Yezidi narrative and pledged to protect them. Since the tribal connection runs much deeper on the identity ladder than the political relations with some Kurdish parties, this can be the best tool of survival for the Yezidis in Syria.

6.6. POLITICAL IDENTITIES

In areas where Yezidis did not constitute a large community, they have largely refrained from political activities out of fear of possible repercussions. But as we have seen in the Kurdagh in the 1930s and to a lesser extent in the Wadi al-Jarrah, individual community leaders did partake in some local governance and administration. These leaders were, however, not religious leaders or clergy; they earned this position through their wealth, reputation, and social skills. Darwish Shamo established himself as the Yezidi leader in the Kurdagh and was subsequently recognized and legitimized by the religious authorities in Sheikhan. Shemo Issa was a community activist and later Kurdish party member, who helped improve the livelihood of his poor community in the Wadi al-Jarrah. He too consulted with the local Yezidi religious authorities before implementing new programs or policies.

But Yezidis in Syria over the past fifty years have been largely apolitical, at least they tried to. In reality, they were forced to react to political decisions and developments, which affected their physical livelihood as well as their spiritual needs. One way of reacting to the daily challenges was to retreat and live in isolation. From a religious angle, this did not always work in Syria as they were unable to stay off the government's and Islamists' radar. And more so on the ground: even in the remote areas of the Kurdagh and the Jezira, their otherness haunted them and caused them harm, mostly from their Arab/Muslim neighbors. They were stigmatized as Yezidis.

In addition, they were also considered outcasts as Kurds; and while they were perhaps able to hide their religious affiliation, their Kurdishness was an obvious fact and important cause for their discrimination. However, when Muslim Kurds rallied behind one of the many Kurdish political parties, Yezidis remained on the outside. They did, however, support the PKK.

Generally, they followed this "wait and see" approach because of concerns for the community at large, which was too scattered and too small to master any kind of support network against the overwhelming political enemy. It should also be remembered that many members of the Syrian Yezidi community had issues with their residence status and citizenship, and any kind of political engagement with the opposition would have made the life for the individuals and their families even harder. Thus, Yezidi political identity before the civil war can be best described as reactive, passive, and slightly opportunistic.[53]

The Syrian uprising and the following civil war brought significant changes to the political world of the Yezidis. One immediate gain was President Asad's announcement in April 2011 in which he outlined a naturalization process for the stateless Kurds. Between 60 and 70 percent of the Yezidis in the Jezira were affected by the earlier decision to strip many Kurds of their citizenship. Thus, the move by the government was welcomed. However, doubts about its implementation and underlying consequences remained.

From a practical perspective, the revolution and civil war had disrupted government authority and installations in many areas. Public institutions, such as local civil registries and courts, were no longer operating, and the official rule of law has been suspended. While on a first look, the decree seemed attractive and beneficial, it was difficult to say how many Kurds/Yezidis actually may take advantage of the decree. McGee surveyed Syrian Kurdish refugees living in camps in Iraqi-Kurdistan. Ninety four percent of those claiming to have been registered as *ajanib* tried to take advantage of the decree with a very high success rate of 98 percent. Of those Kurds considered *maktum*, only 7 percent tried to benefit from the law and three-fourths of those still had no citizenship.[54] The discrepancy is understandable considering that the decree forty-nine targeted a priori the ajanib and not the maktum. Issa stated that from the Yezidi villages in the Wadi al-Jarrah near Qamishli many *ajanib* applied for citizenship and subsequently obtained the necessary documents.[55] It must be noted that the government still has a strong presence in the administration of Qamishli, and thus, access to these institutions is easier than in areas where the government faulted and handed over the authority to the Kurds or rebels.

And although the numbers from McGee's study sound impressive, we must also note that full citizenship in most cases has not been acquired yet. Among the reasons for the delay is obviously the ongoing war, but also Kurdish suspicion of ulterior motives in the government's decision to grant this right to the Kurds now. The move was also interpreted as an attempt by the government to appease the Kurdish sector of not joining the opposition. And finally, the president's decision affected only a minority of Kurds who resided mainly outside of the government-controlled territory. For the majority of the Syrian Kurds, their situation has not been improved.

Generally speaking, the decisions as well as the following developments have elevated the political status of Yezidi Kurds. Yezidis in the Jezira are now heavily involved in political activities as are those in Efrin. Both groups were politicized by the PKK and PDKS activities in the 1980s and now by opposition activists and the Syrian government's response to them. This is why the younger generation usually supports the larger issue of Kurdish nationalism and not a specific Yezidi agenda. On the other hand, the older generation and religious leadership still promote the mantra of keeping a lower profile. They think it is better for a small and vulnerable community without any inside and outside connection to remain quiet and to avoid taking sides in any conflict.[56]

Also only a few Yezidis participated in the activities of the new administration and of the Kurdish parties, a fact that might be used against them in the future because it is interpreted as a sign of not being committed to the cause and of possibly hiding connections to the old regime. This is obviously incorrect: while, for example, the new political elites do not address the issue of mass emigration, the Yezidi philanthropic society Shams do go to the villages to talk to the families and find out about the grievances and the reasons why all the young people want to leave.[57]

The political landscape in the Syrian Yezidi territories is dominated by the Democratic Union Party or Partiya Yekitiya Demokrat (PYD), a Kurdish political party affiliated with the PKK and cochaired by Salih Muslim and Asiya Abdullah. However, other parties and alliances exist with significantly less power and influence. The KNC (Kurdish National Council) is nominally the representative body of the Syrian Kurds, but it excludes the PYD. They do have a working relationship with the SNC (Syrian National Council), the main opposition framework, which recently has had tremendous losses in terms of recognition and acceptance among the Kurds for their failure to remove the word Arab from the country's official name and changing it to Syrian Republic. For a short while, an alliance between KNC and SNC seemed possible and was regarded as the only change to diminish the influence of the PYD.[58] Among the main complaints against the PYD were the tactical cooperation with the Asad regime, the unilateral decision-making in the three cantons, the use of violence in quelling Kurdish protests, and the enforcement of the general conscription law.

Three territories in northern Syria were declared an autonomous zone under the name of Rojava or Western (Kurdistan). These territories have a majority of Kurdish inhabitants, but other ethnic and religious minorities live there too. The three cantons of Efrin, Kobani, and Jezira include almost all Yezidi villages. During the formative weeks of Rojava, KNC and PYD collaborated and formed the Kurdish Supreme Committee as the governing and administering body of the cantons. They also established the People's

Protection Units or *Yekineyen Parastina Gel* (YPG) and the Asayish as a local police force.

The new political ideal was realized with the creation of local councils being in charge of local affairs. Less central government and more public participation was the motto, which was picked up by the coalition Movement for a Democratic Society or *Tevgera Civaka Demokratik* (TEV-DEM), currently the main political leadership platform. TEV-DEM includes local volunteers, activists, and professionals from all major ethnic and religious groups in Rojava, among them many Yezidis. In all major cities, towns, and villages, TEV-DEM promoted the idea of self-government through local councils.

A different approach to Kurdish politics, however, must be noted within the various Yezidi territories. In Efrin, where the PYD has an overwhelming approval and support rate, other Kurdish political parties are less visible and operate on a smaller, individualized level. Arguably, this makes Yezidis there less concerned about political diversity and varying political goals. The PYD and their military wing, the YPG, explicitly recognized the Yezidis as an important part of the Kurdagh community, and many Yezidis in return found a new political home with them. In the past, younger Yezidis, especially university students, expressed their solidarity with PKK and Kurdish nationalism; however, family, village, and regional support groups kept them in check and worked on measures of coexistence instead. Now, there is no more wavering, especially when the front lines with the Islamic radicals are next to the Yezidi villages. Voices of dissent or opposition to the PYD and canton administration cannot be heard. This is not surprising considering the political support granted to Yezidi organizations and the accomplishments of Yezidi activists aligned with the PYD.

The political idea behind the Rojava model is not seeking independence from Syria, but to have locals in charge of local affairs and in control of local resources. While the local councils are mostly elected bodies, the government of the three cantons is comprised of appointed officials, many of which have a party affiliation and a specific identity background. Another challenging stipulation is the 40 percent women quota. But for the first time in Syrian history, the Yezidis were recognized as an official, independent entity. Three seats were reserved for them in the legislative council in Efrin, and in the executive council, the portfolio of foreign affairs was awarded to Suleyman Ja'far. Abd al-Qadir Hasko was appointed deputy minister for health and Abd al-Rahman Shamo deputy of the director for religious affairs. Burhan Abdi was appointed deputy minister for religious affairs in the Jezira Canton.

The canton government issued a constitutional statement or social pact describing the self-rule of the three cantons, which recognizes all ethnic groups like the Kurds, Arabs, Syriac (Assyrian, Chaldeans), Turcoman, Armenians, and Chechnyans. As a religious group, the Yezidis were not mentioned here, but they received attention later in the document. Relevant sections in this document describe the position of the Yezidis in Rojava[59].

Paragraph 3, section 3 states that the Jezira canton is a joined region between the Kurds, Arabs, Syriac, Armenian, and Circassian people. It respects the religions of Islam, Christianity, and Yezidism. The relations between the different groups are built on the principle of mutual coexistence and brotherhood.

Paragraph 32 states that all citizens have freedom of religions and belief. It is not allow to politicize religion or to exploited religion as a tool to incite division or strive.

Paragraph 33, Section 4 states that the Yezidi religion is autonomous. The pact allows all of its followers to regulate their social and religious lives as well as their personal status law.

Paragraph 94, Section 1 states that this contract is built on the principle of secularism. Section 2 talks about the absolute freedom of belief. The administration respects all religions and sects and guarantees the freedom of expressing religious feeling as long as they don't violate public order.[60]

6.6.1. Local Councils in the Jezira Region

All Yezidi villages in the Jezira are currently within the autonomous zone. Some are located very close to the frontline with IS or JN and are in a precarious situation. But in many cases, the political changes instigated by the PYD and implemented by TEV-DEM are now bearing fruits. Self-administration is now practiced in many Yezidi villages through a local council of elected members. Surprisingly, this novel idea did not require much time to be successful.

On November 12, 2012, the people of the Yezidi village of Zeydiya voted for their local council. The PYD council member Sheikhmus Ahmad addressed the villagers and talked about the recent developments and events in the area, and Sabri Efrini, member of TEV-DEM, talked about the importance of the councils. The villagers then elected thirty-three members representing several Yezidi villages north of Hasake.[61]

A meeting was held in the Yezidi village of Otelje in December 2012 to discuss the attempts of the local Yezidi community to organizing themselves into a council. They met at the famous cemetery Diyare Feleke with representatives from the People's House in Tirbespi and the Aliyan Regional Council. Farhad Khalti from TEV-DEM briefed the attendants on the latest events and stressed the importance of organizing the Yezidi society in light of the current dangers and threats against them. He called: "We tell everyone that we exist and we are here on our land." This plea included another warning about the growing number of emigrants, who ultimately will lose their identity and weaken their community.

On February 15, 2013 a local council of eight Yezidi villages in the Hasake region was founded. The representatives met in Gumar Gharbi to finalize the formation of the council. This move was in line with the policies of the self-administration and thus supported by TEV-DEM. The council included the following villages: Tell Aswad Fawqani, Tell Aswad Tahtani, Gumar Sharqi, Gumar Gharbi, Tell Teyr, Um al-Jafa, Jdeyda, and Antariya. The move was initiated by Sabri Efrini, a representative from TEV-DEM. After observing a minute of silence to honor the martyrs and discussing the conspiracy against Ocalan, Efrini talked about the importance of the council and the role it plays for the local representation, administration, and protection of the villages. At the end of the meeting, the villagers elected fifteen representatives from the eight villages.[62]

On February 23, 2013 several local organizations and civic institutions, including Yezidi representatives, signed an agreement to form a local joint council in the city of Tirbespi. The council included thirty members: ten Kurds, ten Arabs, five Assyrians, and five Yezidis.[63] It was charged with organizing the service sector and not to interfere with political or military decisions. One week later, on March 1, 2013, Tirbespi was liberated from the government control and the joint council for self-administration took over. They made sure that social and economic services continued. On March 13, 2013 they held their inaugural meeting where every group was given the podium to address its concerns. Faris Shamo represented the Yezidi community.[64] The joint council made the following decisions:

1. Naming the council Local City Council
2. Electing Supervisory Board with six members (two Kurds, two Arabs, one Assyrian, and one Yezidi—Kan'an Ali)
3. Forming three service committees each with six members to supervise the seventeen departments
4. Weekly progress reports from the boards
5. Forming a security committee to coordinate with the Asayish police.

The thirty members were distributed among the different committees according to the formula: two Kurds, two Arabs, one Assyrian, and one Yezidi.[65]

On February 17, 2014, another meeting was held in Gari Rash (Tell Aswad) that was attended by many of the villagers. Here, Sheikhmus Ahmad from the PYD talked about the conspiracy against Ocalan, the leader's philosophy and the efforts of the self-administration to defeat the conspiracy. He also said that the struggle for his liberation will continue and that his philosophy will be applied in Rojava. Raghida Khalil from the PYD women's department talked to the villagers about the role of women in the fight for freedom and said that Ocalan had the same vision for women.[66]

6.6.2. Local Councils in the Kurdagh/Efrin Region

Earlier in 2012, on February 23, locals in Qestel Jindo gathered for a meeting to elect their representatives of the popular council as part of the self-administration policy in the Efrin Canton. They appointed Gharib Hasso as their representative, who stressed the importance of the councils for the Kurds and the Yezidis. Only through the councils can they play a role in the new Syria. His slogan resonated well with the villagers when he said: "Every time we were working for someone else's interest, and we were killed for this. But this time we will not shed our tears for someone else, but for our will." [67] He also referred to the age-old division between the Yezidi Kurds and Muslim Kurds and referred to Ocalan and his interest in the Yezidis for a way to overcome these divisions. Later, Shirin Jamal spoke about the important role of women in the councils.

On May 14, 2012, a group of Yezidi elders gathered at a meeting facilitated by the Yezidi Association in Syria and West Kurdistan in order to discuss the situation of the community and to revive the practice of their customs. Suleyman Ja'far, president of the association, led the discussion and talked about the TEV-DEM movement and its efforts to defend the rights of Kurds in Syria under the banner of the self-administration project. TEV-DEM gave the Yezidis lots of attention and helped protecting them from the ongoing attacks in the civil war. The attendants formed several committees, such as a committee for reconciliation that works on the basis of peaceful conflict resolution and the people's strength to solve local conflicts and issues. It was also agreed that delegations should visit the Yezidi villages and encourage the formation of a popular committee there.[68]

A follow-up meeting was held a month later in Efrin. On November 9, 2012, TEV-DEM organized another meeting in Basufan where Jamil Efrini talked about the role the organization plays in protecting the minorities and defending their rights. He also stressed the importance of self-defense against regime attacks or any intervention in the Kurdish region; and he referenced the attacks on Qestel Jindo and warned the villagers about their vulnerable position so close to the front line at Deyrat Izza. See map on page 19.

A month later, on December 10, 2012, the elders gathered again in Ghezewiye, among them Sheikh Huseyn Brimo and Sheikh Muhammad Kalo and Sheikh Omer Hamqadio as well as Suleyman Ja'far, the president of the Yezidi Association. They discussed the general situation in the region and the Yezidi situation in particular. Since the meeting coincided with the religious holiday of the Eida Ezid (here referred to as Feast of Fasting), the discussion included religious instructions as well as a lecture by Sheikh Huseyn on the importance of fasting in Yezidism, and Sheikh Muhammad Kalo talked about the Yezidi religious holidays. Suleyman Ja'far ended the meeting with an explanation of the political situation of the Kurds in Syria.[69]

On December 26, 2012, the popular council of the Sherew region held several meetings in the villages of Shadhere, Ghezewiye, and Iskan. The TEV-DEM representative Arif Sheikho talked about the changing role of the Kurds in the revolution. In his statement, he referenced only the threats from the government and not the Islamist militants, denouncing the cut off supplies and services and the economic blockade against the Kurdish territories.[70] Apparently, Yezidi specific issues were not discussed at the meeting.

Regular elections for city councils were held on September 10, 2015, and the top two candidates were appointed codirectors. Of the villages with significant Yezidi population, only Qatma and Basuta have the status of a town or baladiya. The other villages are part of the administrative structure of other towns.[71] Six Yezidis have been appointed to these councils as part of a quota.

From a rare field trip to Azaz a city close to the Efrin Canton, at the end of 2014 it was reported that a dozen individual Yezidis were still living in this city currently under control of the Northern Storm, a rebel militia affiliated with the Islamic Front (not ISIS and not JN). According to the report, they were tolerated by the militia and the local population and no animosity against them existed. The sectarian strife, instead, is directed against the Shia and Alawite population, who were not regarded as Muslims.[72]

By now, Yezidism as a religion and an identity has established a place in the social pact and in the larger political landscape of Rojava. Yezidis are encouraged to participate in the formation of the councils and other forms of the self-administration. For the first time in Syria Yezidis obtained a legal status in the cantons of Jezira and Efrin. They are free to practice their religions and to administer their own socioreligious affairs, such as marriages, divorces, inheritance cases, and death. Rojava officials maintain good relations with the Yezidi communities by attending their holidays, acknowledging their customs, and honoring Yezidi contributions to the protection of Rojava. In Efrin, one Yezidi lawyer, Hisham Ahmado, was appointed to the seven members of the People's Court, where he works on implementing a new personal status law for the Yezidis.

It must be noted, however, that is was relatively easy for the Kurdish parties to exploit the Yezidis as a soft target and to use their narrative for their own purposes. The political propaganda of the PYD does not aim at converting the Kurds to their "original" religion, but to generally strengthen Kurdish culture and the collective Kurdish identity. Yezidis are well aware of this balancing act between recognition and appropriation of their religion. But while Iraqi

Yezidis, and in particular the Mir, distanced themselves from political monopolization, the Syrian Yezidis almost completely adopted the political narrative of the PYD. In contrast, the Sheikhan Yezidis in Iraq consider the PYD and subsequently the PKK a political rival. They all were keenly aware of the important historical function of Yezidism in the construction of the Kurdish identity at large. It is now common knowledge to identify the Yezidis as the original Kurds, and that prior to the Islamization of the Kurds, all were Yezidis. This boosted Yezidi confidence and group esteem enormously, because they now enjoy the feeling of belonging and acceptance. The secular nature and ideology of the PYD certainly supported these claims, more so than traditional Kurdish parties who have to consider their predominant Muslim constituency.

In the areas that comprise the four cantons of self-administration, one must note the improved perception and increased participation of Yezidi representatives in the political and administrative affairs. Perhaps because of their balanced approach toward building relations with other interest groups, they are now accepted as a partner in the formation of new social, religious, political, and educational institutions. Differences between the two regional groups, however, remain.

But as part of their survival strategy, Yezidis living in areas of cohabitation with other sects practiced this type of peaceful and productive collaboration in their villages. For example in the village of Mizgeft, the Yezidi majority lives alongside Christian and Muslim families or in Tell Khatun where we find a mixed Yezidi-Muslim population. In Drechik, this coexistence includes Yezidis and Muslims who are both ethnic Kurds and Arabs. In one case, this mutual acceptance was even elevated into an admiration of Yezidis by the other groups. According to them, it is the Kurdish national movement that values the Yezidis and gives them hope.[73]

6.7. VIOLENCE AND IMMIGRATION

Peaceful coexistence is, however, only the smallest denominator, whereas even in the recent past the same Yezidi villages experienced harsh economic discrimination from the government and local Kurdish/Muslim landowners as well as social stigmatization. These conditions led to a significant decrease in the number of Yezidi inhabitants of those villages and turned former majorities into minorities. Large numbers of Yezidis left their villages and immigrated to Europe. In addition to the above-mentioned reasons, Yezidis are becoming increasingly afraid of rapidly growing militant Islamic groups and eminent attacks, clashes, and discriminations by them. The following is a list of reported cases of attacks against Yezidis and Yezidi villages related to the civil war.

A Yezidi woman from Qestel Jindo, Zarifa Horik Rashid, was killed alongside her three children and two nephews, while her sister-in-law was critically injured when unknown men entered their house on June 6, 2012. The bodies were found in a nearby lake.

For two days in late October 2012, militants from Azaz, believed to be part of the Free Syrian Army,[74] attacked the village of Qestel Jindo, which is located only five kilometers to the north. However, the frontline between the militants and the People's Protection Units (YPG) was right outside the village and heavy clashes erupted between the two camps and resulted in several civilian (Yezidi) casualties. While this could have been described as yet another clash between two rival militias, it must be noted that the attackers described the villagers as unbelievers and infidels, clearly indicating an anti-Yezidi, sectarian aspect in their attack. Yezidi community leaders in Syria, among them Sheikh Said Hado from the Yezidi House in Qizlacuq and the Roj Charitable Association, denounced the attack on the helpless civilians. They also demanded assurances from the Free Syrian Army (FSA) to respect and protect the religious minorities in Syria.

On December 9, 2012, the Yezidi Fatih Sheikh Miro from Tell Tewil near Hasake was abducted by terrorists, and a ransom of 1.5 million SP was demanded. When his relatives demanded to know whether he was still alive, they found his dead body on the following day.

On August 17, 2013, the village of Asadiya near Ras al-Ayn was attacked by ISIS. Two inhabitants of the village, Ali Biru and his brother Murad Sadu Biru, were kidnaped and killed. Shams Nuri, the widow of Ali, recounted the event: "Men with long beards came one thirty in the morning demanding that we would leave our homes, which we refused to do. Half an hour later they came back with heavy weapons and started attacking the village. Our guys were defending the village but at one point we all had to leave. Then, my brother-in-law was killed and another villager injured and my husband captured. The next morning they sent us his body." The people in the village believed that they were targeted because they did not want to convert to Islam. From Asadiya they fled to another near by Yezidi village, but this village was attacked too and they had to continue fleeing all the way to Tell Sakhr.[75]

On August 21, 2013, 50-year-old Hassan Khabur was killed by a roadside explosion planted by al-Nusra Front on the road to Lazqa near Ras al-Ayn. With him two of his coworkers died, the Arab Taha Turki and wounded Ahmad Mahmud.[76]

On 29 August 2013 a suicide attacker drove into an YPG checkpoint near Amuda. Among the seven people killed, all belonging to the local guards, was one Yezidi (Salman Khalil Nayif) from Hesheri. Another Yezidi boy, Rizan Ibrahim Krim from Bur Said was injured in the attack.[77]

In mid-September 2013, the village Cava was attacked by Islamist militants and later liberated by YPG. In the process, all inhabitants fled the scene and found refuge in neighboring Yezidi villages.

On September 20, 2013 government air strikes were conducted against the village of Basuta near Efrin, which is largely inhabited by Yezidi families and older people. No casualties were reported, only physical damage to the homes and fields. Earlier the same month, Aleppo's mostly Kurdish neighborhoods like Sheikh Maqsud, Bustan Pasha, Siryan Qadim, and Siryan Jadid were attacked and among others a young Yezidi woman was killed. The FSA on that day attacked the regime forces in downtown Aleppo and was able to capture several regime soldiers. Among them was a Yezidi conscript from Hasake who apparently was released later.[78]

On May 1, 2014, the Syrian air force attacked the Yezidi villages of Kimar and Sokhanek in the Efrin region; however, no casualties were reported.[79]

At the end of May 2014, ISIS (or JN) carried out a coordinated attack on the villages west of Serekaniye (Ras al-Ayn). They were able to take over several villages, including the Yezidi villages of Teleliye, Tell Khanzir, and Tell Banat. After YPG repelled the attack and push the militants back, they discovered that the mills and grain storages were destroyed and, in Tell Eliye, several civilians were massacred.[80] It was unclear, however, if these were indeed Yezidis or refugees. Most Yezidi families had left the area prior to the attack.

On November 19, 2014, Jabhat an-Nusra issued an ultimatum to YPG in Basufan to withdraw from territory they considered under their control. Earlier YPG built trenches in the fields near Basufan and Deirat Izza and the local population was complaining about the loss of land, first to Harakat al-Hazm, as the more moderate rebel forces, and after their complaints were not answered, they talked to JN, who immediately confronted YPG and issued the ultimatum in order to restore the status quo, as otherwise they would consider this a declaration of war. Interestingly, this incident was reported by the Kurdish Democratic Party of Syria or Partiya Demokrat a Kurdistane li Suriye (PDK-S – el-Parti), a Kurdish political party and rival of the dominant PYD.[81]

On December 28, 2014 a checkpoint near the largely Yezidi town of Qatme near Azaz was attacked and three YPG fighters as well as four Arab civilians were killed. Seventeen people were wounded.

Leaving Syria, the homeland, where Yezidis just received recognition and a status upgrade, is still a viable, but controversial, option. For one reason, they may escape from the war zone. But, living abroad, after all, no longer has this negative stigma, especially when formerly emigrates relatives report back or visit telling stories of material gains and religious freedom.

To coordinate the activities abroad and to support the political work inside Syria in collaboration with the two Yezidi Houses in Efrin and Jezira, two lobby organizations were founded in German exile where most of the Syrian Yezidi refugees settled. One organization, the Syrian Yezidi Assembly or *Hevbendiya Ezidiyen Suriye* (HES), which was founded in July 2013, sees itself as the sole representative of Syrian Yezidis at home and in exile.

On June 29, 2014, the HES organized a conference on minority rights, especially Yezidi rights, in the semi-autonomous cantons in Rojava (Western Kurdistan) in Syria. Many Kurds, Arabs, and Germans attended.

The HES also sent a delegation to Jezira Canton and the Region of Southern Kurdistan to offer help for the people from Sinjar who had to flee there from the terror attacks of August 3, 2014. The visit was coordinated with the Yezidi House in Siegen, the Kaniya Sipi Organization, and 140,000 Euros were brought to buy supplies and aid for the Yezidis over there.

There is regular communication and visits between the two houses in Efrin and Jezira and the Yezidi organizations in Germany such as HES, Kaniya Sipi, and the Yezidi House in Siegen. They discuss political and financial support among these Yezidi groups in order to support and defend the Yezidi rights in these territories. They also say that the door is open for any other Yezidi to join the organization. This is interpreted as an invitation for other Syrian Yezidi organizations to operate under their umbrella. However, there are growing concerns that HES might co-opt other organizations and does not value political pluralism.

These concerns were mainly echoed by a second Syrian Yezidi organization, The Syrian Yezidi Council or *Encumena Ezdiyen Suri* (EES), which was established in March 2012 with its seat in Bielefeld, Germany. Confrontations between the two organizations quickly arose. While HES is closely linked to the PYD, EES wants to remain politically neutral. According to its constitution, it defines the council as follows:

The EES is a basically a political council that seeks to defend the cultural, social, and political rights of the Syrian Yezidis according to the Human Rights Charter, international law, and within the framework of the Syrian state. The council believes in the institution of the modern civil state on the basis of the separation of religion and state and on the basis of democracy and freedom and justice and equality for all national, ethnic, religious, and linguistic groups. It calls for full gender equality without discrimination. The council also rejects all forms of racism, violence, and terrorism regardless of their sources and motives. It works on the main principles of peace and security and coexistence between all elements of Syrian society and its diverse ethnic, religious, and intellectual people and groups.[82]

It is also important to record the position of EES regarding issues of Yezidi identity. EES describes the Yezidis as followers of a unique religion, but they are ethnical Kurds. For EES, the Civata Ruhani (the Spiritual Council) in Iraq under the leadership of the Mir and the Baba Sheikh is considered the highest authority. Ultimately, EES sees itself as a bridge between the Yezidis in the homeland and in the diaspora. Its members are committed to civil, peaceful protest as a means to work for change. Politically, they are close to the KNC as well as Barzani's KDP in Iraq, similar to the Yezidi leadership.

Some of these positions are in stark contrast to the philosophy of HES. Both organizations operate in Germany as well as in Kurdistan, lobbying, delivering aid, promoting Yezidi issues, building alliances with local partners, and strengthening their support network. However, one must note the clear advantage of HES over EES. HES is closely linked to the PYD/PKK and fully supports the successful model of self-administration, while EES connects better with the Iraqi Yezidis and opposes many measures by the canton administration, in particular, the conscription law. According to EES, it illegally recruits women and minors. HES (and other local Yezidi organizations like the Mala Ezdiya in Efrin and the Mala Ezdiya in the Jezira) vehemently oppose the (perceived) claim to sole representation of EES citing the lack of elections, the residence of abroad, and its engagement with the KNC as the main factors.[83]

However, the division among the exile groups matter less to the villages in Syria. On the ground, they need to forge their own alliances and networks. As such, they promote religious tolerance and goodwill for cooperating with the other ethnic and religious groups in the three cantons.

On November 22, 2014, another meeting was held in Zeydiya where representatives from the Arab tribes, and the Christian and Yezidi groups got together to form a committee to solve disputes among them and to avoid any fighting between the two groups.[84] Prisoners of the Asayish were to be released and a truce was agreed upon.

Otherwise, Yezidi families find themselves stuck between the fighting parties and their vulnerable situation which might be exploited to the benefit of those groups. For example, in Hasake, Yezidi families live mostly in the neighborhoods along the front line between the Syrian army and the YPG, such as the Airport neighborhood, the New Post quarter, or the Khabur villas. YPG calling upon those families to leave their homes and move to the part of town under their control arguing that the regime will soon abandon their location and allow ISIS to take over. The Yezidi families could only be protected when they would move over. To increase the pressure on the Yezidis, YPG stated that they know their names, places, addresses, and phone numbers.[85]

The small Yezidi community in Syria is divided spatially, religiously, economically, and of course politically. The latter comes as no surprise when considering how apolitical the community was for the entire existence until recently. The constant fear of further attacks led to a widespread depolitization of an already marginalized community.[86] "We don't want to criticize either the government or the opposition yet, since we don't know who will prevail," according to a 50-year-old Yezidi from Qizlacuq.[87] This uncommitted attitude helped the community to survive in a hostile environment. Retreat, silence, secrecy, pragmatism, and an overall low-key attitude to foreign relations summarize the political agenda of the community until the outbreak of the revolution and civil war.

It is thus also not uncommon to hear nonconfrontational statements when asked to describe their role in the ongoing war. They would not condemn the Syrian government absolutely and would not support the PYD-led self-administration wholeheartedly. Staunchly avoiding taking side and staying out of conflict agendas were the key to preserve their existence. This does not mean that individuals may participate in either side's activities. Thus, we find Yezidis actively engaged in the PYD; for example, the PYD representative in Germany is Yezidi and so is the current minister for foreign affairs in the Efrin Canton. In fact, one of the two main organizations for Yezidis abroad, the HES, is very closely affiliated with the party. And other Yezidis vehemently oppose this collaboration and favor a closer relationship with the Kurdish parties from Iraq and the Kurdish National Council. The latter even reserved five seats for the group, one of which is held by Sheikh Bedi Mamo, a well-known religious leader from Qizlacuq.

This uncommitted, or some say wishy-washy attitude, served them well over the past five years. However, was what served them better is the fact that most Yezidi villages were located within the self-administered territory or the three cantons. Here, for the first time in history, they have the chance to develop a political agenda. The political agenda covers important questions of alliances, loyalties, and origin, creating a conundrum of conflicting new identities.

Among the major political discourses is the unsettled question of ethnic origin and belonging with three contrary opinions: Are the Yezidis ethnic Arabs, Kurds, or a separate Yezidi ethnicity? The Syrian Yezidi writer and activist Fermaz Gharibo summarized the Syrian position (which of course is opposed to the Iraqi-Yezidi position). Gharibo sees the mirids and pirs all supporting the Kurdish ethnicity. Only among the sheikhs is one lineage, the Qatanis, who upholds the claim of Arabness. In Iraq, this opinion is more popular than in Syria where the Qatani sheikhs are in a minority and the frontline of daily persecution was drawn between Arabs and Yezidis.[88] Thus, no Syrian Yezidi would support this idea. Instead they mostly favor the Kurdish option, especially those who are affiliated or supporters of the PYD.[89] As mentioned before, both the PKK and its Syrian branch, the PYD, adopted the position that the Yezidis were the original Kurds. The third option of a separate Yezidi ethnicity was born among the communities in Armenia and has not gained substantial support among the Yezidis in Syria.

6.7.1. Sinjar in August 2014

For over a decade Yezidis from Syria looked at their fellow Yezidis in Iraq with a sense of envy due to the accomplishments and achievements the community made after the fall of Saddam's regime. They did recognize the heavy price Iraqi Yezidis had to pay to become a politically recognized minority with reserved seats (number unclear) in the Iraqi parliament and five in the Kurdish regional parliament. According to the Syrian Yezidi understanding of the events on the other side of the border, things went relatively well, thanks to the (sometimes overwhelming) support by the KDP and the Kurdistan government. And they stated this even in the summer of 2014.

However, things changed drastically on August 3rd, 2014. After the betrayal of the Peshmerga and their subsequent withdrawal from Sinjar, the Yezidi villages in the area became defenseless against the powerful attack by Islamic radical militants from IS or how they were called locally, Da'sh. Like Yezidis all over the world, the Syrian community watched with horror the brutal scenario that unfolded in the wake of the initial attack. The genocide against the Sinjar community brought the violence of the war to an unprecedented level. Thousands were killed, hurt, kidnaped, humiliated, and forced to flee to the Sinjar mountain.

However, after they were able to consolidate their weak position on the mountain, Yezidis organized the military resistance to the siege, first with help from other Kurdish militias, the YPG from Syria[90] and the HPG from Turkey,[91] and then relying heavily on Yezidi-only fighting units. Two battalions were especially successful in repelling Da'sh attacks on the remaining Yezidi sanctuary and shrine in Shingal, the Sherfedin shrine. The Heza Parastina Shingal (HPS) or Shingal Protection Force under the leadership of Qassim and Heydar Shesho as well as the Yekineyen Berxwedan Shingal (YBS) or Resistance Unit Shingal under Sheikh Khalaf stood their ground for weeks against multiple attacks and without proper supplies and weaponry. They and other Yezidis from Iraq and Syria called for an immediate arming of the general Yezidi population in order to protect themselves from the eminent Da'sh attacks and massacres. On the frontline, the units included fighters from various backgrounds—PKK, YPG, Yezidis, Peshmerga, tribal forces. Yezidi volunteer fighters from Syria also joined their ranks. Despite their high spirits, they all complained about lack of weapons.

Aside from the human tragedy within Sinjar, there were also thousands of Yezidis from the area who fled their villages and sought shelter with their Syrian brothers and sisters. Most Sinjar refugees went to Dohuk and Zakho, but a significant number crossed into Syria and registered at the official UN camps or found refuge in the Yezidi villages near Hasake and Qamishli. Estimates speak of 5,000 Sinjari refugees now living in Syria, which quickly became a logistic and financial burden for the small local community. Aid organizations, especially from among the diaspora in Germany, collected money and donations to be distributed to the families and ease the burden. All major Yezidi organizations, federations, houses, and associations in Germany contributed financially and with donations in kind. They sent many trucks to Turkey and beyond with aid for the refugees. On one occasion, a joint HES/PYD delegation brought over 130,000 euros and dispatched eight trucks filled with food and aid to the villages in Tirbespi.[92]

The events in Iraq reminded the Syrian Yezidis about their own vulnerable situation. And although their own situation had improved, especially for those living in the three cantons, the overall atmosphere was still poisoned by the civil war, IS ideology, government military operation, and Kurdish infighting. Certainly, the Yezidis were now generally acknowledged as victims of IS, and the international community started to deliver aid to the refugees. But the Yezidi community was far from having a unified position on how to address these challenges.

At an international conference in Vienna organized by KAICIID (the Saudi-based King Abdullah Bin Abdulaziz International Centre for Interreligious and Intercultural Dialogue), the Yezidis were represented by Brin Said Tahsin Beg, grandson of the Mir, who aside from stressing the urgency of supporting the Yezidis, made a point of preserving the leadership of the Mir's family over all Yezidi communities.[93] This triggered an automatic rebuttal from the Syrian community, in particular, from the HES.

That the plight of the Iraqi Yezidi is dominating the public discourse, is evident by the statement of the US government which highlighted all the atrocities against the Yezidis in Iraq but failed to mention the Syrian case.[94]

However, there are also examples of Syrian Yezidi benefits from Iraq. In the collective town of Sharia, where many Yezidis from Syria sought refuge, forty-five Yezidi women from Syria received training in the Kurdish language, Yezidism, and sewing for six months. Over the past five years, several thousand Syrian Kurds fled to Kurdistan Iraq and the Sharia Mujamma alone hosted more than fifty Yezidi families.[95]

6.8. LAND AND ECONOMY

As mentioned before, Syrian Yezidis live in two separate areas, Kurdagh/Efrin and the Jezira and three diferent cantons. Although now politically connected, the spatial distance created a disconnected community, disconnected not only from each other, but also from other Yezidis communities in Turkey, Iraq, or Armenia. The arbitrary drawing of borders and shifting of frontlines disrupted the evolution of strong communities and left the remaining Yezidis on the Syrian side weak and vulnerable. In addition, there is little interaction between the two Syrian communities who in theory could support each other. Syrian law and the realities on the ground prevented the Yezidis from moving to the other territory and from forming strong supportive bonds. As a result, stereotypes built on misunderstandings and ignorance were frequently applied, and even a certain distrust runs between the two communities who accuse each other of heresy and assimilation into mainstream Islamic society. Not surprisingly, these frontlines are carried over into the diaspora where little contacts (marital relations) are noted. However, recently, a rapprochement is noted with religious collaboration between the two Yezidi Houses in Efrin and Amuda (Jezira).

This dichotomy was also noticeable in the economic and business sphere where an obvious gap between Efrin and the Jezira must be observed. Yezidis in Efrin have a long track record of economic integration and success. Efrin is a very fertile area known for its olive trees and oil mills. Yezidis in the Jezira settled there much more recently, switching from pastoralism to farming. However, because the political situation, they were never able to prosper or consolidate their land. On the contrary, because they are at the bottom end of the food chain, they were the first to be deported and to lose their land. Yezidi villages in the Jezira cannot provide support and security; they are too small and too scattered. Thus, many had to abandon their farms and villages and move to the cities where they continue to struggle making a living. In addition, several anti-Kurdish measures by the government with regard to citizenship, land ownership, and financing contributed to the economic hardships of the Jezira community.

In 2008, Kurds (Yezidis) from Merkeb near Amuda took possession of open land (laid their hands on it), but were subsequently sued by Kurdish (non-Yezidi) landowners who stipulated that foreigners were not allowed to own land in the SAR. The Yezidis did not have the right papers; they were maktum/ajanib.

The economic blockade of the Kurdagh region led to price hikes and shortages in resources, food, spare parts, etc. The tight economic situation was further worsened by increased taxes, which forced some of the local factories and mills to close down. The remaining mills are working nonstop to provide the necessary flour; however, prices for a kilo of flour have gone up from 3 SP to 25 SP.[96]

On October 9, 2012 Mahmud Salo Jarki from Khirbet al-Banat was kidnaped and a huge ransom was demanded for his release. Other non-Yezidi residents from the area of Serekaniye were also targeted in a kidnaping campaign and among them were landowners, lawyers, and businessmen. Extorting ransoms from the families became a lucrative business opportunity for local gangs often affiliated with Islamist militias. In the nearby village of Qizlacuq, the inhabitants decided to form a local committee to organize patrols and to protect the village from kidnapers and thieves. A total of twenty-four young men were signed up to do day-and-night patrols around the village.[97]

Property and land owned by Murad Darwish, a Yezidi from the Yezidi village in al-Mukhtale near Serekaniye who immigrated to Germany, was looted and later confiscated by militants from the FSA (Ahrar al-Sham) on the ground of his Yezidism; they also accused him of heresy. Local administration stood up for his rights and issued legal statements denouncing the illegal appropriation of property; however, the militia did not pay heed to such statements.[98] However, seizure, confiscation, or simply stealing of property of families who have left the country have become quite frequent.

Syrian Yezidis suffered economically, but it was especially hard for those in the Jezira. What helped their survival was the tight social fabric of kinship and religion. In areas of larger Yezidi concentration, they were able to provide for a better livelihood than in those regions where single Yezidi families were scattered among other identity groups. The Efrin region still sees Yezidi cohesion in villages with exclusive or majority Yezidi population. In the Jezira, this was not the case, mostly due to the small number of Yezidis and the distance between the villages. Restrictive official economic policies as well as unusual weather conditions[99] contributed to the economic hardship of the Jezira Yezidis. However, they were still able to muster large sums of money necessary for paying bribes to smugglers and officials to send their family members abroad. The creation of cantons and self-administration aimed to provide equal access to all people and communities living within this territory; however, provisions are scarce and the war economy has other priorities.

NOTES

1. For a detailed analysis of the Yezidi creation story, see Spät (2002).
2. Spät (2002): 28.
3. Kizilhan (1997): 117.
4. The author over the past 20 years conducted many formal and informal interviews and conversations with Yezidis from all areas. Almost all mentioned sed u hed as the fundamental dogma of their religious identity.
5. See Yezidi Identity Inventory.
6. See Pierret's analysis of the 50 years of cooperation between state and Sunni authorities (2012): 83–106.
7. Maisel (2013): 36–39.
8. White (2011): 154.
9. Tejel (2009): 9.

10. See the Terrier Plan and its provision in Tejel (2007): 93–108.

11. Tork Dalalyan, "The Construction of Kurdish and Yezidi Identities Among the Kurmanj-Speaking Population of the Republic of Armenia," in Changed Identities: Armenia, Azerbaijan, Georgia, Heinrich Boell Foundation, ed. Tbilisi (2012), 177–201.

12. The example of the Serbs, Croats, and Bosnians is often referred to: three distinct religions speak the same language but live in three different nations. Along this line, Yezidis refused to be grouped with the Kurds into one nation although they speak the same language.

13. Dalalyan (2012): 181–182.

14. Mass emigration to Europe concerns Kurdish authorities in Efrin. Video report for Al-An TV, Jenan Moussa, August 30, 2015 available at https://www.youtube.com/watch?v=e_98zJlGDVs , accessed September 4, 2015.

15. Ferman usually refers to decrees by the Ottoman Sultans; however, in the Yezidi context it translates into massacre.

16. During countless informal conversations with Syrian Yezidis this was the general perception.

17. Alarabiya with AFP. "Syrian refugees drown on their way to Greece." http://english.alarabiya.net/en/News/2013/03/21/Syrian-refugees-drown-on-their-way-to-Greece.html (accessed June 5, 2016).

18. Behzad Yakhmaian: Syria's Civil War and the World's Oldest Refugee. The Globalist, February 11, 2014.

19. This statement was repeated during many conversations with Syrian Yezidis who migrated to Germany.

20. Average age 30 years, 44 percent women and 56 percent men; 87 percent mirids, 8 percent sheikh, and 5 percent from the pir caste.

21. The following organizations participated in the leadership meeting on February 23, 2014 in Celle, Germany: Yezidi European Society, HES, Siegen, Sulingen, Wesel, Osterholz-Scharmbeck, Oldernburg, Nienburg, ZYD, Leer, Komela Kaniya Sipi, Hameln, Kalkar, Hessen, Heidekreis, FEK, Celle, Saarland, Emmerich, Delmenhorst, Augsburg, Bremen, Bielefeld, and Essen. See report about this meeting at www.ezidipress.com/?p=1509

22. Abkommen zwischen der Regierung der Bunderrepublik Deutschland und der Regierung der Arabischen Republik Syrian über die Rückführung von illegal aufhältigen Personen, July 14, 2008.

23. See letter from the German Ministry of Interior to Zentralrat from January 23, 2012.

24. See Zentralrat der Yeziden in Deutschland, Offener Brief, August 11, 2009.

25. Kai Weber, "Überfall im Morgengrauen: Landkreis Hildesheim schiebt kurdische Yeziden nach Syrien ab," Nds-fluerat.org. http://www.nds-fluerat.org/5557/pressemitteilungen/ueberfall-im-morgengrauen-landkreis-hildesheim-schiebt-kurdische-yeziden-nach-syrien-ab/ (accessed June 5, 2016).

26. Zerdesht Ja'far, letter to the editor, 2008.

27. Rasho, Muhammad. "Mithaq al-'aqd al-ijtima'i lil-idara al-dhatiya al-dimuqratiya." www.alhewar.org. http://www.ahewar.org/debat/show.art.asp?aid=433651 (accessed June 5, 2016).

28. Firatnews, November 25, 2013. http://ar.firatajans.com/news/akhr-l-khbr/ftth-dr-lyzydyyn-fy-qry-bswfn.htm

29. Bahzani4. "Li awal mara al-diyana al-izidiya tudras fi al-madaris al-rasmiya." www.bahzani.net. www.bahzani.net/services/forum/showthread.php?95923 (accessed June 5, 2016).

30. Bahzani4. "Gharbi Kurdistan tabda bi-tadris madat al-diyana al-izidiya fi afrin." www.bahzani.net. www.bahzani.net/services/form/showthread.php?97657 (accessed June 5, 2016). A copy of the official appointment letter is published too.

31. Videos of the celebrations were posted on Youtube, and there one can see the performance of various rituals as well as the diverse Kurdish-Syrian decoration.

32. Interview with Sheikh Shamo October 13, 2011, published in lalishduhok.com.

33. Firatnews, December 17, 2011.

34. I was unable to get answers to the importance of the year 612.

35. Firatnews, April 16, 2013

36. Hawarnews, February 13, 2014.

37. The political and religious activities of Yezidi activists are noted by their adversaries and held against them. Sheikh Mlehan's daughter, for example, was kidnaped on May 15, 2014 for ransom and to exert pressure on the Yezidi leader. Another girl from the neighboring village of Gondor was kidnaped in late 2013 for similar reasons; however, her name has not been revealed to the public.

38. Firatnews, September 23, 2012. http://ar.firatajans.com/news/akhr-l-khbr/jtm-fy-qry-qzl-jwkh-llkrd-lydhydyyn-b-mwd.htm

39. TEV-DEM: Tevgera Civaka Demokratik or Movement for a Democratic Society, the ruling political coalition in the self-administration areas of Rojava.

40. Hawarnews, January 5, 2014. www.hawarnews.com/index.php/component/content/article/9313-2014-01-05-06-48-24?tmpl

41. Hawarnews, May 6, 2014.

42. Firatnews, April 17, 2013.

43. Amed, Xebat. "Ijtima' li-hizb al-itihad al-dimuqrati fi qariay Dugerka." http://www.pydrojava.net/ar/index.php/tamazight/2502-2014-04-19-18-43-13 (accessed June 5, 2016).

44. Hawarnews, July 8, 2013. http://www.hawarnews.com/index.php/2013-02-14-17-53-15/4216-2013-07-08-13-24-55

45. As pointed out earlier, the ethnic affiliation of Armenian Yezidis has changed. Now they regard themselves as ethnic Yezidis, a unique form that is different from the other Armenian Kurds, who are Muslims and who preserve their Kurdishness.

46. The current aspirant to the Mirship, Anwar Muawiya al-Umawi, points to an official decree which was issued in 1980 by the Iraqi government and appointed Bayazid Ismail, Anwar's paternal uncle, as Mir of all Yezidis. According to Anwar, Mir Tahsin Beg should be referred to only as the guardian of Sheikh Adi's shrine. Furthermore, he accuses him of treason and of usurping the Mirship from his side of the family.

47. See Anwar Muawiya's side of the story published in Matar (2003): 211–243.

48. Rudaw, "al-Barzani radda ala Mir Tahsin: La ahad yastati' an yazhar hawiya al-izidiyin." Rudaw.net. www.rudaw.net/arabic/kurdistan/211020144 (accessed June 5, 2016).

49. Statement issued by the Yezidi Supreme Spiritual Council (2010).

50. Sirianews, "al-qabd al ab wa waladahu li-irtikabihim jarima sharaf." http://www.syria-news.com/readnews.php?sy_seq=127157 (accessed June 5, 2016).

51. Amnesty International: Iraq: Amnesty International appalled by stoning to death of Yezidi girl and subsequent killings. Public Statement, April 27, 2007, available at www.amnesty.org/en/library/asset/MDE14/027/2007/en/dom-MDE140272007en.htm

52. Hawarnews, March 29, 2014. http://hawarnews.com/index.php/2013-02-14-17-53-15/12085-2014-03-29-10-50-11.

53. Some Yezidis also joined the Ba'th Party, but concurrently gave up their religious identity and affiliation with the community. The editor-in-chief of Tishreen newspaper during the early 2000s was a Yezidi, but referenced it "only by birth" (interview with K. J., May 15, 2006).

54. McGee (2014): 175.

55. Interview with Issa on Jan 15, 2015.

56. Interview with community elders from Tirbespi who recently fled to Germany on October 21, 2013.

57. Rojmaf, "Hijra jama'iya li-abna' al-ta'ifa al-yazidiya al-kurdiya fi suria." Rojmaf.ucoz.net. http://rojmaf.ucoz.net/news/2012-09-19-358 (accessed June 5, 2016).

58. Hossino and Tanir (2012): 15.

59. Efrin became an autonomous canton in January 2014 and held its own elections and built administrative structures. The text of the social pact in the Jezira differs from the one in Efrin. For example, the latter does not specifically mention the Yezidis. See text of the social pact in Efrin: http://cantonafrin.com/ar/pages/Charter%20of%20the%20social%20contract.html

60. The Arabic version of the pact was published at http://www.sotkurdistan.net/index.php?option=com_k2&view=item&id=33965

61. ANF. "Qariyat al-zaydiya fi al-hasaka tushakil majlisaha al-sha'bi." www.afnarabic.com. http://afnarabic.com/akhr-l-khbr/qry-lzydy-fy-lhsk-tshkl-mjlsh-lsh-by (accessed June 5, 2016).

62. Firatnews. "al-qura al-izidiya fi al-hasaka tushakkil majlisaha al-sha'abi." www.sotkurdistan.net. http://www.sotkurdistan.
net/index.php?option=com_k2&view=item&id=23040

63. Agreement between local groups in Tirbespi to form a joint council, Feb. 23, 2013.

64. The other Yezidi members included Mulhem Sinjo, Nadir Osman, Kan'an Ali, and Ziyad Rustom.

65. Firatnews, March 13, 2013.

66. Hawarnes, February 17, 2014. http://hawarnews.com/index.php/2013-02-14-17-53-15/10609-2014-02-17-09-34-48.

67. Firatnews, May 14, 2012.http://ar.firatajans.com/news/akhr-l-khbr/jtm-jmhyry-fy-qry-qstl-jndw-hwl-ntkhbt-lmjls-lsh-by.htm.

68. Firatnews, May 14, 2012.

69. Firatnews, December 10, 2012.

70. Firatnews, December 26, 2012.

71. See the election results at Hawar News, Sept. 12, 2015.
72. Tamimi (2015).
73. See the report by Jabir Jindo about Yezidi perceptions published in the magazine Suwar at http://suwar-magazine.org/ar/programs-details/185.
74. No one claimed responsibility for the attack; but it was widely believed that a radical Islamic militia loosely affiliated with the Free Syrian Army and following their own takfirist agenda, carried out the attack. The FSA strongly denied any involvement and assured the Yezidis that they are considered part of the Syrian mosaic. In the fall of 2012, more elements and brigades from the FSA disassociated from them and began collaborating with the more hard-line Islamist groups such as JN and ISIS.
75. Hawarnews, August 21, 2013. http://hawarnews.com/index.php/component/content/article/43-2013-02-24-21-16-12/5436-2013-08-21-09-55-27.
76. Statement of EES, August 21, 2013: Continuation of Killing and Migration of Yezidi Kurds in Syria, published at http://www.bahzani.net/services/forum/showthread.php?67200, accessed on Sept 23, 2015.
77. Hawarnews, September 4, 2013. http://www.hawarnews.com/index.php/component/content/article/43-2013-02-24-21-16-12/5816-2013-09-04-08-26-02.
78. Bahzani. "Qasf mintaqat al-siryan al-qadim fi Halab." Bahzani.net. www.bahzani.net/services/forum/showthread.php?43469 (accessed June 5, 2016).
79. N.n. "al-nidham yaqsif muhit qariatay saghunak wa kimar fi afrin." www.pydrojava.com. http://www.pydrojava.net/ar/index.php/tamazight/2554-2014-05-01-08-59-44 (accessed June 5, 2016).
80. N.n. "Ras al-Ayn: Ma'arik wa haqa'iq damigha bayna al-YPG wa Da'sh," http://www.all4syria.info/Archive/149822 (accessed June 5, 2016).
81. Telephone conversation with Khalil Huseyn from Afrin, December 25, 2014.
82. Ezidenrat. "Man nahnu?" www.ezidenrat.de; http://ezidenrat.de/?page_id=2 (accessed June 5, 2016).
83. Hawarnews, June 30, 2015, and July 1, 2015.
84. Rudaw, "Tashkil lajnatayn fi al-Hasaka li-itlaq sirah al-mu'taqalin lada quwat al-asayish," www.rudaw.net. http://rudaw.net/arabic/middleeast/syria/2211 20141 (accessed June 5, 2016).
85. Abdo, Ibrahim. "al-A'ilat al-izidiya fi markaz muhafadhat al-hasaka bi-khatr." http://xeber24.org/30564.html (accessed June 5, 2016).
86. Glioti (2013).
87. Ibid.
88. See Fermaz Ghario, Yezidis—National Crisis (September 9, 2010).
89. Apparently, some Yezidis joined the Syrian Communist Party. See Gharibo (2013).
90. Yekineyen Parastina Gel (YPG) or People's Protection Unit, the military wing of the Syrian PYD.
91. Hezen Parastina Gel (HPG) or People's Defense Force, the military wing of the Turkish PKK.
92. Email conversation with T.H., HES member, May 2015.

93. Diyar Al-Khatari, "Mumathil al-amir yusharik fo mu'tamar fiyina," www.bahzani.net. www.bahzani.net/service/forum/showthread.php?95855 (accessed June 5, 2016).

94. Statement by NSC spokeswomen Bernadette Meehan, www.whitehouse.gov/the-press-office/2014/10/31/statement-nsc.

95. Lalish Media Network, Sept. 1, 2013.

96. Hassan Tahsin Nasr, "al-Matahin al-qadima ta'ud ila al-hayat fi Afrin," Tishreen.news.sy. http://tishreen.news.sy/tishreen/public/read/300565 (accessed June 5, 2016).

97. Firatnews, December 16, 2012.

98. Hawarnews, July 8, 2013. http://hawarnews.com/index.php/2013-02-14-17-53-15/4188-2013-07-08-03-43-29.

99. A five-year-long severe drought hit the eastern parts of Syria from 2006 to 2011. Aside from the agricultural failures, it triggered mass migrations to the cities and abroad. See Peter Gleick, "Water, Drought, Climate Change, and Conflict in Syria," Weather, Climate and Society 6 (2014): 331–340.

Chapter 7

Conclusion

Future Challenges

We have seen how over the course of several hundred years, Yezidi religion has emerged as a salient source of identification. Yezidis have established themselves as a recognized, embedded community in parts of Syria. Due to external factors and domestic developments, the identity group, however, split into two communities and built unique local identities. Over time, they adapted differently to external and internal threats, but under the current circumstances of unrest and war, they follow a similar path toward the construction of a unified identity. The two largest obstacles in the formative stage of identity building are the civil war and mass migration. On the other hand, they use the self-administration and the resulting coexistence and tolerance among the various groups within the three cantons to their advantage.[1]

Until very recently, and because of their enhanced vulnerability as a double minority, Yezidis were not equal to other Syrian minorities; however, they were also not discriminated per se. Thus, from the outside it remains an open question whether the Syrian government actively pursued Yezidi discrimination, or if this was rather a local issue with other ethnic, religious, economic, and political interest groups and actors as well as governmental neglect. From a Yezidi perspective this looks different. For them, they saw the daily harassment and many hindrances institutionalized by the bureaucracy. Forced not to follow their religion and dispossessed and denied as farmers and citizens, the Yezidis felt the official stigmatization. Thus, their approach toward reform until the outbreak of the Syrian Revolution and civil war was not aimed at integrating into the larger non-Yezidi Syrian society, but to leave the country as fast and as many as they can. Although they now have the opportunity to participate in the formation of a new political system in the self-administered cantons, many tend to choose emigration to Germany over rebuilding their community in Syria.

It is unrealistic to expect Yezidis in Syria to develop a cohesive and stable identity considering the inconsistent and often traumatic circumstances in their struggle for survival. While studying the process over various periods of time and geographic regions, the ups and downs and incoherent developments must be considered too. Yezidis were forced to react to the daily challenges of inferiority, and in response, created selective and distorted adjustment mechanisms in order to avoid conflict with a hostile environment of ethnic, religious, social, and political adversaries. Their primary goal is still sheer survival, which can be guaranteed only if the Yezidis act unitedly. Internal arguments over identity issues were common, but under the present circumstances it seems imperative to represent the community as a whole. Mir Tahsin Beg offered a compromise in the struggle of identity and loyalty when describing Yezidism as a religion and ethnicity at the same time. He also called for a joint, umbrella organization among the diaspora Yezidis. Only in the diaspora and to a lesser extent in the self-administered cantons have they started entering the phase of redefining their religious and cultural inventory. The Syrian civil war and the Sinjar Massacre served as catalysts for the process of reinventing Yezidi identity.

Among the Yezidi communities inside Syria the fear of an uncertain future is growing, giving raise to the idea of a mass exodus similar to the one of the Yezidi community in Turkey in the 1980s and recently as contemplated by the Sinjar community. These negative feelings toward their home country do not prevent them from supporting other Yezidi communities in need, such as the refugees from Sinjar of whom several thousands stay in camps or live with relatives in Syria. It does however alleviate concerns and anxieties over issues of security, safety, belonging, and rejection, especially when comparing these issues with the situation of their compatriots in the German diaspora.

Another lesson was learned from the events in Sinjar: Yezidis in Syria no longer view the Yezidi experience in Iraq as something to aspire or emulate. For a while it seemed that the Yezidi political and cultural achievements in the Kurdish region and Sinjar could serve as a model and goal for the Syrian communities to achieve. But certainly after Sinjar, Syria's Yezidis came to the conclusion that they have something equally unique and valuable in their self-administered cantons. Here, they participate as ministers, directors, military leaders, teachers, administrators, and council members representing their distinct community. Furthermore, their legal rights and religious identity have been recognized officially in the constitution. The Peoples Protection Units (YPG) include many Yezidi fighters, both men and women, and they fight to protect these political achievements. When YPG and PKK fighters (and among them Yezidis) came to rescue the Iraqi Yezidis, the hierarchical order was reversed. In the past, the Syrian Yezidis used to live on the margins and looked toward Iraq as the center of Yezidism. Now Syria's Yezidis have something to offer too: military protection and self-administration.

Thus, alongside their Muslim and secular Kurdish brethren, Syria's Yezidis have now found themselves a better place on the sociopolitical ladder. In particular, the revoking of the citizenship law helped many to become more grounded. Likewise, the self-administration introduced civil marriages in order to combat sectarianism, and Yezidis may benefit from this decision because it will lift the dominance of Islamic personal statute rules over their lives. Certainly, this improved position is recognized only on a regional level and is dependent on the outcome of the civil war and the revolution. So far, the Syrian government has not made any concessions to the Yezidis. They look at them only as part of the Kurdish block. And so do many Yezidis, who combine their ethnic origin and identity with the religious affiliation. Playing the Kurdish card has served them well until now.

It has also eliminated one member from the list of Yezidi enemies. Most anti-Yezidi attacks were committed by Muslims, in the past Kurdish Muslims, who constituted the majority of their neighbors. Nowadays it is fair to say that the Syrian Kurds are more aware of their Yezidi neighbors and in many instances respect and recognize them as equals, especially when stressing the common religious origin. While Kurdish Sufism has contributed to this change of mind, we must also credit the growing secularism among the younger generation. And after the PKK and PYD accepted the idea of a Yezidi origin of the Kurds, this label became part of the official political discourse.

The previous Yezidi fear of the violent, ignorant, and racist Arab-Muslim has now transferred to generally despise radical and violent Muslims who commit genocide against the Yezidis. Looking at the attacks in Sinjar, but also against the Syrian Yezidi villages of Qestel Jindo, Cava, or Asadiya, remind us that this threat is real and current. The perpetrators of those threats and attacks are loosely defined as da'sh, takfiristis, salafists, or radical Islamists. It makes no difference to the Yezidis whether these Islamists belong to Jabhat al-Nusra or IS. Both have attacked Yezidis in Syria. The ISIS focuses strongly on the village of Dabiq, as a place for executions, videos, and direction of their military campaign[2]. Dabiq, in Islamic eschatology, is viewed as a place of Armageddon or the end of days where the final battle between Muslims and the unbelievers is fought. Dabiq is only ten miles away from the Yezidi villages in the Kurdagh.

Yezidi identity has been described as an identity of hiding, fear, and victimization. Recent history supports this argument: the 74th ferman against the community is only one year old, and the next attack can occur any time. To communicate and define such a negative, traumatic identity is difficult.

However, the recent events in Iraq and Syria also witness the emergence of a new Yezidi identity, one that can be described as assertive—yes, we want to build something new, innovative—we participate in the self-administration and one that is pragmatic—we will leave Syria if necessary, we are open to reform—we can redefine religious dogmas and traditions. While Yezidis remain a double minority in Syria, Iraq, or Germany, they have embraced the uniqueness of their community's fate.

NOTES

1. Jindo (2014) has Yezidis from the three cantons comment on the pros and cons. See Jabir Jindo, "Waqi' al-ta'ifa al-izidiya fi Suria tazayud al-mukhawuf ba'da ma'sat Shingal," [in Arabic], in *Suwar*, year 3, no. 10 (August 2014): 22–25.

2. *Dabiq* is also the name of the official journal of the Islamic State.

Appendixes

1. List of abbreviations and acronyms of political parties and organizations

Da'sh	Al-Dawla al-Islamiya fi'l-Iraq wa Suria	The Islamic State in Iraq and Syria
EES	Encumena Ezdiyen Suri	Council of Syrian Yezidis
ENKS	Encumena Niştimani ya Kurdi li Suriye	The Kurdish National Council in Syria (KNC)
HES	Hevbendiya Ezidiyen Suriye	Syrian Yezidi Association
HPG	Hezen Parastina Gel	Peoples' Defence Forces
HPS	Heza Parastina Shingal	Shingal Protection Force
ISIS, ISIL, IS	The Islamic State in Iraq and Syria, The Islamic State in Iraq and the Levante	The Islamic State
JN	Jabhat an-Nusra	The Victory Front
PDK	Partiya Demokrat a Kurdistane	Kurdistan Democratic Party (KDP)
PDK-S	Partiya Demokrat a Kurdi li Suriye	Kurdish Democratic Party in Syria
PKK	Partiya Karkeren Kurdistan	Kurdistan Workers' Party
PYD	Partiya Yekiti ya Demokrat	Democratic Union Party
SCP	Al-Hizb al-Shuyu'i al-Suri	Syrian Communist Party (SCP)
SNC	Al-Majlis al-Watani al-Suri	The Syrian National Council (SNC)
TEV-DEM	Tevgera Civaka Demokratik	Movement for a Democratic Society
YBS	Yekineyen Berxwedan Shingal	Resistance Unit Shingal
YNK	Yekitiya Niştimani ya Kurdistane	Patriotic Union of Kurdistan (PUK)
YPG	Yekineyen Parastina Gel	Peoples' Defence Units

2. Glossary of words related to Yezidism

Agha	Honorary title for rich landowners
Ajanib	Foreigner, citizenship category in Syria
Aqaliya	Minority
Asabiya	Group solidarity
Baba Sheikh	Religious Leader of the Yezidis
Basimbar	Red and white bracelet
Batizmi	Yezidi religious holidays, celebrated in the Syrian Jezira and neighboring areas
Berat	Small rocks and charms from Lalish
Beyt	Religious hymn
Biraye akhrete	Brother in the afterlife
Bisk	Cutting-the-hair ceremony
Charshemasor	Yezidi new year
Chile havine	40 days of summer fasting
Chile zivistane	40 days of winter fasting
Chivate ruhani	Supreme Spiritual Council
Di'a/niza	Yezidi prayers
Feqir	Religious title for a pious, ascetic man
Feto	Annual fees paid by Yezidi laymen to their clerics
Kaniya sipi	The White Spring in Lalish
Khawarij	Those who move out. Early Islamic opposition movement which declared their Muslim enemies infidels. Today the word is used to describe terrorists.
Kherqe	Special woolen outfit worn by Feqir
Kleja	A special sweet bread served during New Year celebrations
Kochek	Religious title, pious man, foreseer
Krive	Godfather during circumcision
Madh'hab	Islamic school of law
Maktum	Unregistered. Citizenship category in Syria
Mes'haf Resh	The Black Book, a Yezidi sacred text
Me'na	Religious text, legend
Michewir	Guardian of a local Yezidi shrine
Millet	Officially recognized religious community in the Ottoman Empire
Mir	Secular leader of the Yezidis
Mirid	Layman, one of the three Yezidi castes
Mukhtar	Village elder or leader
Newroz	Kurdish New Year
Peshimam	Clergyman, bearer of a high religious office
Pir	Clergyman, one of the three Yezidi castes
Qewal	Hereditary caste of learned, pious men who memorize, perform, and interpret the sacred texts
Qewl	Sacred poems
Rojiyen Khodanen	Holidays in honor of the pious ancestors
Rojiyen Sheshims	Holidays in honor of Sheshims
Sed u hed	The socioreligious caste segregation
Serisal	Yezidi New Year
Sevik	Special sourdough bread served at Batizmi

2. Glossary of words related to Yezidism

Agha	Honorary title for rich landowners
Shari'a	Islamic Law
Sheikh	Clergyman, one of the three Yezidi castes
Sinjaq	Yezidi religious symbol or idol representing Tawsi Melek
Ta'ifa	Sect
Taj hilla	Religious holiday among the Yezidis in Kurdagh
Tariqa	Brotherhood, community of Sufis
Tawsi Melek	The Peacock Angel
Tawusgeran	Annual tour of the sinjaq to the various Yezidi communities
Umma	Islamic nation
Khwede	God
Zawiya	Sufi shrine

Bibliography

Abdo Ali, Muhammad, Jabal al-Kurd "Afrin"—Dirasa tarikhiya, ijtimaiya thaqafiya; [Kurdagh "Afrin"—A Historic, Social and Cultural Study], [in Arabic], Sulaymaniyah: Mudiriyat al-Tab` wa-al-Nashr, 2009.

Abdo Ali, Muhammad, al-Diyana al-Izidiya wa'l-Izidiyun fi Shamal Gharb Suria [The Yezidi Religion and the Yezidis in Northwest Syria], [in Arabic], Halab: Dar Abd al-Munim, 2008.

Abkommen zwischen der Regierung der Bundesrepublik Deutschland und der Regierung der Arabischen Republik Syrien über die Rückführung von illegal aufhältigen Personen, [in German], July 14, 2008, published at https://dejure.org/dienste/vernetzung/rechtsprechung?Gericht=OVG%20Saarland&Datum=10.06.2010&Aktenzeichen=2%20A%2013/10, accessed September 22, 2014.

Acikyildiz, Birgül, *The Yezidis: The History of a Community, Culture and Religion*, London: I.B.Tauris, 2010.

Acikyildiz, Birgül, "The Sanctuary of Shaykh Adi at Lalish: Centre of Pilgrimage of the Yezidis," in *Bulletin of SOAS*, vol. 72, no. 2 (2009), pp. 301–333.

Ackermann, Andreas, "Yeziden in Deutschland: Von der Minderheit zur Diaspora", [in German], in Paideuma: Mitteilungen zur Kulturkunde, 49 (2003), pp. 157–177.

Ackermann, Andreas, "Kontinuitat und Wandel der yezidischen Identitat in Deutschland: Eine vorläufige Bestandsaufnahme", [in German], in Denge Ezidiyan, vols. 8+9, December 2001, pp. 10–12.

Agreement between local civic groups in Tirbespi to form a joint council, February 23, 2013.

Ali, Rozad, "Bidayat al-yaqzha al-qawmiya wa bawadir nashat siyasi al-murafiq fi mintaqat Jabal al-Kurd Afrin 1919–1957," [The Beginning of National Awareness and Sign of Political Activism in the Jabal al-Kurd Region, Afrin (1919–1957)], [in Arabic], *Hiwar*, vol. 64, October 2011, pp. 22–35.

Allison, Christine, "Unbelievable Slowness of Mind": Yezidi Studies, from Nineteenth to Twenty-First Century," *The Journal of Kurdish Studies*, vol. 6, 2008, pp. 1–23.

Allison, Christine, *The Yezidi Oral Tradition in Iraqi Kurdistan*, London: Curzon Press, 2001.

Aloian, Zourab, "Shaikh 'Adi, Sufism and the Kurds'", accessed at http://www.penkurd.org/englizi/zorab/zorab-SheikhAdi-Sufizm.html

Altug, Seda, *Sectarianism in the Syrian Jazira: Community, land and violence in the memories of World War I and the French mandate (1915–1939)*, PhD thesis, University of Utrecht, 2011.

Arakelova, Victoria, "The Hereafter in the Yezidi Beliefs," *Iran and the Caucasus*, vol. 16, 2012, pp. 309–318.

Arakelova, Victoria, "Sufi Saints in the Yezidi Tradition I: Qawlē Husēyīnī Halāǰ," *Iran and the Caucasus*, vol. 5, 2001, pp. 183–192.

Asatrian, Garnik and Viktoria Arakelova, The Religion of the Peacock Angel: The Yezidis and Their Spirit World, Routledge, 2014.

Bachmann, Walter, *Kirchen und Moscheen in Armenien und Kurdistan,* [in German], Leipzig: J.C. Heinrichsche'se Buchhandlung, 1913.

Barakat, Marwan: Jabal Laylun fi maraat al-tarikh: bahth jiuluji tarikhi athari ijtima'i mawathaq [Laylun Mountain in the Mirror of History: A documented, geological, historical, archaeological and social study], [in Arabic], Dar Abd al-Mun'im, Aleppo, 2006.

Bar Hebraeus, *Chronology.* Ed. Paul Bedjan, translated by E. Budge, 2 vols., Oxford, 1932.

Baveniroda, "Al-Ezidiyun wa'l-jughrafiyat al-makan fi Suria," [The Yezidis and the spatial geography in Syria], [in Arabic], May 2, 2009, http://baveniroda.zikforum.com/t230-topic#241.

Bell, Gertrude, *The Desert and the Sown*, Dutton, 1907.

Bengio, Ofra and Gabriel Ben-Dor (eds.), *Minorities and the State in the Arab World*, Boulder, CO: Lynne Rienner Publishers, 1999.

Benninghaus, Rüdiger, "Friedhöfe als Quellen für Fragen des Kulturwandels: Grabkultur von Yeziden und Aleviten in Deutschland mit Seitenblick auf die Türkei", [in German], in Langer, Robert; Motika, Raoul; Ursinus, Michael (Hrsg.): Migration und Ritu-altransfer: Religiöse Praxis der Aleviten, Jesiden und Nusairier zwischen Vorderem Orient und Westeuropa, Frankfurt am Main u.a.: Peter Lang Verlag, 2005, pp. 247–288.

Biro, Hassan, "al-Hizam al-'Arabi – Dirasa siyasiya qanuniya," [The Arabic Belt – Legal, Political Study], [in Arabic], published at http://all4syria.info/Archive/53030, on September 1, 2012, accessed October 10, 2015.

Bittner, Maximilian, *Die heiligen Bücher der Jeziden oder Teufelsanbeter*, [in German], Vienna: Denkschriften der kaiserlichen Akademie der Wissenschaften, 1913.

Bou-Nacklie, N.E., "Les Troupes Speciales: Religious and Ethnic Recruitment, 1916–46," *International Journal of Middle East Studies,* vol. 25, 1993, pp. 645–660.

Cardinal, Monique, "Religious Education in Syria: Unity and Difference," in *British Journal of Religious Education*, vol. 31, no. 2, March 2009, pp. 91–101.

Castellino, Joshua and Kathleen A. Cavanaugh, *Minority Rights in the Middle East*, Oxford: Oxford University Press, 2013.

Celil, Celile, "Mythologie, Kult und zwei heilige Bücher der Yazidi", [in Arabic], in *Yazidi: Gottes auserwähltes Volk oder die "Teufelsanbeter" vom Jebel Sinjar, Irak*, eds. Axel Steinmann and Karin Kren, Katalog zur Sonderausstellung, 30. April - 27. September 1998, Vienna: Museum für Völkerkunde, 1998, pp. 35–54.

Celil, Ordixane and Celil, Celile, *Zargotina Kurda*, [in Kurdish], Moscow: Nauka Publishers, 1978.

Dalalyan, Tork: "Construction of Kurdish and Yezidi Identities among the Kurmanj-Speaking Population of the Republic of Armenia," in *Changing Identities: Armenia, Azerbaijan, Georgia*, ed. by Heinrich Boell Foundation South Caucasus Regional Office, Tbilisi: Heinrich Böll Stiftung, 2012, pp. 177–201.

Damluji, Sadiq, *al-Yazidiya*, [The Yezidis], [in Arabic], Mosul: Matbaʻat al-Ittihad, 1949.

Deshti, Zerdesht, "Ezdiyen Kurdaxe", [The Yezidis from Kurdagh], [in Kurdish], *PIRS*, vol. 6, no. 2, 1995, pp. 28–30.

Directorate of Education in Hassake, Letter to Principals, no. 4723/4623, September 17, 2008.

Drower, E.S., *Peacock Angel: Being Some Account of Votaries of a Secret Cult and Their Sanctuaries*, London: J. Murray's, 1941.

Dulz, Irene, Siamend Hajo and Eva Savelsberg, "Persecuted and Co-opted – The Yezidis in the 'New Iraq,'" *The Journal of Kurdish Studies*, vol. 6, 2008, pp. 25–44.

Febvre, Michele, *Teatro della Turchia*, Bologna, 1683.

Final Statement of the Second Conference of the Yezidi Association in Western Kurdistan and Syria, March 10, 2013.

Fisk, Robert, *The Great War for Civilisation: The Conquest of the Middle East*, New York: Vintage, 2007.

Fragiskatos, Peter, "The Stateless Kurds in Syria: Problems and Prospects for the Ajanib and Maktumin Kurds," *The International Journal of Kurdish Studies*, vol. 21, nos. 1+2, 2007, pp. 109–122.

Frank, Rudolf, *Scheich 'Adi, der große Heilige der Jezidis*, [in German], Berlin, 1911. (Türkische Bibliothek, vol. 14)

Frayha, Anis, "New Yezidi Texts from Beled Sinjar, 'Iraq,'" *Journal of the American Oriental Society*, vol. 66, 1949, pp. 18–43.

Fuccaro, Nelida, "Kurds and Kurdish Nationalism in Mandatory Syria: Politics, Culture and Identity," in *Essays on the Origins of Kurdish Nationalism*, ed. by Abbas Vali, Costa Verde, CA: Mazda Publications, 2002, pp. 191–217.

Fuccaro, Nelida: *The Other Kurds: Yazidis in Colonial Iraq*, London, New York: I.B. Tauris, 1999.

Fuccaro, Nelida, "Communalism and the State in Iraq: The Yazidi Kurds, c. 1869–1940," *Middle Eastern Studies*, vol. 35, no. 2, 1999, pp. 1–21.

Fuccaro, Nelida, "Ethnicity, State Formation, and Conscription in Postcolonial Iraq: The Case of the Yazidi Kurds of Jabal Sinjar," *International Journal of Middle East Studies,* vol. 29, no. 4, 1997, pp. 559–580.

Fuccaro, Nelida, "A 17th Century Travel Account on the Yazidis," *Annali*, vol. 53, no. 3, 1993, pp. 241–253.

Gharibo, Fermaz, "al-Izidiyun – Azmat al-Qawmiya," [The Ezidis – National Crisis], [in Arabic], published September 20, 2010 at www.doxata.com/aara_meqalat/4622.html, accessed June 14, 2015.

Gharibo, Fermaz, "al-Izidiyun al-Suriyun – wahdat saff wa ikhlas," [The Syrian Ezidis – United ranks and sincerity], [in Arabic], essay posted on www.bahzani.net/services/forum/showthread.php?56334, accessed June 14, 2015.

Gharibo, Fermaz, "Al-Ezidiyun fi Suria, al-qism al-awal," [The Syrian Ezidis – Part Two], [in Arabic], May 12, 2009, published at http://www.hekar.net/modules.php?name=News&file=print&sid=2847, accessed May 11, 2014.

Gleick, Peter, "Water, Drought, Climate Change, and Conflict in Syria," *Weather, Climate and Society*, vol. 6, 2014, pp. 331–340.

Glioti, Andrea, "Yazidis Benefit From Kurdish Gains in Northeast Syria, published http://www.al-monitor.com/pulse/tr/originals/2013/10/syria-yazidi-minorities-kurds.html#ixzz3oZjHBpLz, accessed August 15, 2015.

Goldsmith, Leon, "Syria's Alawites and the Politics of Sectarian Insecurity: A Khaldunian Perspective," *Ortadoğu Etütleri*, vol. 3, no. 1, July 2011, pp. 33–60.

Guest, John S., *Survival among the Kurds: A History of the Yezidis*, London, New York: Kegan Paul, 1993.

Hasibi, Muhammad Abu as-Saʿud al-, "Mudhakkirat," [Memories], [in Arabic], in *Tarikh Bilad ash-Sham fi-l-qarn at-tasiʿ ʿashar* ed. by Suhayl Zakkar, Damascus: Dar al-Fikr, 1982, pp. 281–316.

Helberg, Kristin, "In der Heimat, doch bedroht", [in German], *TAZ*, no. 7793, October 14, 2005.

Hilal, Muhammad Talib, *Dirasat ʿan Muhafazat al-Jazira min al-nahiya al-qawmiya waʾl-ijtimaʾiya waʾl-siyasiya*, [A Study of the al-Jazira Governorate with regards to national, social and political issues], [in Arabic], 1963, n.p.

Hossino, Omar and Ilhan Tanir, *The Decisive Minority: The Role of Syria's Kurds in the Anti-Assad Revolution*. A Henry Jackson Society Report, March 2012, p 16.

Hourani, Albert Habib, *Minorities in the Arab World*, London: Oxford University Press, 1947.

Ibn Taymiyya, "Risalat al-ʿadawiya," [Epistles of the Adawiya], [in Arabic], in *Majmuʿat ar-rasaʾil al-kubra*, vol. 1, Cairo, 1906/1323.

Issa, Chaukedin, Telim Tolan and Sebastian Maisel, *Das Yezidentum – Religion und Leben*, [in German], Oldenburg: Denge Ezidiya Verlag, 2007.

Issa, Chaukedin: "*Shemo Meke Shemo Issa: His Life for the People,*" obituary read at funeral on August 31, 2006.

Ja'far, Zerdesht: Where is the Mir when these things are happening to the Yezidis in Afrin? Letter to the editor, January 25, 2008 at http://www.kaniya-sipi.de/modules.php?name=News&file=article&sid=2341

Jindo, Jabir, Waqi al-taʾifa al-izidiya fi Suria tazayud al-makhawuf baʾda maʾsat Shingal, [The Situation of the Yezidi Sect in Syria - Increased fear after the Shingal tragedy], [in Arabic], in Suwar Magazine, vol. 10, w.d., downloaded at www.suwar-magazine.org/ar/programs-detail/185/

Al-Jarrad, Khalaf, *al-Yazidiya waʾl-Yazidiyun*, [Yezidism and the Yezidis], [in Arabic], al-Ladhiqiya: Dar al-Hiwar, 1996.

Joseph, Isya, *Sacred Books and Traditions of the Yezidis*, Boston: Gorham Press, 1919.

Jullien, R.P.M., *Sinaï et Syrie. Souvenirs bibliques et chretiens*, Lille: Desclee de Brouwer, 1893.

Jum'a, Nuri al-: handwritten letter to the minister of justice via the prosecutor in Hasake, May 2, 1993.

Khalo, Muhammad, "Beyambur – the Epic of Kurdish-Arab Brotherhood," [in Arabic], esyria.sy/ehassakeh, published April 21, 2013, accessed June 15, 2015.

Khoury, Philip, *Syria and the French Mandate: The Politics of Arab Nationalism, 1920–1945*, London: I.B.Tauris, 1987.

Khuri, Fuad, *Imams and Emirs: State, Religion and Sects in Islam*, London: Saqi, 2014.

Khuri, Issam, "Taqdir al-Izidiya, Din Allah al-Mughib fi Suria" [Assessment of the Yezidis, Hidden Religion of God in Syria], [in Arabic], in Al-Hiwar al-Mutamadin, no. 1529, April 23, 2006, published at http://www.ahewar.org/debat/show.art.asp?aid=62940, accessed October 2, 2013.

Kizilhan, Jan Ilhan, *Die Yeziden. Eine anthropologische und sozialpsychologische Studie über die kurdische Gemeinschaft*, [in German], Frankfurt/M.: Verlag Medico International, 1997

Kreyenbroek, Philip, *Yezidism in Europe – Different Generations speak about their Religion*, Wiesbaden: Harrasowitz, 2009.

Kreyenbroek, Philip, "History in an Oral Culture: The Construction of History in Yezidi Sacred Texts," *The Journal of Kurdish Studies*, vol. 6, 2008, pp. 84–92.

Kreyenbroek, Philip and Khalil Jindy Rashow, *God and Sheikh Adi are Perfect: Sacred Poems and Religious Narratives from the Yezidi Tradition*, Wiesbaden: Harrasowitz, 2005.

Kreyenbroek, Philip, *Yezidism – Its Background, Observances and Textual Tradition*, New York: Edwin Mellen Press, 1995.

Kumaraswamy, PR, "Problems of Studying Minorities in the Middle East," in *Alternatives: Turkish Journal of International Relations*, vol. 2, no. 2, 2003, pp. 244–264.

Kurdwatch, *Der Aufstand von Qamishli – Beginn einer neuen Era für die Kurden Syriens?*, [in German], Kurdwatch Report No. 4, Berlin, 2009.

Kurdwatch, *The Amuda Cinema Fire of November 1960*, Kurdwatch Report No. 2, Berlin, 2009.

Lammens, Henri, "Le massif du Gabal Sim'an et les Yézidis de Syrie", *Mélange de la Faculté Orientale*, vol. 2, 1907, pp. 365–96.

Leezenberg, Michiel, *Political Islam among the Kurds*, Paper originally prepared for the International Conference "Kurdistan: The unwanted state", March 29–31, 2001, Jagiellonian University, Cracow, Poland, 2001.

Lescot, Roger, "Le Kurd Dagh et le mouvement Mouroud", *Studia Kurdica*, vol. 1–5, 1988, pp. 101–126.

Lescot, Roger, *Enquête sur les Yezidis de Syrie et du Djebel Sindjar*, Beyrouth: Libraire du Liban, 1938.

Lynch, Maureen and Perveen Ali, *Buried Alive, Stateless Kurds in Syria*, Report written for Refugees International, January, 2006.

Maisel, Sebastian, "Syria's Yezidis in the Kurdagh and the Jezira: Building Identities in a Heterodox Community," *The Muslim World*, vol. 103, January 2013, pp. 24–40.

Maisel, Sebastian, Doppelte Minderheit – Die syrischen Yeziden im Spannungsfeld von Religion und Ethnizität, [in German] unpublished master thesis, Leipzig University, 1997.

Matar, Salim, The Controversy of Identities – Arabs, Kurds, Turkmen, Syriacs, Yezidis. The Fight of Belonging in Iraq and the Middle East, [Jadal al-Hawiyat – Arab, Akrad, Turkman, Sirian, Yazidiya. Sira' al-Intima'at fi'l-Iraq wa'l-Sharq al-Awsat], [in Arabic], London: Saqi, 2003.

McGee, Thomas, "The Stateless Kurds of Syria – Ethnic Identity and National I.D.," *Tilburg Law Review*, vol. 19, 2014, pp. 171–181.

Menzel, Theodor, "Ein Beitrag zur Kenntnis des Sindschar und seiner Bewohner. Aus Ewlija Tschelebis grossem Reisewerke [Sijahat-name]", in: *Meine Vorderasienexpediton 1906 und 1907* by Hugo Grothe, Leipzig: K.W. Hiersemann, 1911, pp. 194–211.

Mir Tahsin Beg, "Wir müssen uns auf unsere eigenen Kräfte besinnen" [in German], in Denge Ezidiyan, vols. 6+7, 1997, pp. 59–60.

Murad, Jasim E., *The Sacred Poems of the Yazidis: an Anthropological Approach*. PhD thesis, University of California, Los Angeles, 1993.

Nga Longva, Anh and Anne Sofie Roald (eds.), *Religious Minorities in the Middle East: Domination, Self-Empowerment, Accommodation,* Leiden: Brill, 2011.

Omarkhali, Khanna, "The Status and Role of the Yezidi Legends and Myths," *Folia Orientalia*, vols. 45–46, 2009–2010, pp. 197–219.

Omarkhali, Khanna, "Names of God and Forms of Address to God in Yezidism with the Religious Hymn of the Lord," in *Manuscripta Orientalis*, vol. 15, nos. 1–2, 2009, pp. 13–24.

Omarkhali, Khanna, "On the Structure of the Yezidi Clan and Tribal System and its Terminology Among the Yezidis of the Caucasus," *The Journal of Kurdish Studies*, vol. 6, 2008, pp. 104–119.

Ortac, Serhat, Sheikh Adi – Mythos und Wirklichkeit, [in German] 2005, n.p., accessed at www.yeziden-colloquium.de

Othman, Abd al-Rahman Haji, "The Martyrs are the builders of the Nation," published March 16, 2008 at www.tirejafrin.com/site/sh-1973.htm, accessed August 23, 2015.

Othman, Pir Mamo, "Die Beziehungen des Sufismus zum Yezidentum," [in German] published at www.yeziden/de/beziehungen_sufismus.0.html#top, accessed October 8, 2015.

Patton, Douglas, "Badr al-Din Lu'lu' and the Establishment of a Mamluk Government in Mosul," *Studia Islamica*, vol. 74, 1991, pp. 79–103.

Perdrizet, Paul, "Documents du XVIIe siècle relatifs de Yezidis", *Bulletin de la Société de Géographie de l'Est*, 1903, pp. 281–306 and 429–45.

Petition for HE President Bashar al-Asad by the delegation from Hasake Province, April 5, 2011.

Pierret, Thomas, "The State Management of Religion in Syria: The End of 'Indirect Rule'?" In: Middle East Authoritarianisms: Governance, Contestation, and Regime

Resilience in Syria and Iran, ed. by Reinoud Leenders and Steven Heydemann, Redwood, CA: Stanford University Press, 2012, pp. 83–106.

Pinto, Paulo, "Sufism among the Kurds in Syria," *Syrian Studies Association Newsletter*, vol. 16, no. 1, 2011.

Roj Journal, vol. 69, June 2009, published by el-Party: Kurdish Democratic Party in Syria, Jezira Branch.

Rondot, Pierre, "Les Kurdes de Syrie", *La France méditerranéenne et africaine*, vol. 1, no. 4, 1938, pp. 81–126.

Salo, Siban, "al-Batizmi – tuqus tastamir sabat ayam," [Batizmi Rituals Continue for Seven Days], [in Arabic], published on January 1, 2015 at www.bahzani.net/services/forum/showthread.php?97587, accesses on Sept 9, 2015.

Savelsberg, Eva and Siamend Hajo, "Ten Years of Bashar al-Asad and No Compromise with the Kurds," *Syrian Studies Association Newsletter*, vol. 16, spring 2011, pp. 6, 32–34.

Savelsberg, Eva, Siamend Hajo, and Irene Dulz, "Effectively Urbanized: Yezidis in the Collective Towns of Sheikhan and Sinjar," *Etudes Rurales*, vol. 186, 2010, pp. 101–116.

Schulz, Aniko, *Die besonderen traditionellen Regeln der Partnerwahl der Yeziden und deren Auswirkung auf die Integration*, [in German], Master thesis, Universität Hannover, 2009.

Seetzen, Ulrich Jasper, *Tagebücher: Tagebuch des Aufenthalts in Konstantinopel und der Reise nach Aleppo 1802–1803*, [in German], Olms Georg AG, 2012.

Selim, Yasser Fouad and Eid Mohamed (eds.), *Who Defines Me: Negotiating Identity in Language and Literature*, Newcastle Upon Tyne: Cambridge Scholars Publishing, 2014.

Shamo, Dakhil, "Lamha an mazarat Afrin," [Short account on the shrines of Afrin], [in Arabic], *Majallat Roj*, vol. 6, n.a., pp. 124–128.

Sheikh Khalaf, Khodayda, "Ziyara 'anda'l-Yazidiya fi Suria", [A Visit with the Yezidis in Syria], [in Arabic], *Nur Lalish* vol. 11, 2004, pp. 19–20.

Sileman, K. and K. Jindy, *Ezdiyati* [Yezidism], [in Kurdish], Baghdad, 1979.

Sinclair, Christian and Sirwan Kajjo, "The Evolution of Kurdish Politics in Syria," Middle East Research and Information Project, published at www.merip.rog/mero/meir08311#_3 on August 31, 2011, accessed September 8, 2013.

Siouffi, Nicolas, "Notice sur le Cheikh 'Adi et la secte de Yezidis", *Journal Asiatique*, vol. 8, no. 5, 1885, pp. 78–98.

Spät, Eszter, Following the Peacock – A Documentary, released 2013, available at https://www.youtube.com/watch?v=THdTv2af1bA

Spät, Eszter, Late Antique Motifs in Yezidi Oral Tradition, Piscataway, NJ: Gorgias, 2010.

Spät, Eszter, "Images and Objects of the Supernatural and Sacred Objects Among the Kurdish Yezidis," http://www.personal.ceu.hu/students/09/Eszter_Spat/index.htm, 2009.

Spät, Eszter, "Shahid bin Jarr, Forefather of the Yezidis and the Gnostic Seed of Seth," *Iran and the Caucasus*, vol. 6, nos. 1+2, 2002, pp. 27–56.

Sykes, Mark, "The Kurdish Tribes of the Ottoman Empire", *Journal of the Anthropological Institute*, vol. 38, 1908, pp. 451–486.

Tachijan, Vahe, La France en Cilicie et en Haute-Mesopotamie: aux confins de la Turquie, de la Syrie et de l'Irak, 1919–1933, Paris: Karthala, 2004.

Talay, Shabo, Der arabische Dialekt der Khawetna, II: Texte und Glossar, [in German], Wiesbaden: Harrosowitz, 2003.

Tamimi, Aymenn Jawad al-, "Northern Storm and the Situation in Azaz," Meria Special Report, published on January 7, 2015 at www.gloria-center.org/2015/01/media-specia-report/

Tejel, Jordi, Syria's Kurds. *History, Politics, and Society*, London: Routledge, 2009.

Tejel, Jordi, Le mouvement kurde de Turquie en exil. Continuités et discontinuités du nationalisme kurde sous le mandat français en Syrie et au Liban (1925–1946), Frankfurt, New York: Peter Lang Verlag, 2007.

Tejel, Jordi, "The Terrier Plan and the emergence of a Kurdish policy under the French Mandate in Syria, 1926–1936 (Report)", *International Journal of Kurdish Studies*, vol. 21, no. 1–2, 2007, pp. 93–109.

Van Bruinessen, Martin, "Kurdistan in the 16th and 17th centuries, as reflected in Evliya Çelebi's Seyahatname", *The Journal of Kurdish Studies*, vol. 3, 2000, pp. 1–11.

Van Bruinessen, Martin, "Nationalisme kurde et ethnicités intra-kurdes", *Peuples Méditerranéens*, vols. 68–69, 1994, pp. 11–37.

Van Bruinessen, Martin, Agha, Shaikh and State: the social and political structures of Kurdistan, London: Zed Books, 1992.

Weber, Kai, "Ausländer- und Asylrecht – Praxisrelevante Entscheidungen", [in German], Flüchtlingsrat: Zeitschrift für Flüchtlingspolitik in Niedersachsen, vol. 5, nos. 48/49, December 1997, pp. 126–129.

White, Benjamin, The Emergence of Minorities in the Middle East: The Politics of Community in French Mandate Syria, Oxford: Oxford University Press, 2011.

Winter, Stefen, "Die Kurden Syriens im Spiegel osmanischer Archivquellen (18. Jh.)", [in German], in Siamend Hajo et al., (eds.), Syrien und die Kurden: Vom Osmanischen Reich bis in die Gegenwart, Münster: Unrast Verlag, 2008, pp. 211–239.

Winter, Stefan, "The Province of Raqqa under Ottoman Rule, 1535–1800", Paper presented at the Great Lakes Ottomanist Workshop, Toronto, March 18, 2006.

Urfi, Abdullah, handwritten letter to Abdullah Talbe, minister of justice, August 31, 1993.

Yakhmaian, Behzad, "Syria's Civil War and the World's Oldest Refugee," The Globalist, February 11, 2014.

Yezidisches Forum Oldenburg, Stellungnahme zur Situation der Yeziden in Syrien unter Berücksichtigung der aktuellen Rechtsprechung, [in German], Oldenburg, July 3, 2009.

Yezidisches Forum Oldenburg, Stellungnahme zu der Situation der Yeziden in Nordostsyrien auf Anfrage des VG Magdeburg, [in German], Oldenburg, 2006.

Yusuf, Nidal, "Taj Hilla" al-libas al-tuqusi al-muqaddas [The Taj Hilla – a sacred ceremonial dress], [in Arabic], www.esyria.sy/ealeppo/index.php?p=stories, published January 12, 2013, accessed August 24, 2015.

Yusuf, Nidal, "Darwish Shamo wa al-madrasa al-awlah," [Darwish Shamo and the First School], [in Arabic], http://www.esyria.sy/ealeppo/index.php?p=stories&category=face&filename=201404221322334, published April 22, 2014, accessed September 21, 2015

Zakariya, Ahmad Wasfi, ʿAshaʾir ash-Sham, [The Tribes of Syria], [in Arabic], Damascus, 2007.

Zengi, Dalaur, "Min dhakirat al-sahafa al-kurdiya: wathaʾiq min arshif majallat hawar" [From the Kurdish Media Memory: Documents from the Archive of Hawar Journal], [in Arabic], http://www.yekiti.nl/html/erebi/dilawer1.htm, 2006.

Zentralrat der Yeziden in Deutschland, Offener Brief an das Bundesministerium des Innern, [in German], August 11, 2009.

Index

Adi bin Musafir, Sheikh, 34–36, 41–42, 44–49, 56, 58, 61, 65–66, 68–70, 72n7, 73n23, 77–80, 103, 112n5
afterlife. *See* reincarnation, 52, 58, 170
Ahl al-Kitab, 8, 81, 130
Ajanib, 98–99, 101–2, 115n67, 143, 158
al-Asad, Bashar, 107–11, 133
al-Asad, Hafiz, 27, 103, 133
Aleppo, 14, 18, 22, 25–26, 28, 36, 77–82, 84–85, 87, 89–90, 97, 100, 136, 151–52
Amuda, 22, 24, 26, 84, 99, 101, 107, 110, 134–36, 141, 151, 158
Angels, 43–44, 64–65, 72n5, 74n41
Arab belt project, 29, 99, 121
Arabization, 21, 28, 33, 97, 108, 139.
   See also Arab Belt project
Armenia:
   Yezidis in, 17, 31n14, 31n16, 38–40, 49, 53–54, 56, 58, 62, 80, 86, 122–23, 155, 161n44
Asabiya.
   See also group solidarity, 11–12, 54
Assembly Festival.
   See also Cejna Cemaye, 51, 56–57, 60–61
Assyrians, 9, 15, 28, 86, 147,

Baba Sheikh, 17, 48–51, 58, 78, 94, 111n1, 139–40, 153

Bahzani, 31n16, 42, 51, 87, 97, 138
Barzani, Masud, 95, 107, 138, 153
Barzani, Mulla Mustafa, 92
Bashiqa, 31n16, 41–42, 51, 96–97, 138
Basufan, 19–20, 22–23, 68–70, 99, 125, 131–33, 140, 148, 152
Ba'th Party, 2, 17, 93, 97, 99–100, 107, 110, 122, 129, 138, 140, 162n52
Batizmi, 57, 61–62, 7n34, 122
Bedirkhan Brothers (Jalalat and Kamuran), 89–90, 138
Berat stones, 50, 58, 62
Beyt Far.
   See also Khirbet Qanafir, 44–46, 77–78
Biraye akhrete (Brother of the Hereafter), 52
Bisk ceremony, 57

cantons, 120, 124, 131–33, 135–37, 144–45, 149–50, 152–55, 159, 162n58, 165–66
caste, 19, 25, 30, 46–53, 55, 58–59, 70, 79–81, 118–19, 127, 131–32, 160n19.
   See also sed u hed
cemeteries, 29, 52, 56–58, 63, 66–68, 73n27, 130, 134, 136, 146
Charshemasor (Yezidi New Year), 56, 67, 69, 133, 136

Index

citizenship, 10, 12–13, 15, 29, 98–99, 101, 109, 111, 119, 141–43, 158, 167

Civate Ruhani. *See* Supreme Spiritual Council

Ciwan Hajo, xi, xii

constitution:
  Rojava, 145, 166;
  Syrian, 98–99, 130, 139

councils, local, 135, 144–47

Damascus; 59;
  Kurdish community in, 14, 85, 103;
  Yezidi community in, 26, 81, 100

Da'sh. *See* The Islamic State in Iraq and Syria

death, 47, 57–58, 130, 149

Decree No. 49, 110, 116n102, 143

devil; 44, 72n4, 80;
  accusations of devil-worship, 33, 37, 110, 129–30

diaspora, xi, 4, 11, 49, 95, 119, 124–29, 153, 156, 158, 166

Diyare Feleke, 29, 104, 136, 146

education; 13, 116n98;
  during French Mandate, 87;
  Yezidi attitudes towards, 23, 47, 63, 83, 102, 110, 123, 133.
  See also mandatory Islam classes

EES. *See* Encumena Ezdiyen Suri (Council of Syrian Yezidis)

Efrin, 18–26, 30, 32n33, 59–60, 65–71, 73n31, 75, 80–81, 84, 87, 89–90, 99, 103, 107, 122, 124, 130–35, 141, 143–49, 152–54, 158–59, 160n13, 162n58

Encumena Ezdiyen Suri (EES - Council of Syrian Yezidis), 153–55, 163n75

Encumena Nishtimani ya Kurdi li Suriye (ENKS - The Kurdish National Council in Syria), 144, 153–54

ENKS. *See* Encumena Nishtimani ya Kurdi li Suriye (The Kurdish National Council in Syria)

ethnicity, 14–15, 120, 122–26, 139, 141, 155, 166

Ezid Festival (Eida Ezid), 55, 57–61, 122

fasting, 55–60, 73n31, 134, 148

Feqir, 51, 58, 67, 71, 73n16, 80–81, 106

Feqira(n), 19–20, 64, 68–70, 133

Ferman.
  See also genocide against Yezidis, 124, 160n14, 167

festivals, 56–58, 60–63

French Mandate; 27, 29
  attitudes towards minorities, 7, 10, 12–14
  relations with Yezidi community, 32n34, 49, 61, 71, 82–87

gender, 3, 153

genocide;
  genocide against Yezidis, xi, 125, 139, 156, 167

Germany; 11;
  diaspora groups in, 11, 17, 25, 94, 104, 125–28, 140, 153, 155–57, 165;
  immigration policies of, 110, 128–29

God, 43–44, 55–57, 60–61, 69, 87, 106

group solidarity (asabiya), 11, 54

Hajo Agha, Hassan, 27, 54, 85, 104, 113n42

Hasake, 23–24, 26, 28, 83–86, 97–101, 106–11, 116n98, 135, 141, 146, 154

Hawar (The Calling), (journal), 83

heresy, accusations of, 35, 78, 158–59

heretics, 3, 9, 33–36, 44, 92, 122, 129

HES. *See* Hevbendiya Ezidiyen Suriye (Syrian Yezidi Association)

Hevbendiya Ezidiyen Suriye (HES - Syrian Yezidi Association), 152–53

Heza Parastina Shingal (HPS - Shingal Protection Force), 156

Hilal, Muhammad Talab, 97–98

honor killings, 126, 140

HPS. *See* Heza Parastina Shingal
    (Shingal Protection Force)
Hussein, Saddam, 95, 128, 156

identity:
    discourse of, xi, xiii, 1–4, 8, 10–17,
        19, 33–34, 50, 54, 57, 75, 82,
        91–92, 97, 102, 108, 117–18, 121,
        159, 165–68;
    ethnic, 138–42, 167;
    Kurdish, 82, 102, 108, 149;
    national, 117;
    political, 142–46;
    religious, 14, 57, 119–20, 122–23,
        129–31, 159n4, 162n52;
    Yezidi, xiii, 4, 43, 46, 92, 101,
        117–20, 122–24, 125–26, 131,
        149, 153, 166–68
Iraq; 5n5, 8, 10, 15, 30n5, 31n11,
        82–83, 92–96, 100, 103, 106–8,
        143, 153, 155;
    Yezidis in, 17, 31n14, 31n16, 39,
        41–42, 49–51, 53, 56–60, 68,
        72, 82, 83–86, 91, 92–96, 96–97,
        113n36, 120–21, 124, 127–28,
        131, 133, 138–39, 149, 153,
        156–57, 161, 166–68
ISIS. *See* The Islamic State in Iraq and
    Syria
Islam courses, mandatory, 13, 109
Islamic State in Iraq and Syria (Da'sh),
    also ISIS, IS, 14, 96–97, 140,
    151–52, 156–57, 163n73, 167,
    168n2
Issa, Chaukeddin, 50, 85
Issa, Shemo Meke, 104–7, 142

Jabhat al-Nusra (The Victory Front), JN,
    14, 25, 27, 146, 151–52, 163n73,
    167
Jafar, Suleyman, 131–32, 134
Jezira, 21, 24, 26–28, 30, 49, 54, 59,
    61–63, 71–72, 81–84, 86, 91–92,
    97–102, 108, 111, 120–22,
    134–37, 141–46, 152–54, 158–59

JN. *See* Jabhat al-Nusra (The Victory
    Front),

Khaznawi, Sheikh Muhammad Mashuq,
    108
Kherqe, 51, 64, 67, 70–71, 80
Khirbet Qanafir. *See* Beyt Far
Khoybun League, 85, 89, 100, 113n42,
    139
KNC. *See* The Kurdish National
    Council,
Kochek, 50–52
Kreyenbroek, Philip, 34, 38–40, 42,
    112n2
Kurdagh, 18–21, 25, 49, 51, 54, 63,
    65–71, 79, 83, 86–92, 99, 102–3,
    114n53, 121–22, 129–33, 142,
    145, 147–49, 167
Kurdish identity, 102, 149
Kurdish language:
    courses in, 132, 141, 157;
    Yezidi oral traditions in, 38, 40
Kurdish names, 31n17, 140,
Kurdish National Council (KNC), 144,
    153–55
Kurdish national movement, 16, 89–91,
    107–8, 121, 123, 138–39, 150, 155
Kurdish parties in Syria, 17, 102–3,
    107–8, 142, 145, 148, 155

Lalish, 17, 35, 41, 46, 49–52, 56–57, 60,
    62, 67, 72n7, 77, 94–95, 97, 112,
    120, 127, 133–37
land ownership, 10, 110, 158
leadership, religious: 48–52, 144;
    in Efrin, 69–70, 88, 135;
    in Iraq, 62, 93–95, 124, 131, 153,
        156–57;
    in the Jezira, 71–72, 106, 135

Maktumin, 98–102, 111, 115n67,
    116n98, 1443, 158
marriage:
    marriage endogamy, 30, 32n33, 43,
        47, 55, 119;

Index

marriage relations within the Syrian Yezidi community, 59, 81, 110, 129–30, 149, 167;
marriage restrictions for maktumin and ajanib, 101–2
massacres, xi, 36, 81, 156
Michewir, 52, 63, 67
migration; 7, 19, 27, 31n14, 53, 82, 100, 108, 124–26, 137, 144, 150–52;
  to Germany, 25, 72, 100, 165
military service; 87, 131;
  mandatory conscription, 81, 83, 113n36, 144, 154
Millet, 8, 30n3, 80–81, 130
minorities:
  construction of concept, 1, 149, 165;
  double, 3, 17–20, 124, 165, 168;
  ethnic minorities in Syria, 2, 14–15, 18, 168;
  hierarchy in Syria, 2–4, 11, 15, 17, 30, 72, 82, 92, 122–23;
  political, 3;
  religious, 55
Mir, 48, 51, 60, 84, 88–90, 114n53, 119, 131, 153
Mir Muawiya Ismail, 93–94, 138
Mir Tahsin Beg, 17, 39, 42n7, 49, 84, 90–91, 93–95, 106, 138–40, 149, 157, 166
Mirid (laymen), caste of, 18–19, 32n33, 42, 47–48, 51–53, 58–59, 62, 71–72, 80, 155
misconceptions, 11, 33
Movement for a Democratic Society (TEV-DEM), 135, 137, 144–48
Mukhtar, 25, 29, 51–52, 86, 99, 101
Muslim attitudes towards Yezidis, 8, 68, 76–77, 81, 95–96, 121, 130, 150, 167

nationalism; 14;
  Arab, 97, 129;
  Kurdish.
  See also Kurdish National Movement, 83, 123, 139, 143, 145

neighbors, 1, 4, 12, 19, 33, 35, 55, 61–62, 77, 81, 97–98, 109, 131, 137, 142, 167

Ocalan, Abdullah, 103, 133, 137, 147–48
Otelje, 27–30, 71, 130, 133, 136, 146
Ottoman Empire, 38, 73n16, 77, 82
Ottomans, 7, 66

Partiya Demokrat A Kurdistane li Suriye (PDK-S - Kurdish Democratic Party of Syria), 99, 100, 115n74, 152
Partiya Karkeren Kurdistane (Kurdistane Workers' Party – PKK), 1, 102–3, 106, 123–24, 128, 132, 142–45, 149, 154–56, 163n90, 166–67
Partiya Yekiti ya Demokrat (Democratic Union Party – PYD), 5, 124, 132–33, 137, 144–47, 149–55, 157, 163n89, 167
Patriotic Union of Kurdistan (Yekitiya Nishtimani ya Kurdistane – PUK), 103, 106, 115n83
PDK-S. *See* Partiya Demokrat A Kurdistane li Suriye (Kurdish Democratic Party of Syria)
Peacock Angel (Tawsi Melek), 36, 44, 55–56, 58, 64, 73n23, 106–7
Peshimam, 58, 72, 136, 140
Peshimam Sileman Omar, 72, 103–6
pilgrimage.
  See also the Assembly Festival;
  Tawaf, 16, 50, 56, 60, 63, 72, 94–95, 120, 127, 133–35
pir, caste of, 19, 32n33, 41–42, 44, 47–55, 58–59, 61, 69–70, 72, 81, 95, 119, 131, 133, 155, 160n19
PKK. *See* Partiya Karkeren Kurdistane (Kurdistan Workers' Party)
population census, 1962, 98, 106, 115n68
prayer, 41, 55, 62–64, 73n21, 136
Prince Anwar Muawiya, 161n45–46

PUK. *See* Patriotic Union of Kurdistan (Yekitiya Nishtimani ya Kurdistane)
PYD. *See* Partiya Yekiti ya Demokrat (Democratic Union Party)

Qamishli; 26–29, 32, 83–86, 99–100, 103, 107–8, 110–11, 143, 156;
   Qamishli uprising, 107–8
Qestel Jindo, 19–20, 31n19, 64, 67–71, 88, 91, 99, 101n48, 133, 148, 151
Qewal, 41–42, 50–52, 56–58, 60, 62–63, 72, 91, 120, 140
Qewl(s), 34, 41–42, 50–52, 57–59, 62–64, 70–72, 133, 137
Qibare, 19–21, 31, 32n5, 51, 64–66, 70–71, 83, 87–88, 91, 99, 103
Qizlachuq, 24, 32n26, 107, 134, 151, 155, 159

Ras al-Ayn (Sere Kaniye), 24, 26–27, 32, 82, 86, 98–99, 110, 136, 151–52
refugees; 3, 20, 22, 83–84, 96–97, 106, 121, 143, 152, 157, 166;
   Iraqi refugees in Syria, 83–84, 106, 121, 156–57
renaming of towns and villages, 20, 22, 108
Rojava, 135, 137, 144–47, 149, 152

sacred books, 37–38
SCP. *See* Syrian Communist Party
Sed u hed, 46, 47, 119, 159n4.
   See also caste
self-administration, 72, 122, 129–34, 141, 146–50, 154, 159, 165, 167–68
Sere Kaniye. *See* Ras al-Ayn
Shamo, Darwish Agha, 49, 71, 87–90, 142
Shamo, Jamil Agha, 49, 84, 89–91
sheikh, caste of; 18–19, 22–26, 32n33, 41, 47–53, 55, 57–61, 63–66, 68–72, 81–82, 93, 103, 118–19, 131–36, 140, 148, 151, 155, 160n19;
   Adani, 49, 69–71, 93;
   Qatani, 49, 69–70, 155;
   Shemsani, 19, 49–50, 69–71
Sheikhan, 17, 37, 41, 49–51, 54, 57, 72n17, 73n32, 84, 88–89, 92, 94–95, 138, 142, 148–49
Sheikh Hassan bin Adi, 49, 52, 77, 79
Sheikh Huseyn Sheikh Hassan Sheikh Brim(o), 69–71, 131, 148
Sheikh Mend, 18, 52, 64–66, 70, 80
Shingal. *See* Sinjar
shrine(s); 16, 21, 40, 45, 51–52, 55–57, 60, 63, 74n39, 77, 93–95, 104, 114n62, 120, 124, 130, 156;
   In Efrin, 21–22, 26, 63, 65–71, 133
Sinjaq, 49–51, 62–64, 73n15
Sinjar (Shingal), 10, 31n16, 35–37, 41, 49, 51, 53, 61, 63, 68, 71, 73n15, 74n39, 78, 82–85, 89, 92–95, 103, 121, 138, 166;
   Sinjar bomb attacks 2007, 96, 140;
   Sinjar massacre 2014, 96–97, 124–25, 138, 153, 155–57, 167
SNC. *See* Syrian National Council
stateless Kurds. *See* Ajanib, maktumin
stereotypes, 33, 81, 158
Sufis, 44–45, 47, 69, 79
Sufism, 16, 79, 102, 167
sun worship, 45, 75, 77–78, 82, 112n5
Supreme Spiritual Council (Civate Ruhani), 49–50, 131–32, 140, 153, 162n48
Syrian Communist Party (SCP), 17, 100
Syrian government, 97–99, 106, 130, 140, 143, 155, 165, 167
Syrian National Council (SNC), 144
Syrian uprising, 1–4, 14, 17, 19, 25, 54, 109–10, 121, 124, 128, 143, 165–67;
   Kurdish reactions to, 141, 143;
   Yezidi reaction to, 154, 166.
   See also Self-administration, 148, 150, 157

Taj hilla, 64–65
Tawaf, 50–52, 63–64, 74n39, 91, 122
Tawsi Melek. *See* Peacock Angel

Tell Khatun, 24, 27–29, 98–99, 104–6, 150
TEV-DEM. *See* Tevgera Civaka Demokratik (Movement for a Democratic Society)
Tevgera Civaka Demokratik (TEV-DEM). *See* Movement for a Democratic Society
Tirbespi (al-Qahtaniya, Qubur Beyd), 22, 26–29, 61, 85–86, 99–100, 104–5, 107, 125, 136, 146–47, 157, 162n62
tribes:
    Arab, 86, 103, 106–7, 142, 154;
    mixed, 28, 36, 54, 141;
    Yezidi, 19, 26, 29, 36, 53–54, 61, 80, 84–85, 89, 112n12, 115n72, 136
Tur Abdin, 54, 61–63, 71, 73n33, 81, 85–86, 104–5, 121
Turkey; 10, 15, 83–85, 94, 98, 102–4, 108, 121, 138, 156;
    Yezidis in, 28–29, 40, 53–54, 63, 104–7, 121, 125–28, 166

values, 54, 126–27, 150
victimization, 92, 122, 167

Wadi al-Jarrah, 22, 24–27, 29, 98–100, 104, 106, 113n36, 116n89, 130, 142–43

women, 47, 56, 61, 66, 73n26, 85, 96, 106, 125, 132–33, 135, 145, 147–48, 154, 157, 160n19, 166

Yazid bin Muawiya (Umayyad caliph), 33, 35, 75, 78, 93, 129
YBS. *See* Yekineyen Berxwedan Shingal (Shingal Resistance Units)
Yekineyen Berxwedan Shingal (YBS - Shingal Resistance Units), 156
Yekineyen Parastina Gel (YPG - People's Defence Units), 25, 120, 137, 144–45, 150–52, 154, 156, 166
Yezidi Identity Inventory (EZI), 126–27
Yezidi Association in Efrin, 132–33, 148
Yezidism; 11, 35, 39, 41–42, 43–47, 52, 54–55, 58, 61–62, 69, 75–81, 85, 91, 95, 102–3, 106, 112n5, 119–22, 125–31, 138, 145, 149, 159, 166–67;
    studies of, 16, 34, 38–40;
    teaching, 87, 106, 133, 135, 157
YPG. *See* Yekineyen Parastina Gel (People's Defence Units)

Zarathustra, 60, 64, 75–76, 137
Zoroastrians, 23, 39, 64, 66, 75–76, 102, 128;
    Yezidis as, 102, 128, 132, 138–39

About the Author

Sebastian Maisel is associate professor for Arabic and Middle East studies at Grand Valley State University. He received his PhD in Arabic and Islamic studies and anthropology from Leipzig University, Germany. As an area specialist of the Middle East, he teaches courses on the diverse cultures and religions of the region as well as Arabic language. His research focus is on social transformation among rural communities and minority groups, for which he conducted field work among the Bedouin tribes in Saudi Arabia, Yezidis in Syria and Iraq as well as Dinka slave soldiers from Sudan. He primarily uses sources that include oral narratives, material culture, and virtual representations. His publications include *The Customary Law of the Bedouins in Northern Arabia* (Peter Lang, 2006), *Yezidism—Religion and Society,* with C. Issa and T. Tolan (Denge Ezidiya 2007), *An Encyclopedia of Life in Saudi Arabia and the Arab Gulf States,* with J. Shoup (Greenwood Press, 2009), *The Kingdom of Saudi Arabia,* with D. Long (University of Florida Press, 2010), and al-'Arabiya al-Mu'asira—*Modern Standard Arabic Integrating Main Arabic Dialects,* with E. Schulz (Hammouda, 2013) and *The Kurds: An Encyclopedia of Life, Culture, and Society* (ABC Clio, forthcoming).

Lightning Source UK Ltd.
Milton Keynes UK
UKHW02n0649161217
314508UK00017B/1309/P

BL 1595 M231y 2017
Maisel, Sebastian, 1970-
Yezidis in Syria